Missions of Love

Volume 13

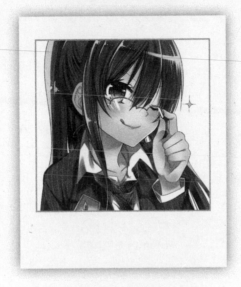

Ema Toyama

Missions of Love
Ema Toyama

Story

The love missions began as research for a novel. In order to take her love to the next level, Yukina initiates a date mission, and chooses Akira to be her boyfriend. To resolve the awkwardness that remained between herself and Shigure after they separated, Yukina tries to tell him her honest feelings, but finds out she was actually talking to his younger brother Hisame!! His twisted affection is new to her, and she wants him to teach her about the dark side of love. Meanwhile, Hisame goes berserk when he learns that Akira and Mami have suddenly gotten a lot closer! Yukina guards Akira from Hisame's fist and gets punched herself!?

Character

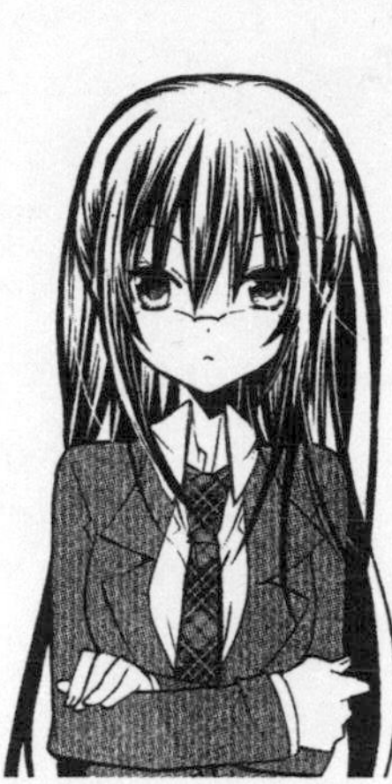

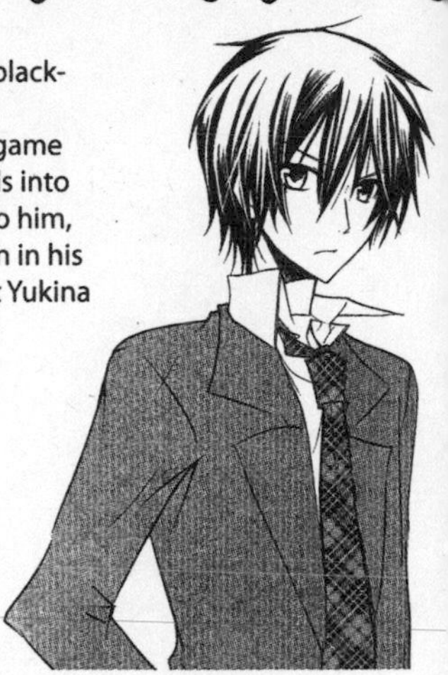

Shigure Kitami
The ever-popular but black-hearted student body president. He made a game of charming all the girls into confessing their love to him, then writing it all down in his student notebook, but Yukina discovered his secret!

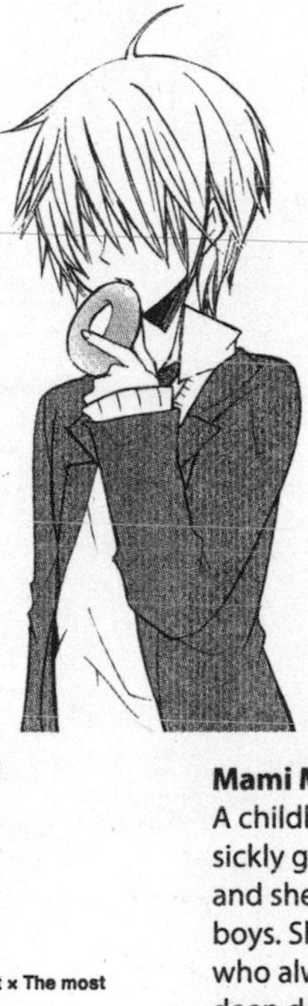

Yukina Himuro
A third-year junior high student who strikes terror in the hearts of all around her with her piercing gaze, feared as the "Absolute Zero Snow Woman." Only Akira knows that she's also the popular cell phone novelist Yupina.

Akira Shimotsuki
Yukina's cousin and fellow student. He loves to eat. He is always nearby watching over her, but he wants Yukina to see him as a man, so he changes his look!

me!

It is time for love.
Secret cellular phone novelist × The most popular boy in school.
Love mission of absolute servitude.

Mami Mizuno
A childhood friend of Shigure's. A sickly girl. The teachers love her, and she's very popular with the boys. She's a beautiful young girl who always wears a smile, but deep down, her heart is black. She recently outgrew her long-held crush on Shigure.

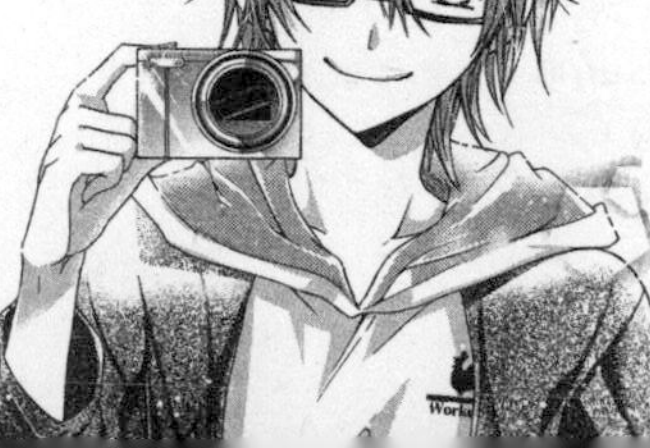

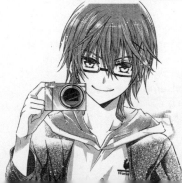

Hisame Kitami
Shigure's brother, one year his junior. He normally attends a boarding school, but is now home for summer vacation. He harbors a twisted affection for Mami.

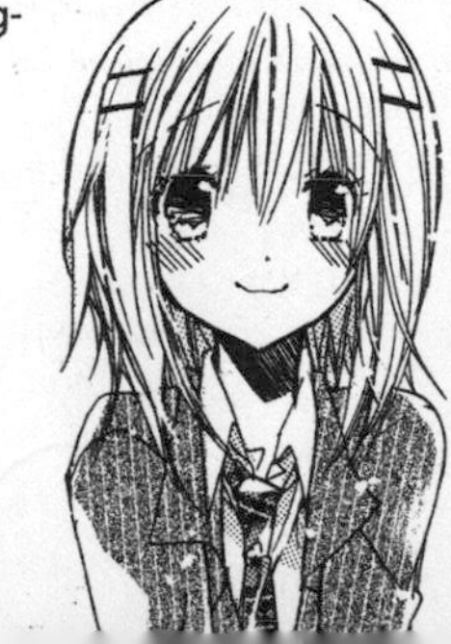

Special Presentation
Graphic Novel Release Countdown Illustrations

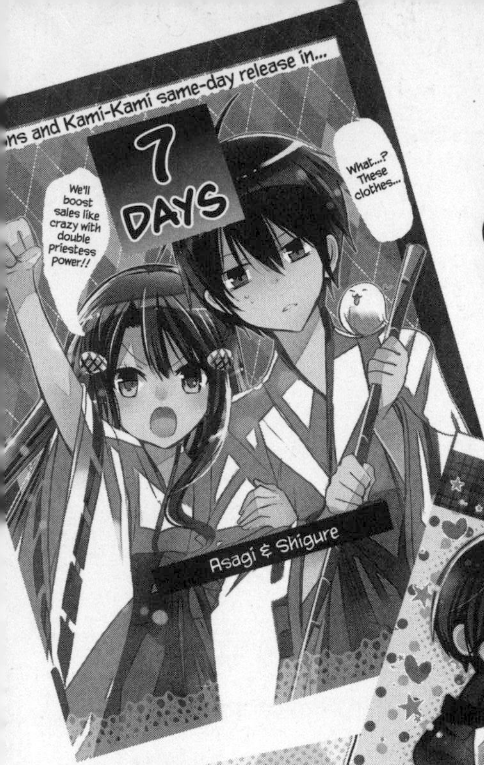
ns and Kami-Kami same-day release in...
7 DAYS
What...? These clothes...
We'll boost sales like crazy with double priestess power!!
Asagi & Shigure

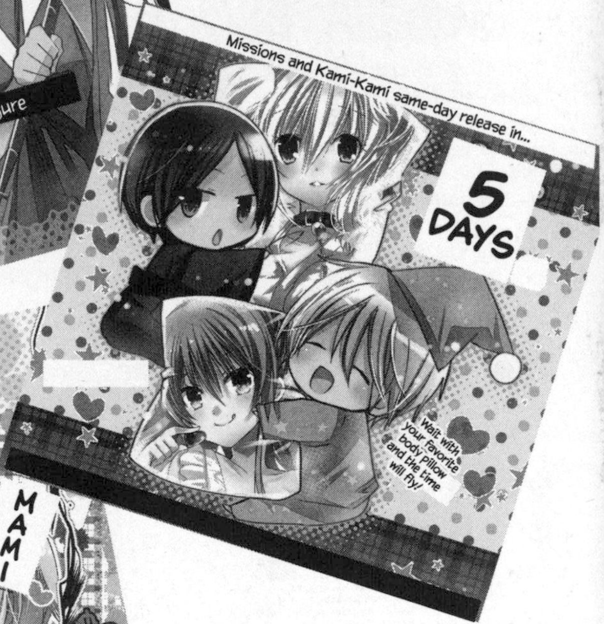
Missions and Kami-Kami same-day release in...
5 DAYS
Wait with your favorite body pillow and the time will fly!

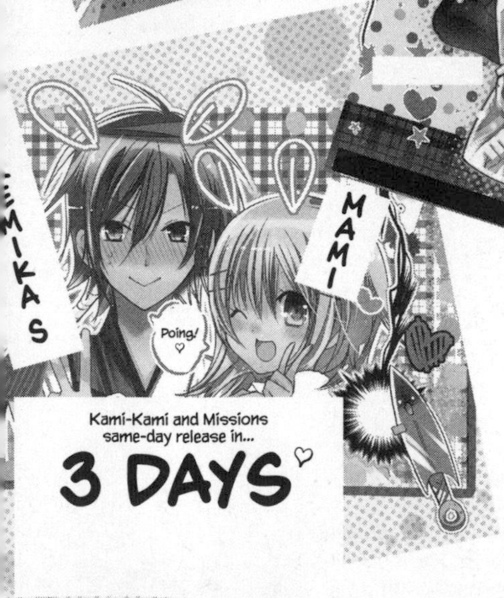
MAMI
Poing! ♡
Kami-Kami and Missions same-day release in...
3 DAYS ♡

It is time for love.
Secret cellular phone novelist × The most popular boy in school.
Love mission of absolute servitude.

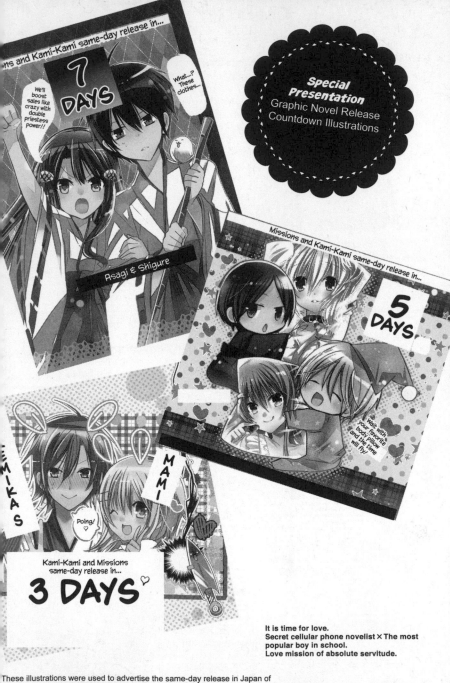

These illustrations were used to advertise the same-day release in Japan of Missions of Love 12 and Kami-Kami Kaeshi 3 on June 13, 2013.

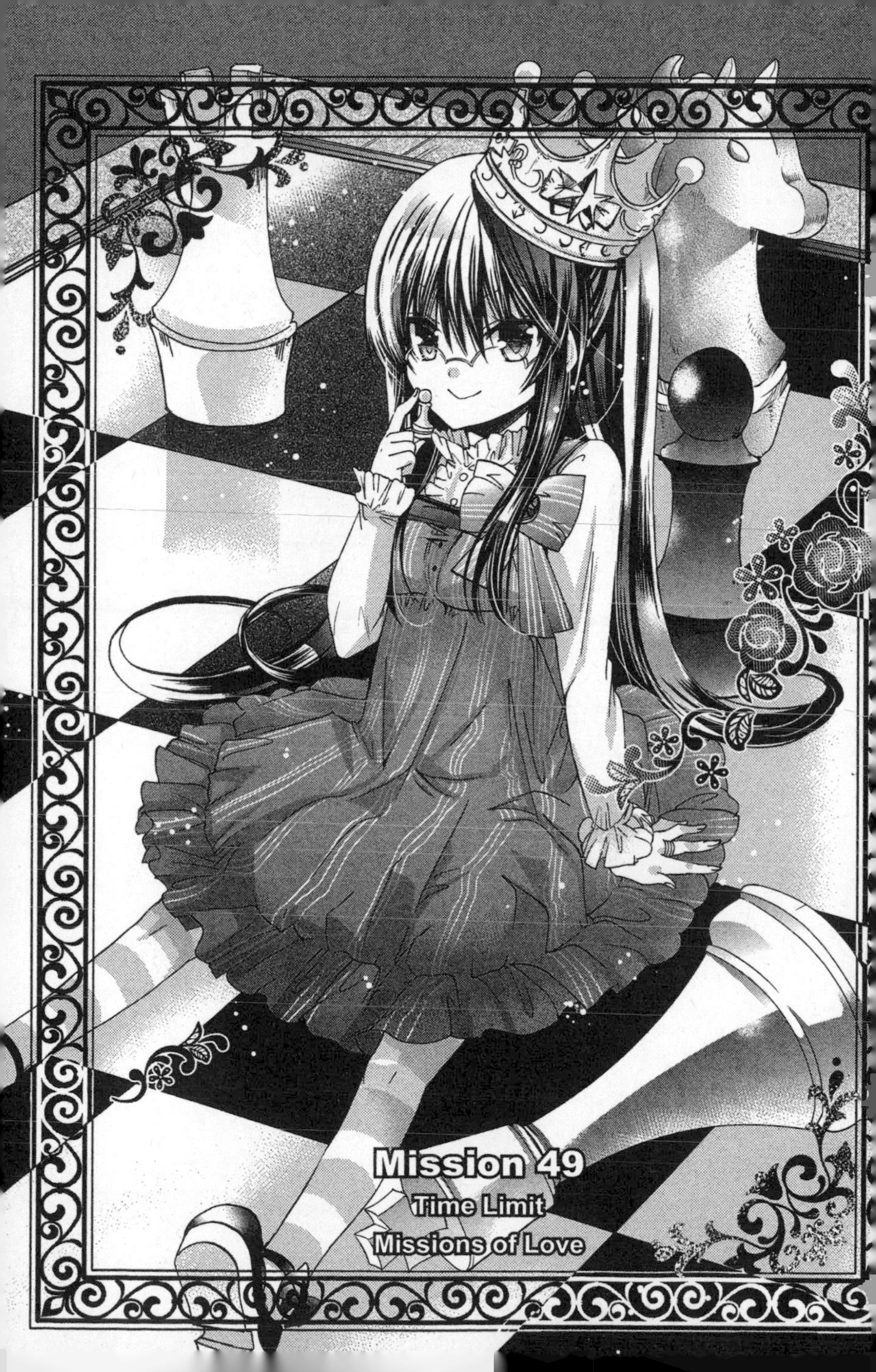
Mission 49
Time Limit
Missions of Love

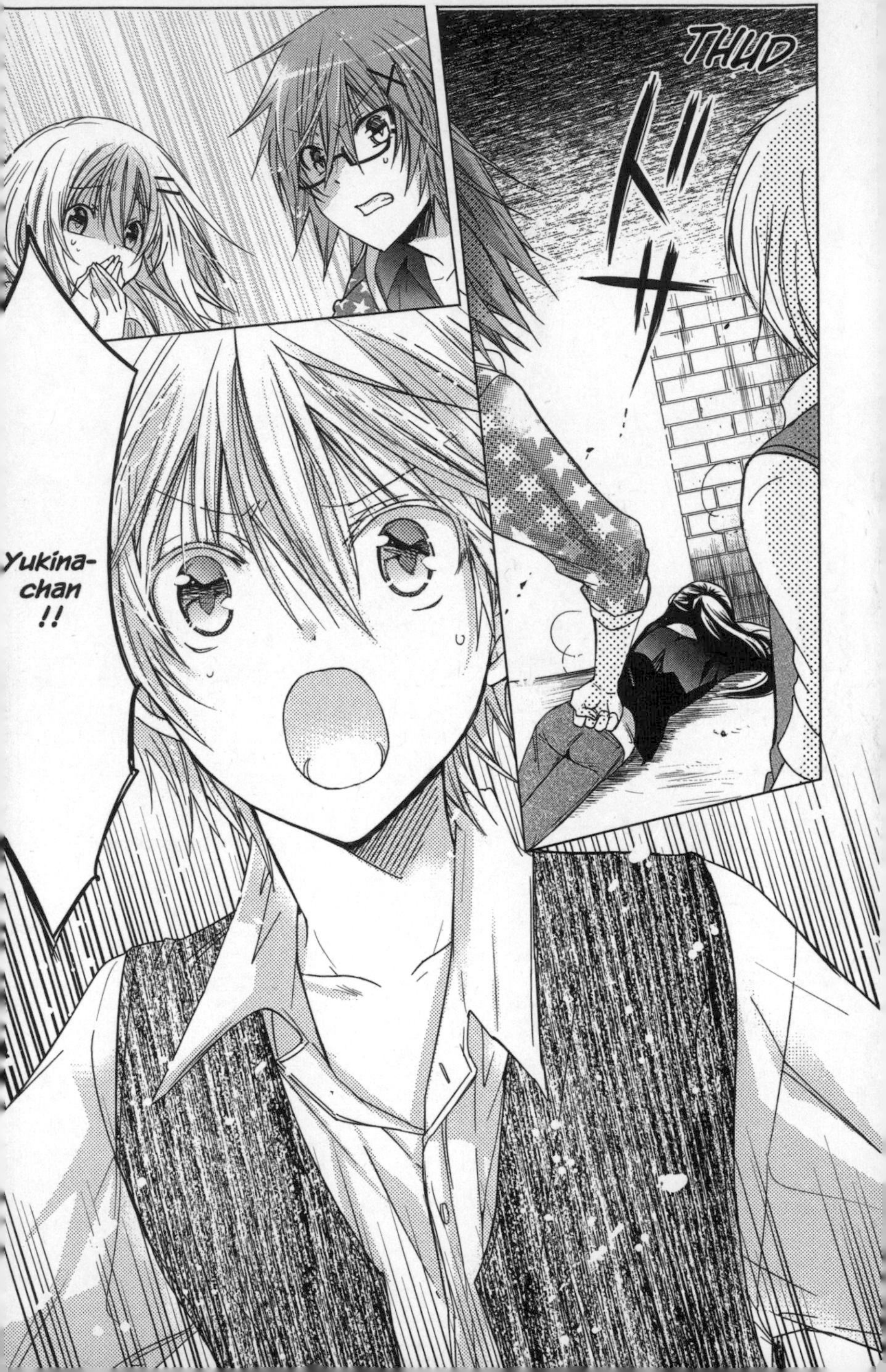
THUD
Yukina-chan !!

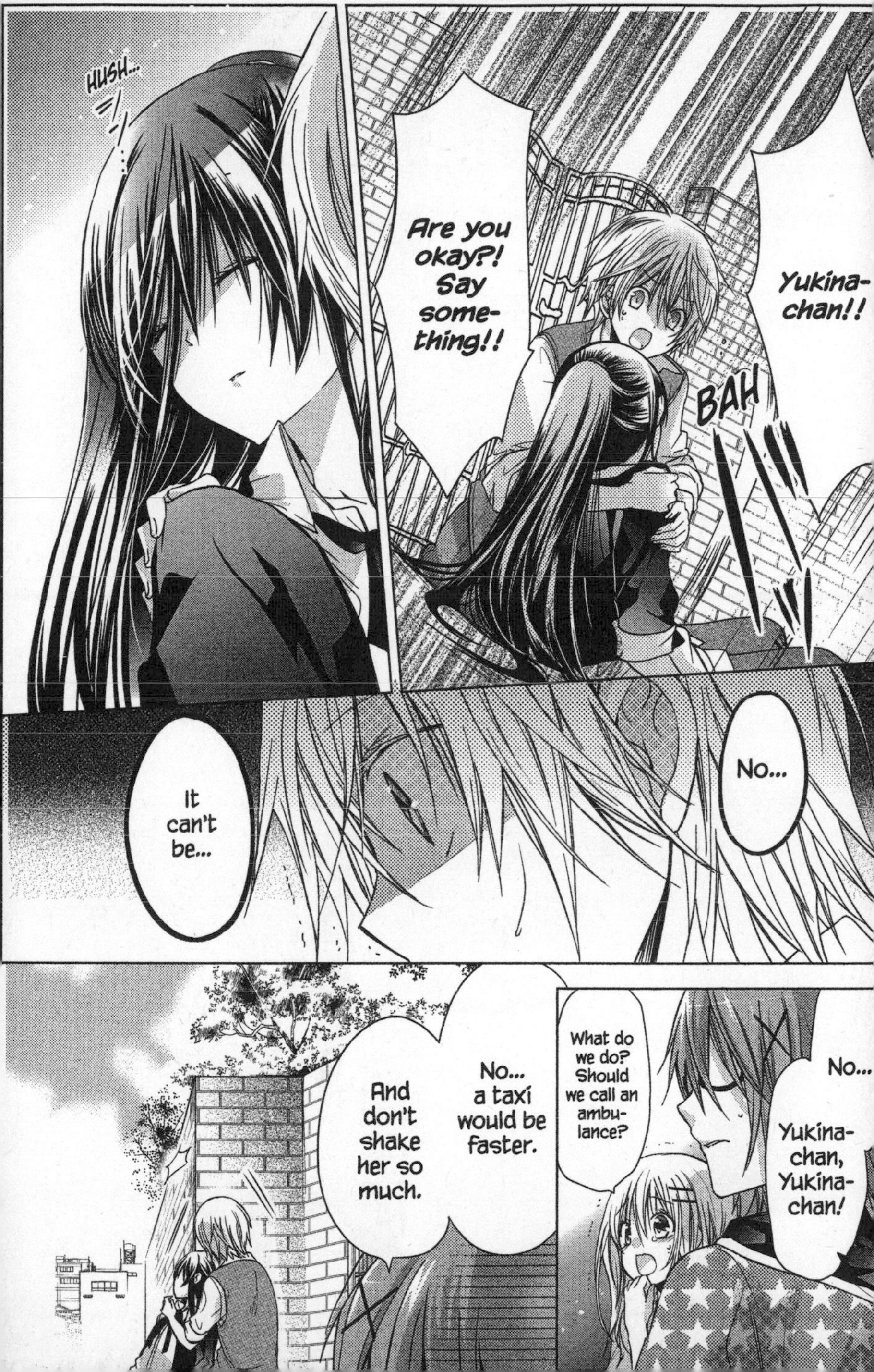
Yukina-chan!!
BAH
Are you okay?! Say something!!
HUSH...
No...
It can't be...
No...
Yukina-chan, Yukina-chan!
What do we do? Should we call an ambulance?
No... a taxi would be faster.
And don't shake her so much.

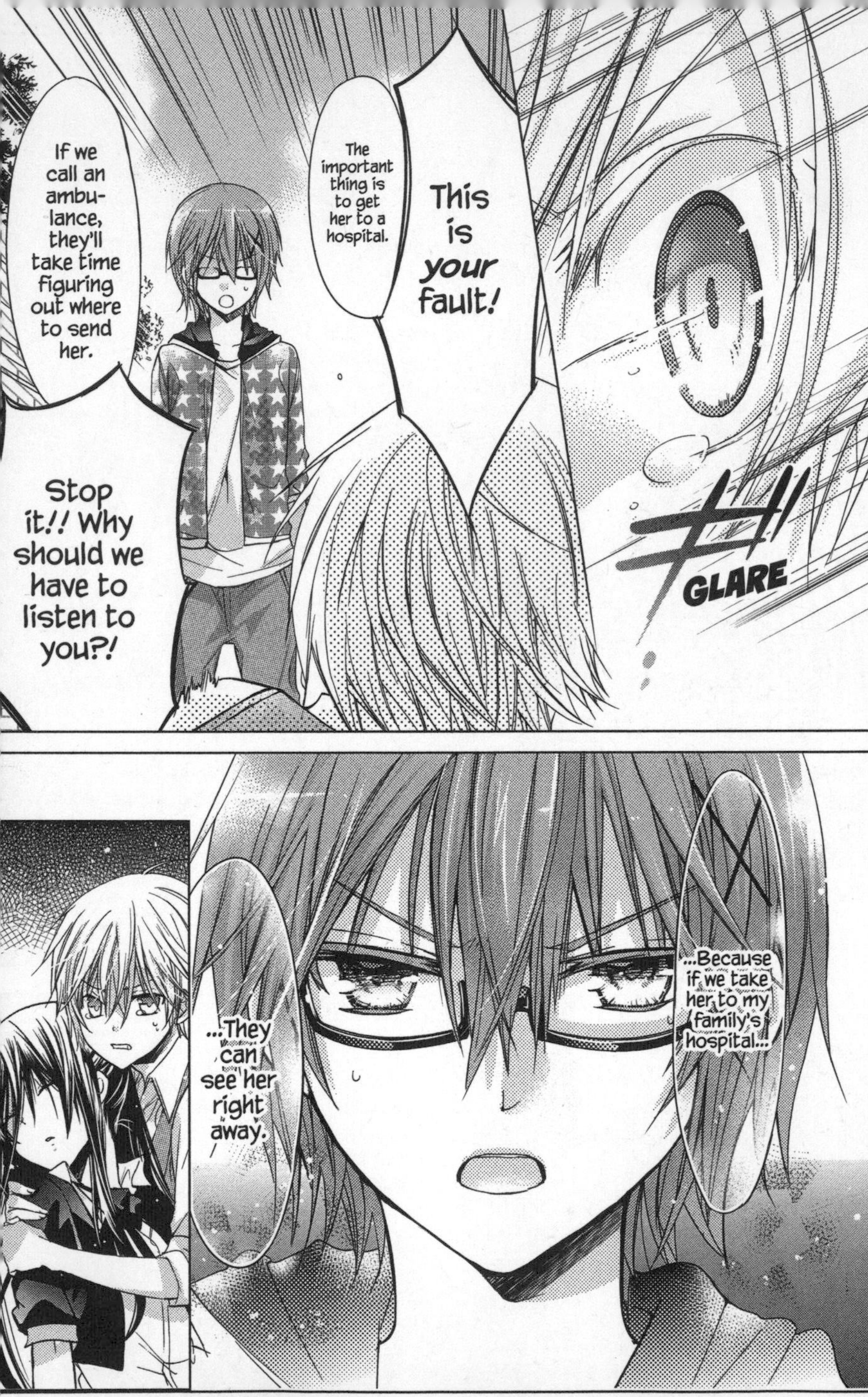
This is your fault!
The important thing is to get her to a hospital.
If we call an ambulance, they'll take time figuring out where to send her.
GLARE
Stop it!! Why should we have to listen to you?!
...Because if we take her to my family's hospital...
...They can see her right away.

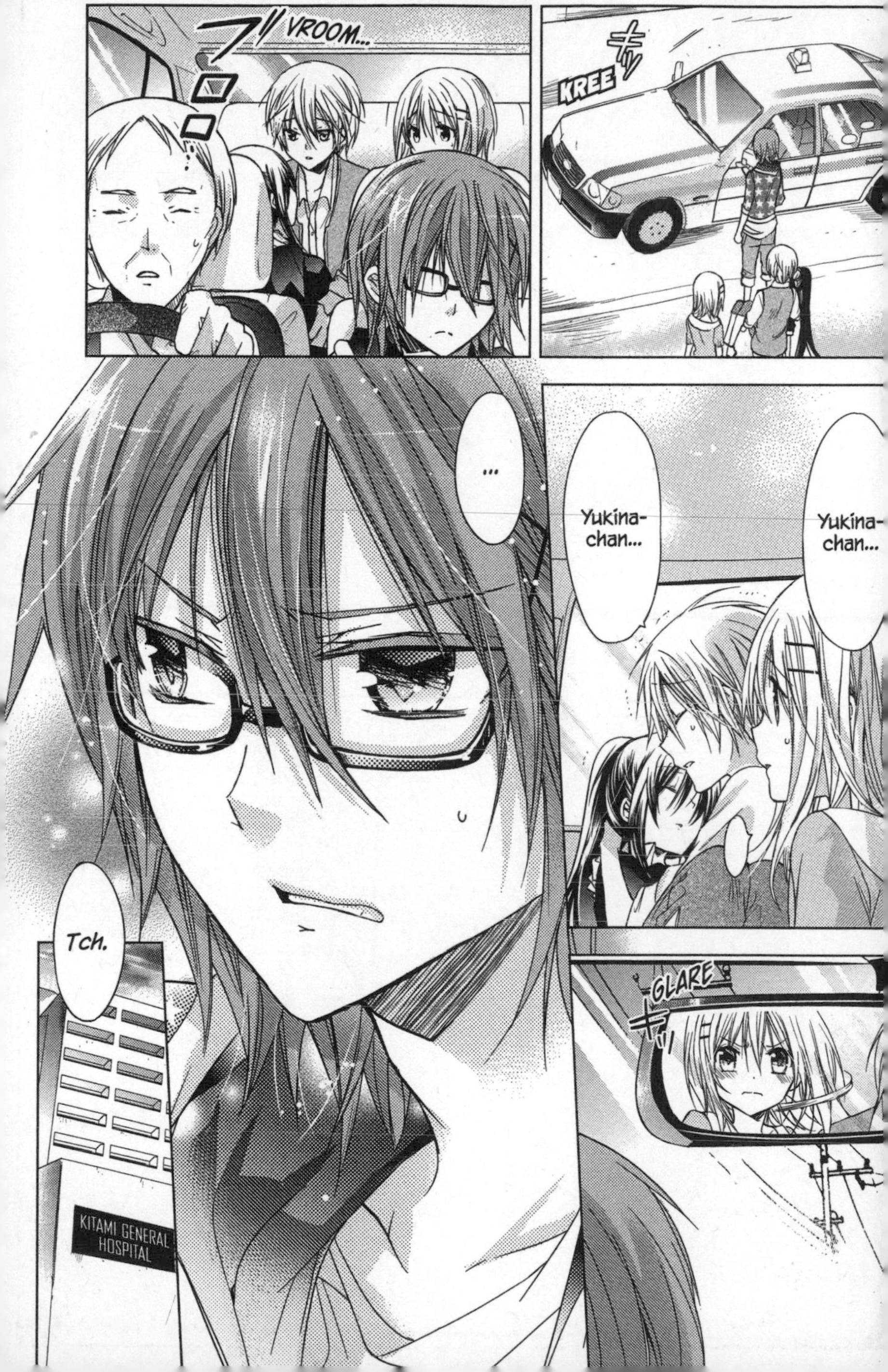
KREE
VROOM...
Yukina-chan...
Yukina-chan...
GLARE
...
Tch.
KITAMI GENERAL HOSPITAL

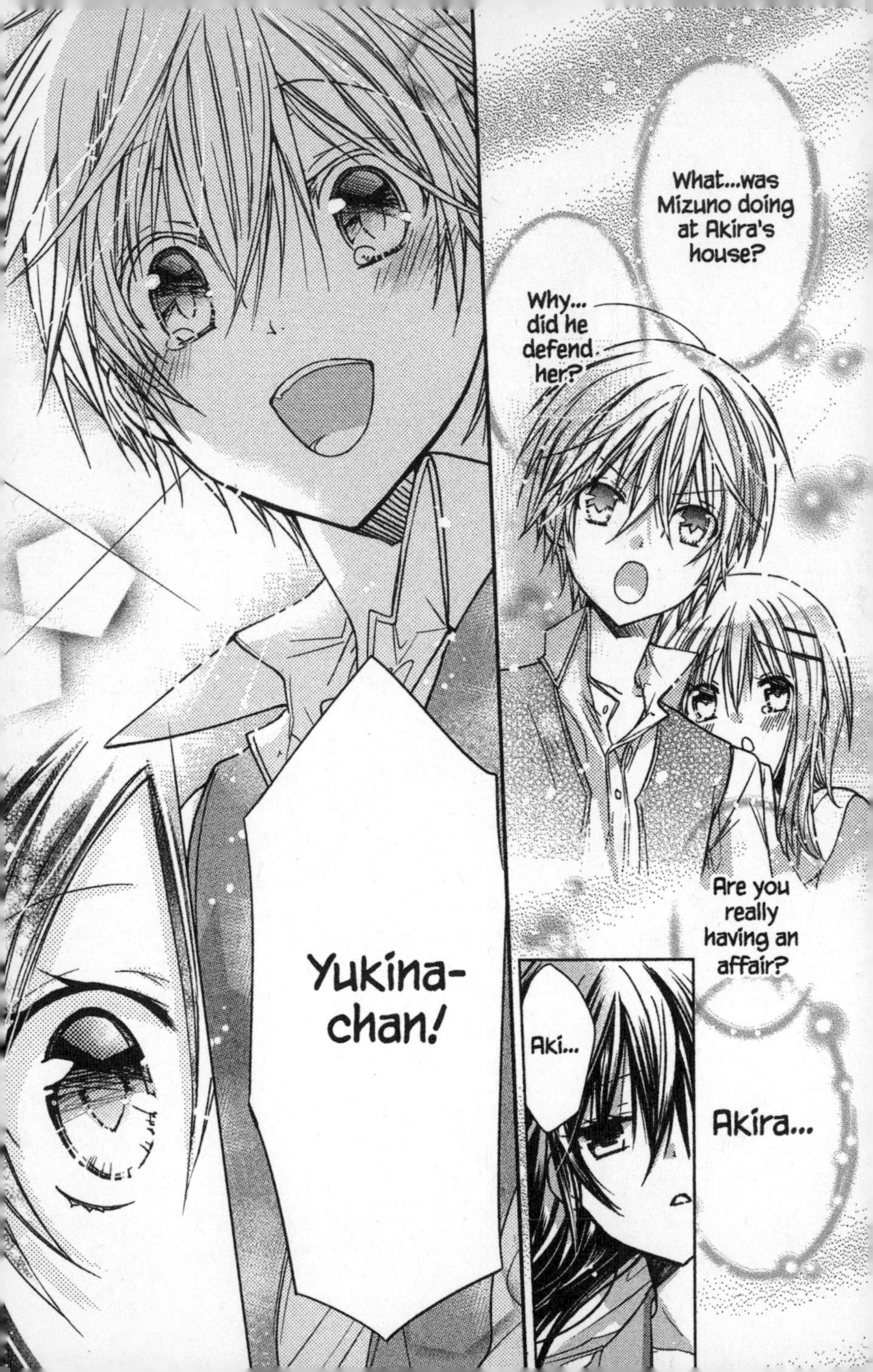

What...was Mizuno doing at Akira's house?
Why... did he defend her?
Are you really having an affair?
Aki...
Akira...
Yukina-chan!

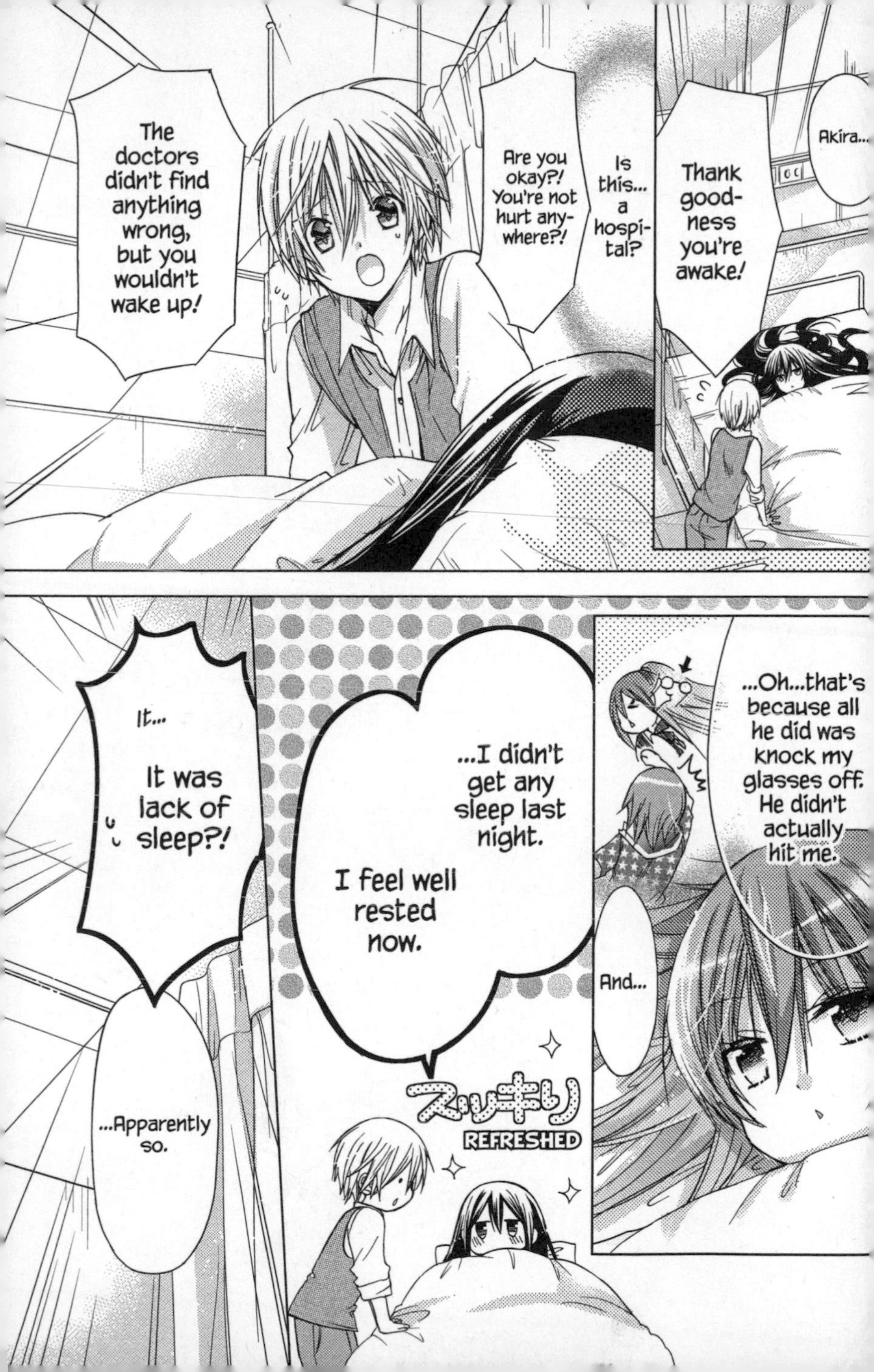
Akira...
Thank goodness you're awake!
Is this... a hospital?
Are you okay?! You're not hurt anywhere?!
The doctors didn't find anything wrong, but you wouldn't wake up!
...Oh...that's because all he did was knock my glasses off. He didn't actually hit me.
And...
...I didn't get any sleep last night.
I feel well rested now.
スッキリ
REFRESHED
It...
It was lack of sleep?!
...Apparently so.

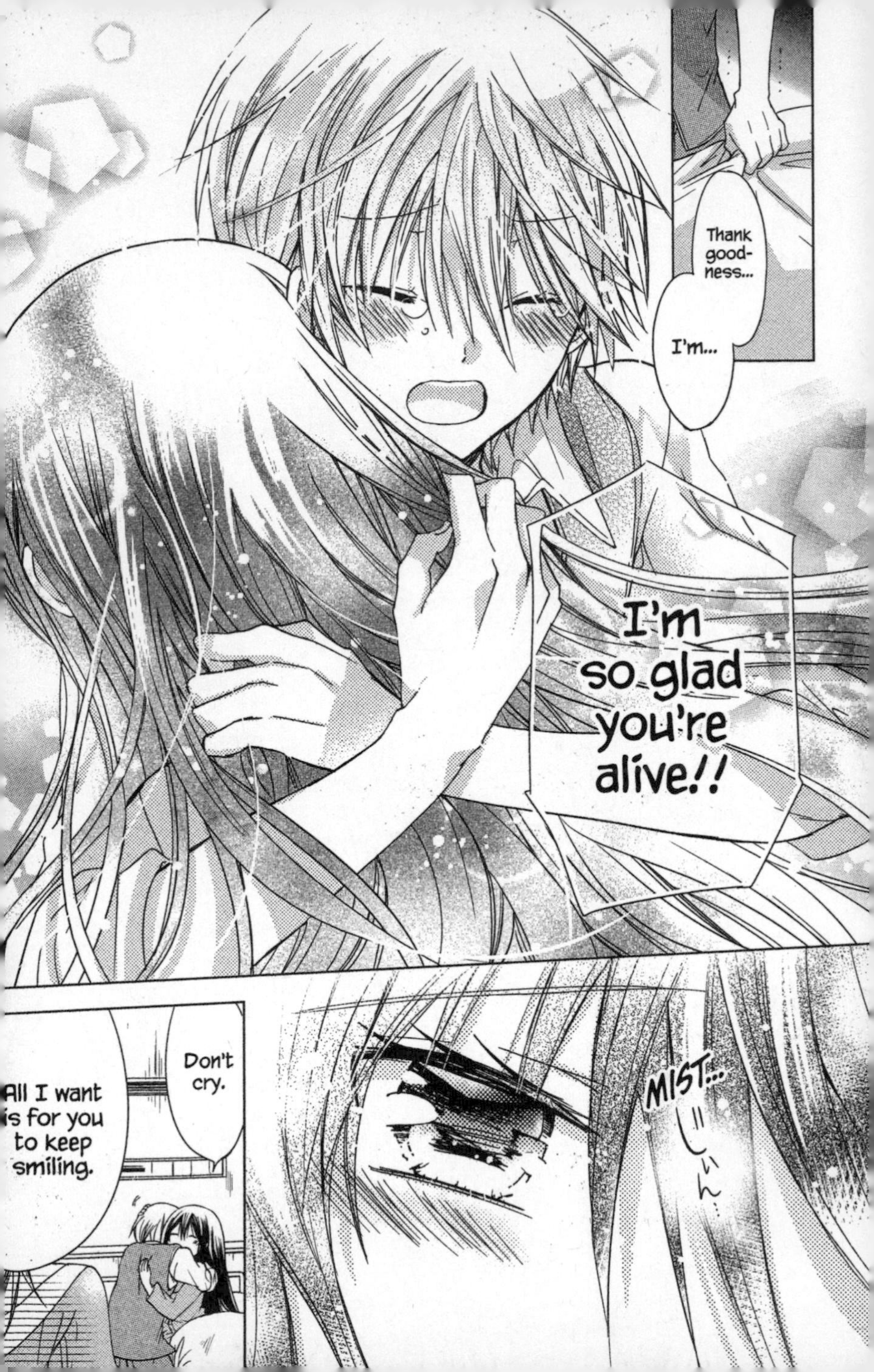
Thank goodness...
I'm...
I'm so glad you're alive!!
MIST...
じいん…
Don't cry.
All I want is for you to keep smiling.

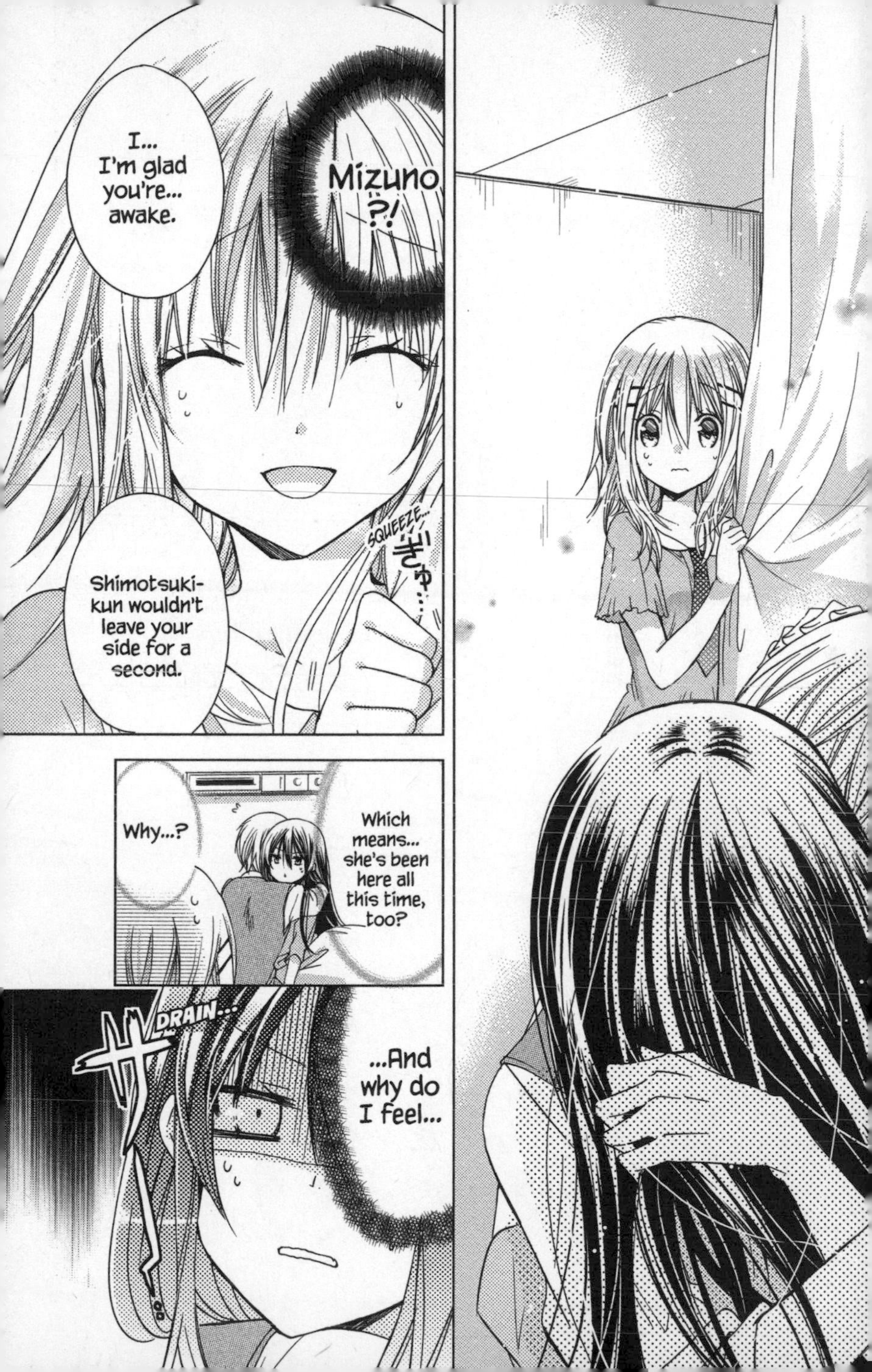
Mizuno ?!
I... I'm glad you're... awake.
SQUEEZE...
ぎゅ…
Shimotsuki-kun wouldn't leave your side for a second.
Which means... she's been here all this time, too?
Why...?
DRAIN...
...And why do I feel...

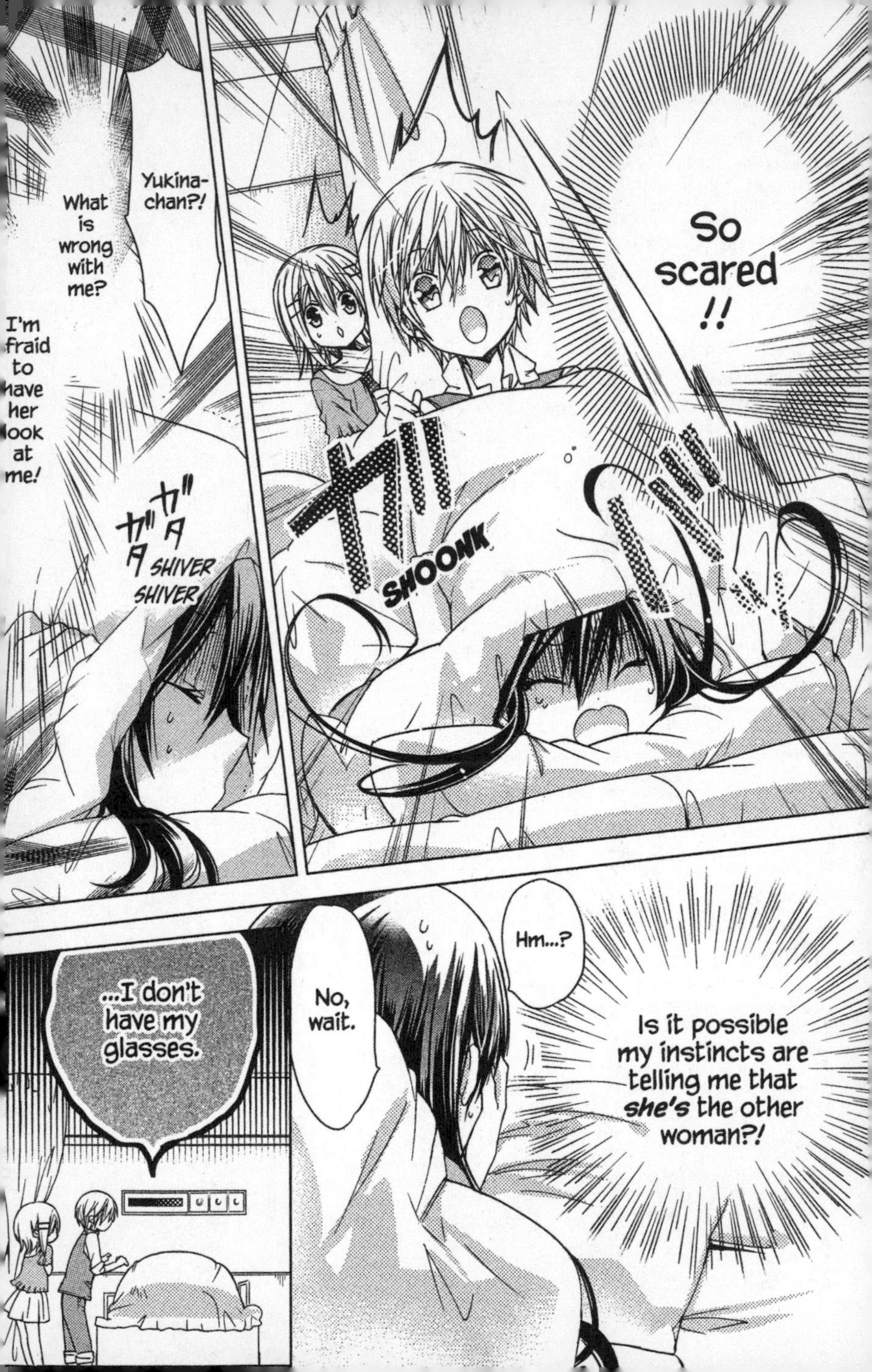
So scared!!
SHOONK
Yukina-chan?!
What is wrong with me?
I'm fraid to ave her ook at me!
SHIVER SHIVER
Hm...?
Is it possible my instincts are telling me that *she's* the other woman?!
No, wait.
...I don't have my glasses.

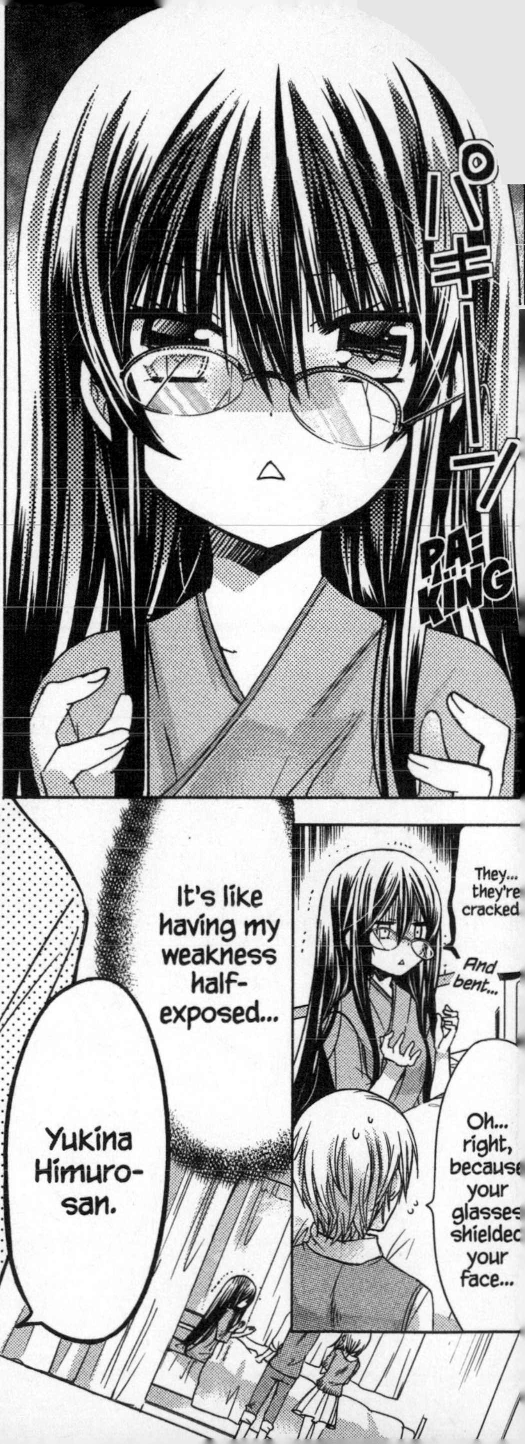
パキーン
PA-KING
They... they're cracked
And bent...
Oh... right, because your glasses shielded your face...
It's like having my weakness half-exposed...
Yukina Himuro-san.

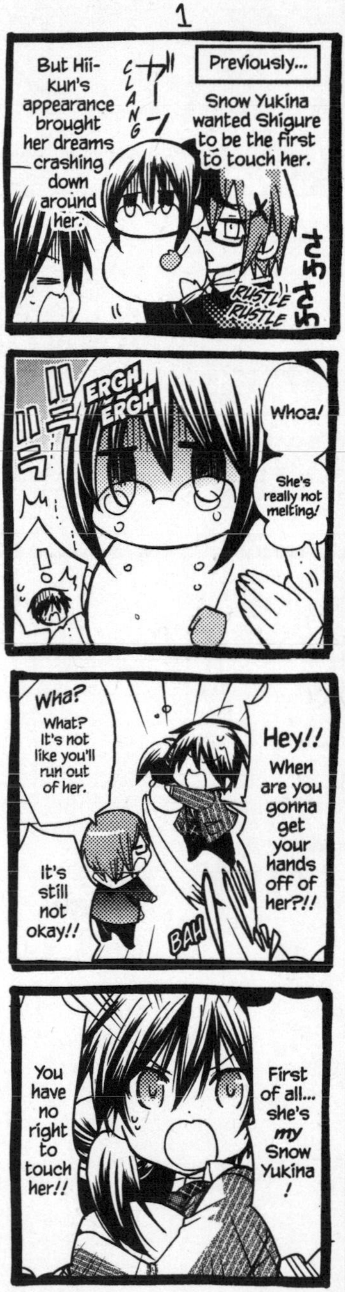
1
Previously...
Snow Yukina wanted Shigure to be the first to touch her.
ガーン
CLANG
But Hii-kun's appearance brought her dreams crashing down around her.
さわさわ
RUSTLE RUSTLE
Whoa!
She's really not melting!
ERGH ERGH
Hey!! When are you gonna get your hands off of her?!!
Wha? What? It's not like you'll run out of her.
It's still not okay!!
BAH
First of all... she's *my* Snow Yukina!
You have no right to touch her!!

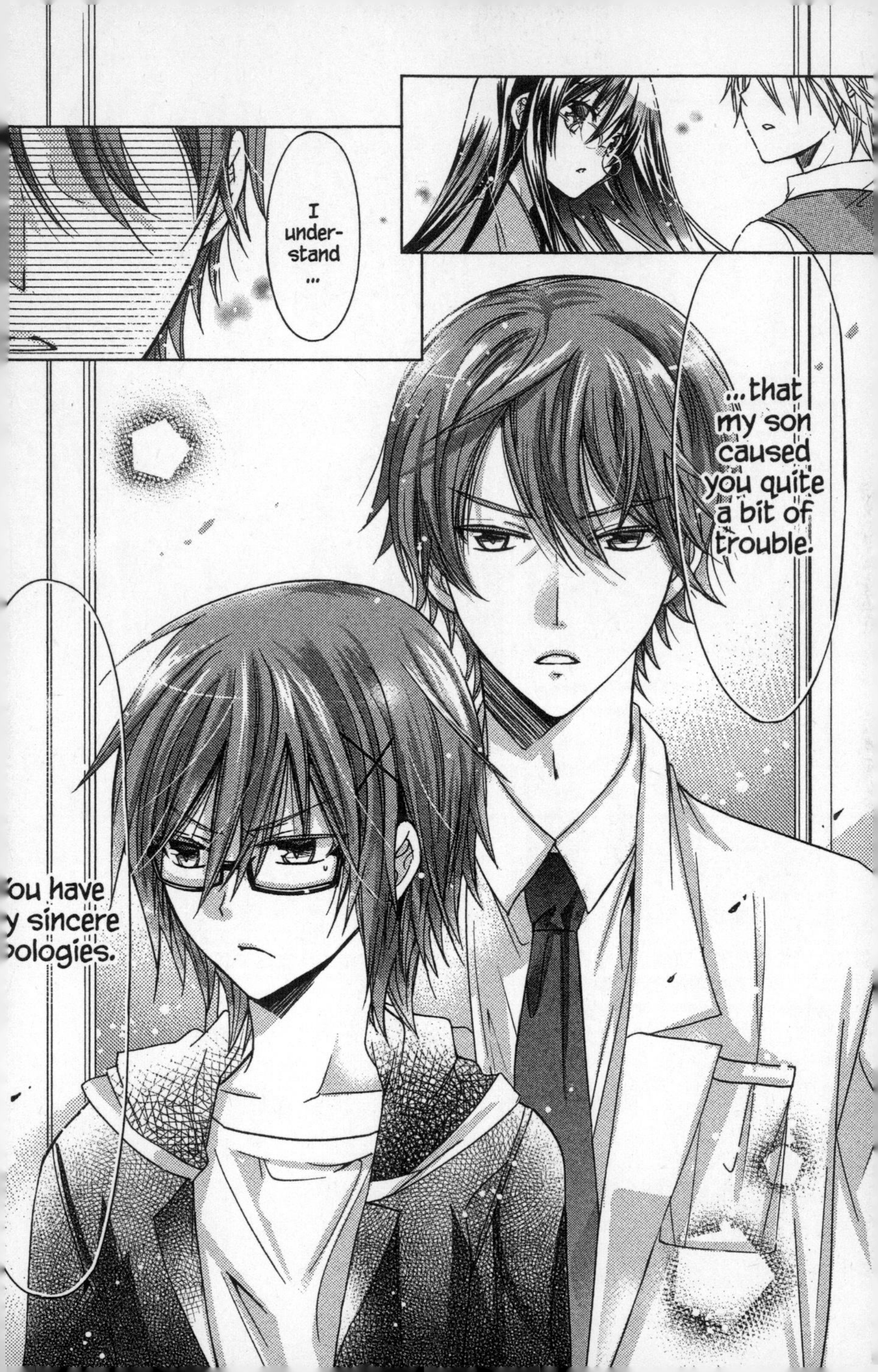
I under-stand ...
...that my son caused you quite a bit of trouble.
ou have y sincere pologies.

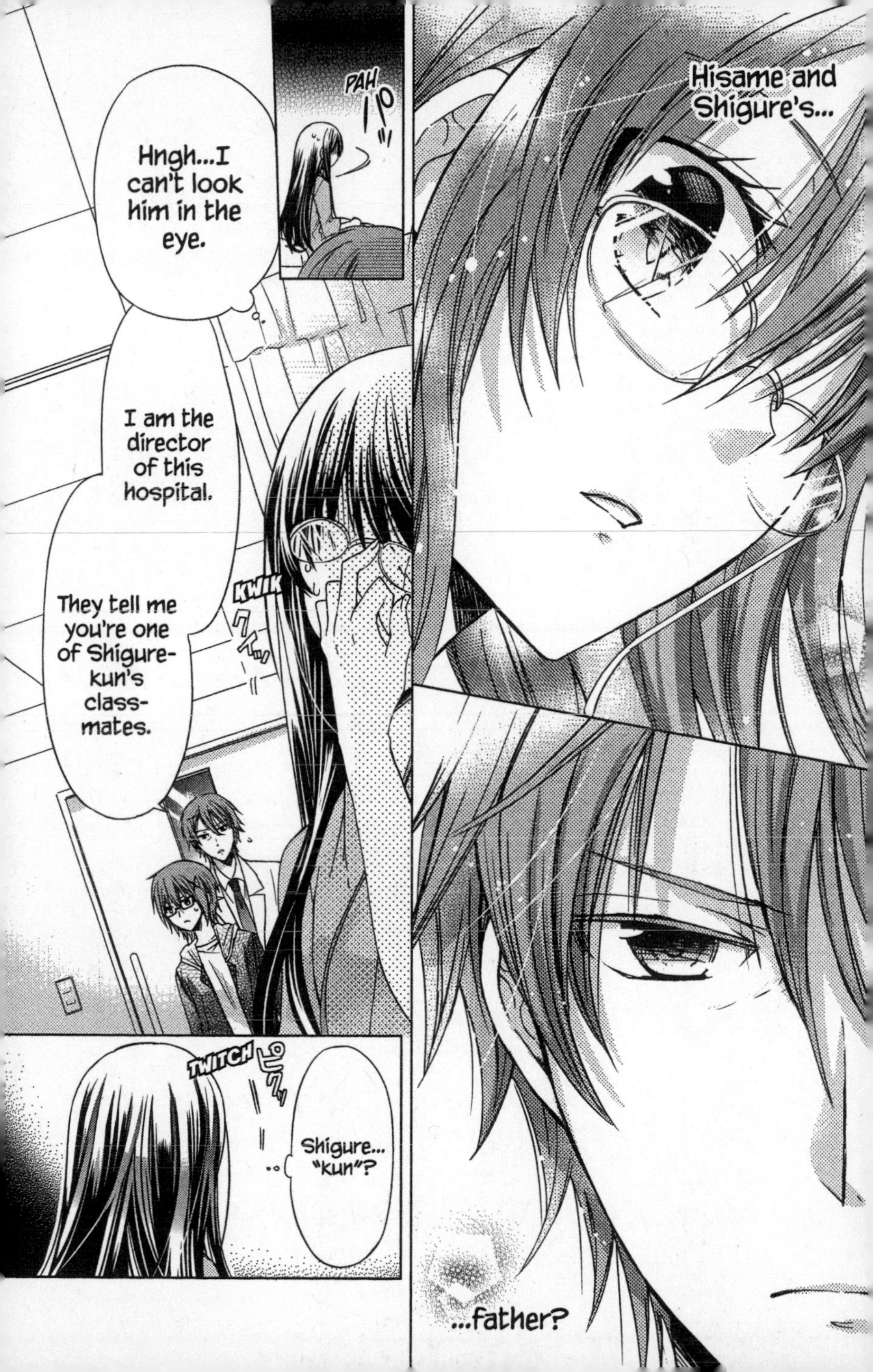
Hisame and Shigure's...
...father?
PAH
Hngh...I can't look him in the eye.
I am the director of this hospital.
KWIK
They tell me you're one of Shigure-kun's classmates.
TWITCH
Shigure... "kun"?

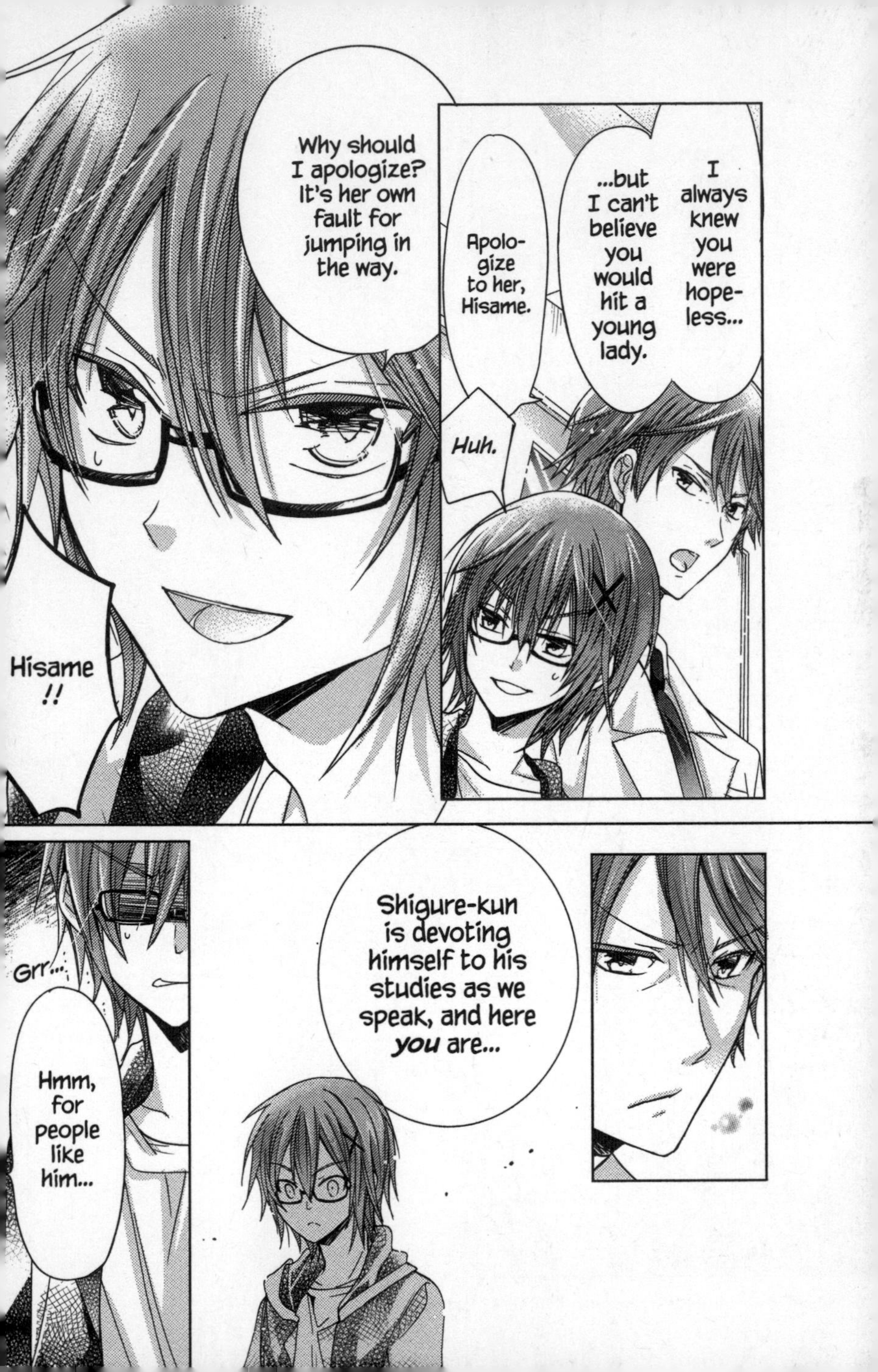
I always knew you were hope-less...
...but I can't believe you would hit a young lady.
Apolo-gize to her, Hisame.
Huh.
Why should I apologize? It's her own fault for jumping in the way.
Hisame !!
Shigure-kun is devoting himself to his studies as we speak, and here *you* are...
Grr...
Hmm, for people like him...

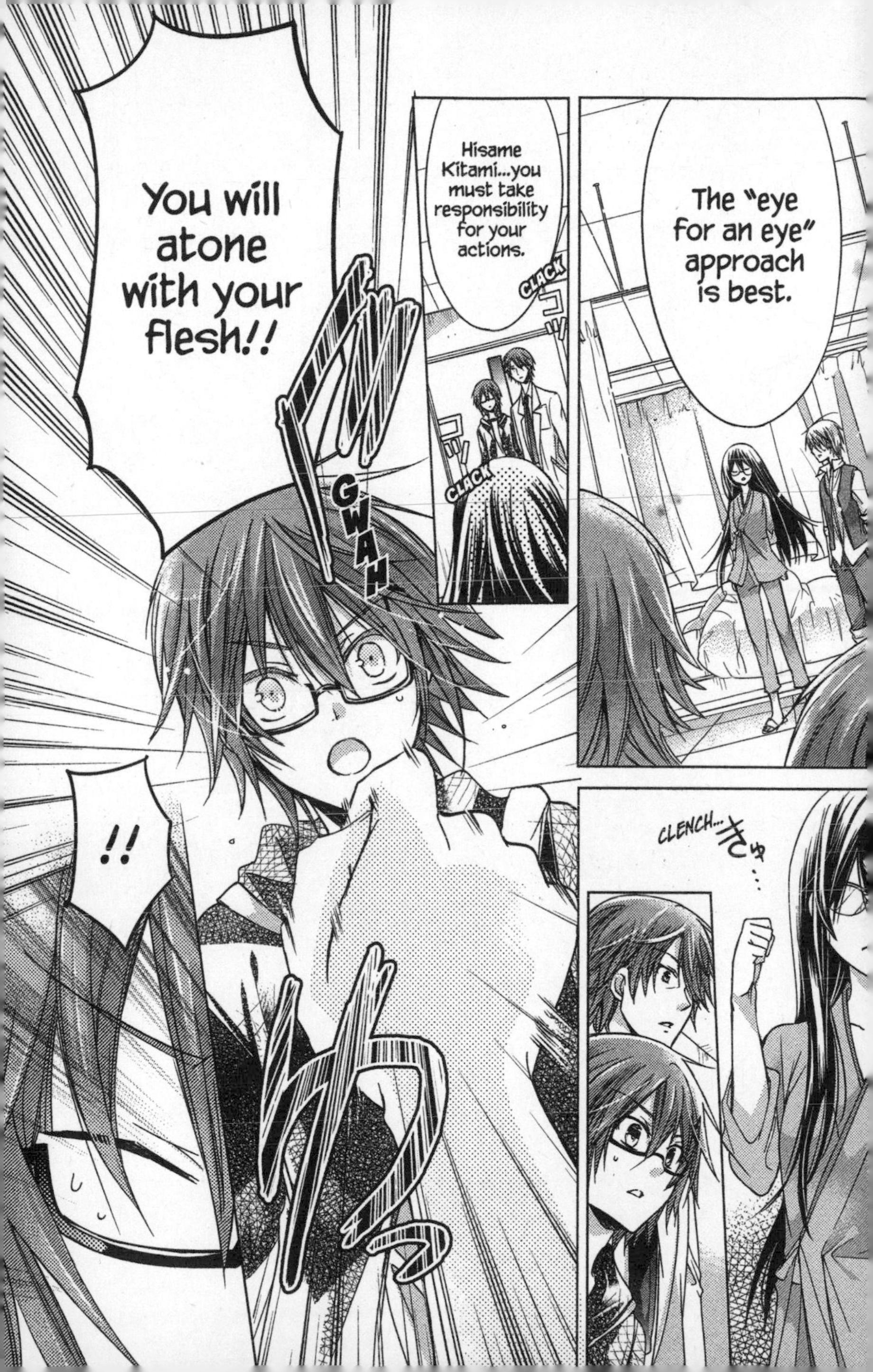
The "eye for an eye" approach is best.
Hisame Kitami...you must take responsibility for your actions.
CLACK
CLACK
CLENCH... きゅ...
You will atone with your flesh!!
GWAH
!!

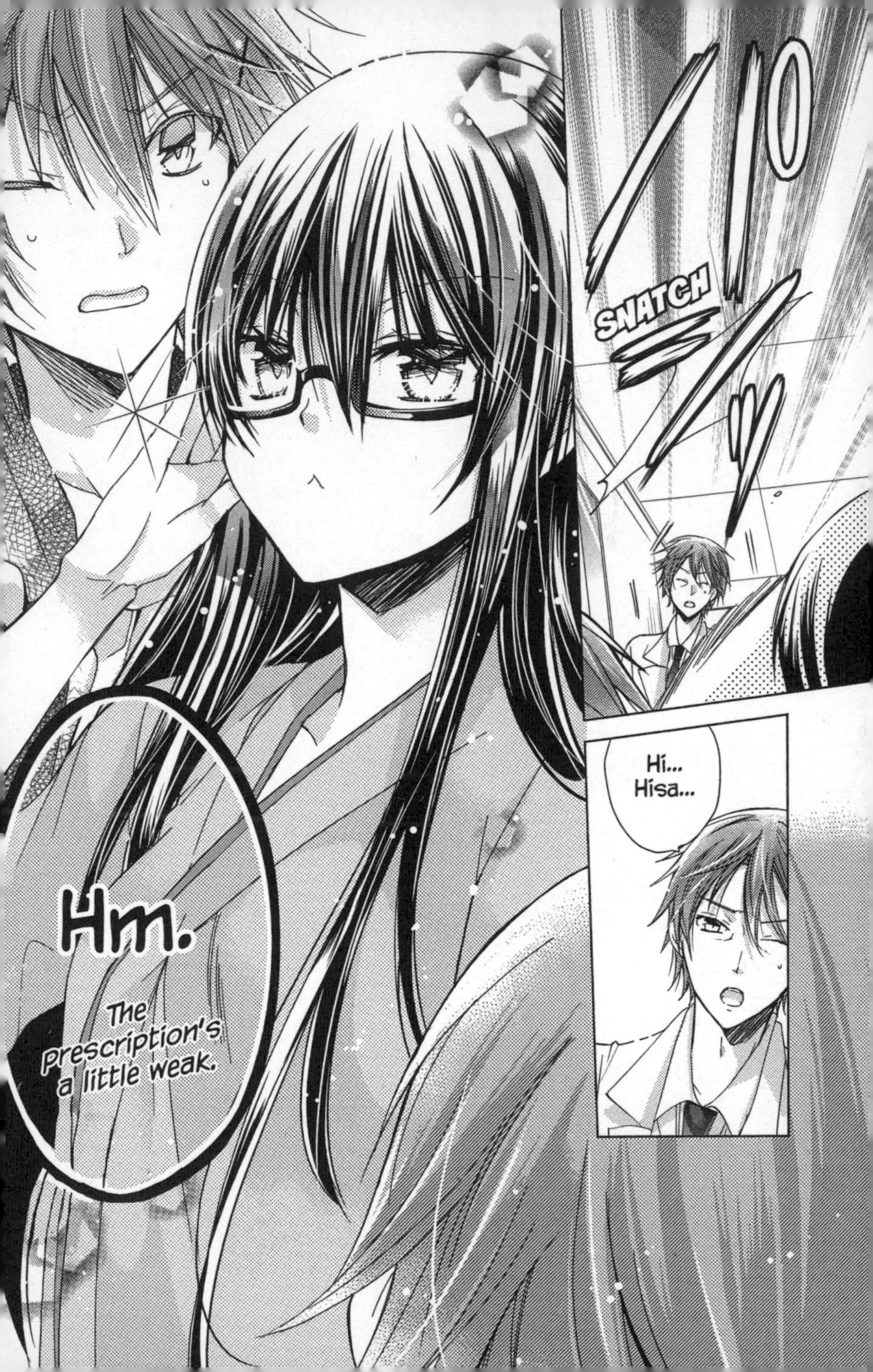
SNATCH
Hi... Hisa...
Hm.
The prescription's a little weak.

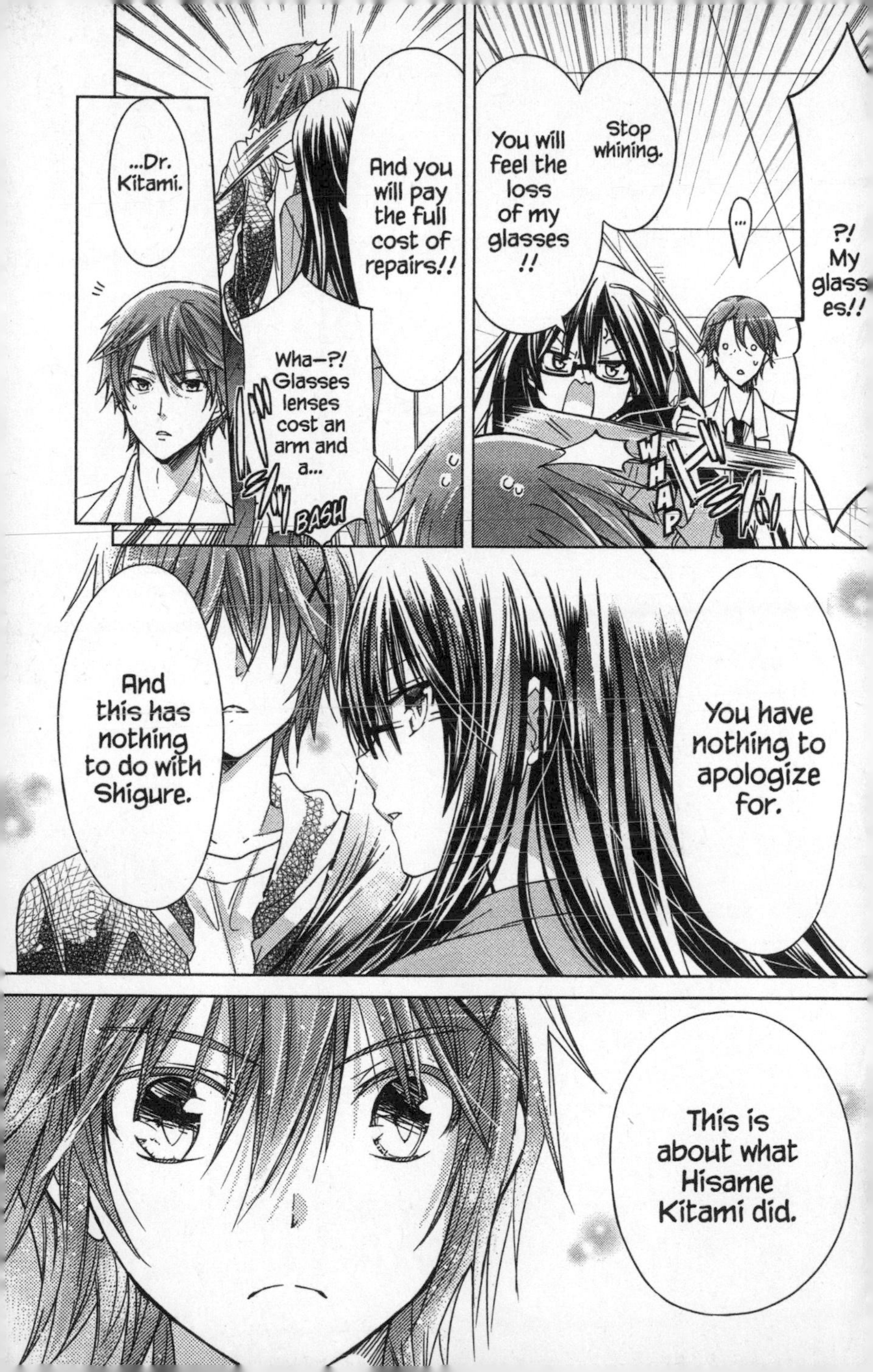
?! My glasses!!
...
Stop whining.
You will feel the loss of my glasses!!
WHAP
And you will pay the full cost of repairs!!
Wha–?! Glasses lenses cost an arm and a...
BASH
...Dr. Kitami.
You have nothing to apologize for.
And this has nothing to do with Shigure.
This is about what Hisame Kitami did.

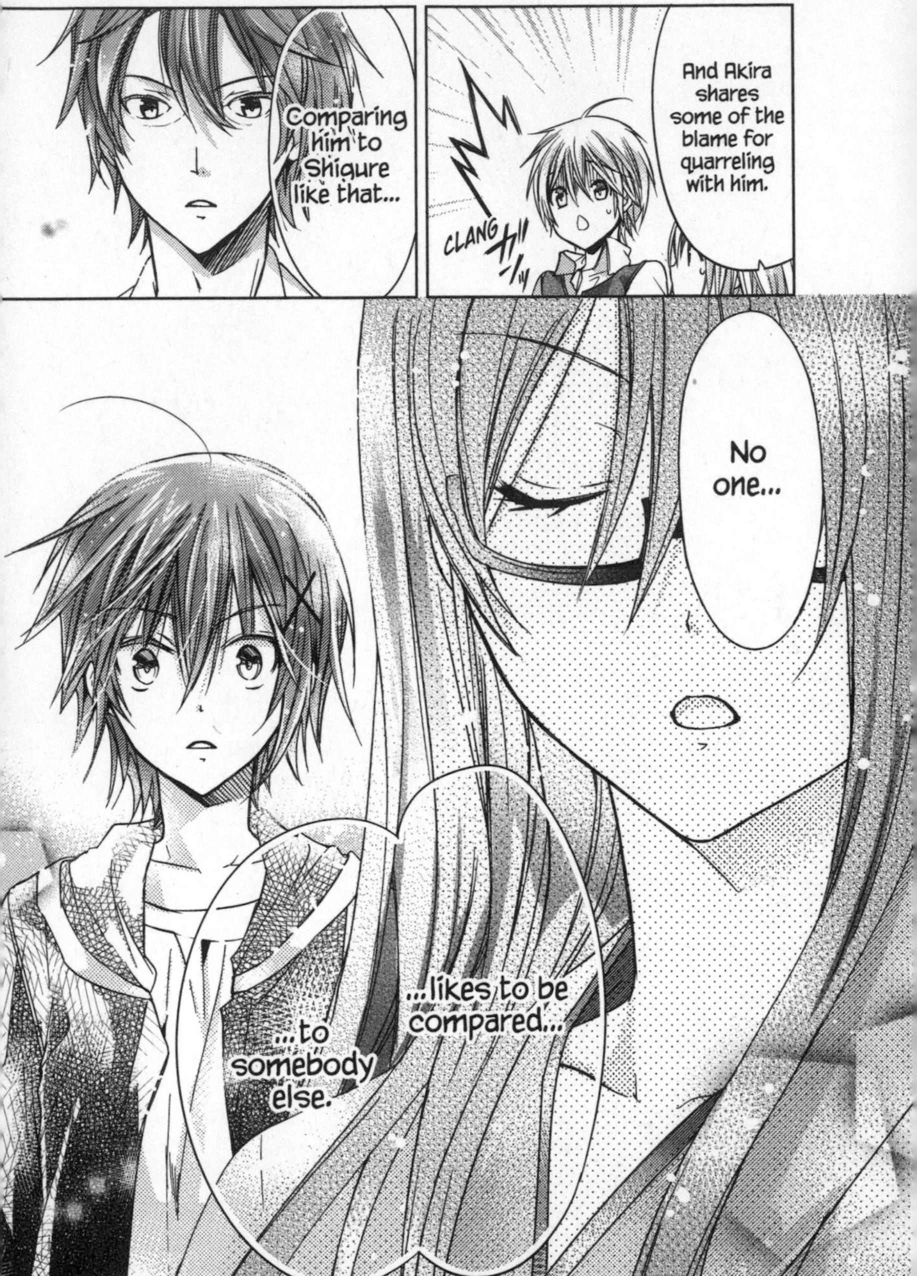
And Akira shares some of the blame for quarreling with him.
CLANG
Comparing him to Shigure like that...
No one...
...likes to be compared...
...to somebody else.

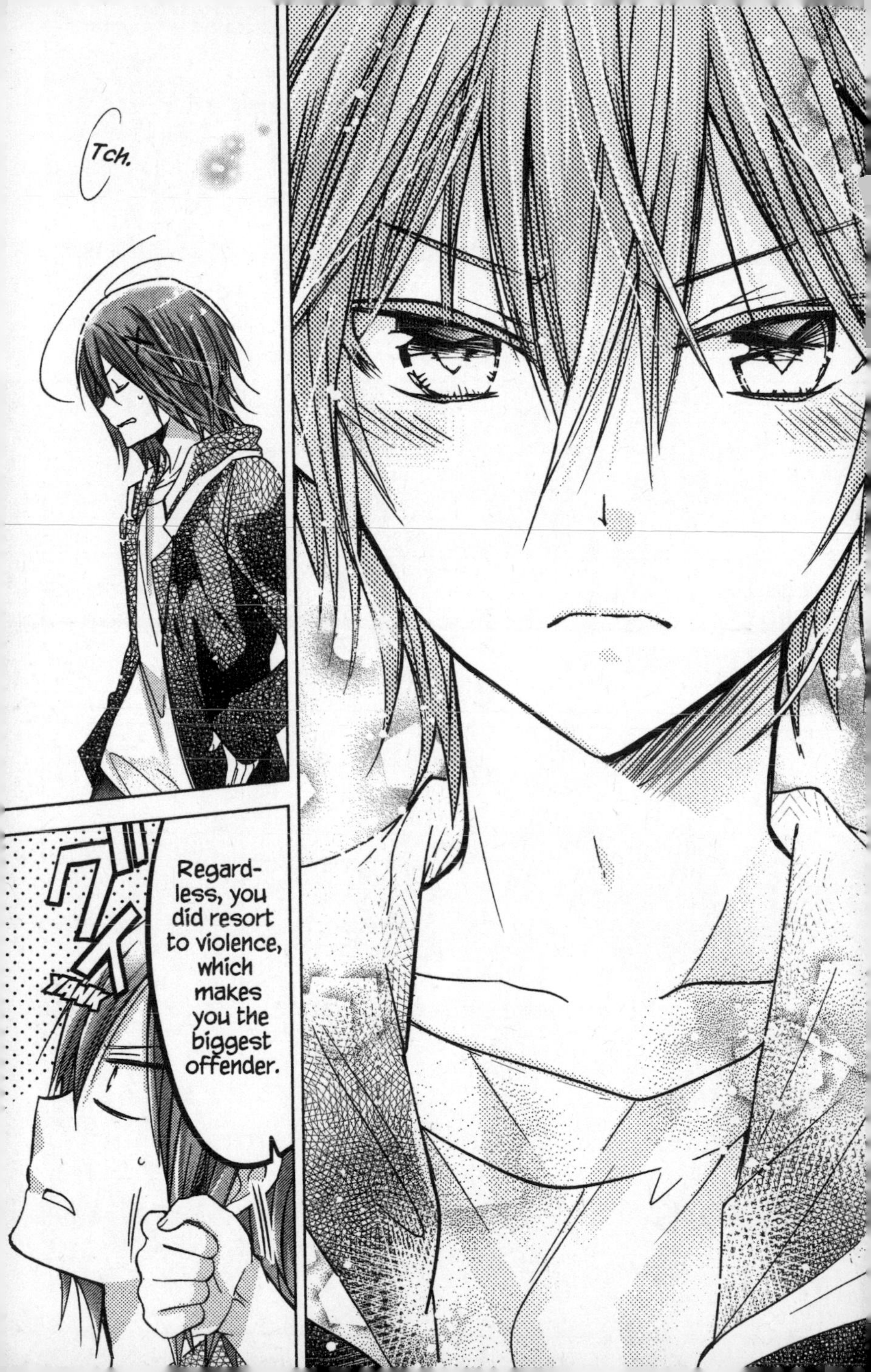
Tch.
Regard-less, you did resort to violence, which makes you the biggest offender.
YANK

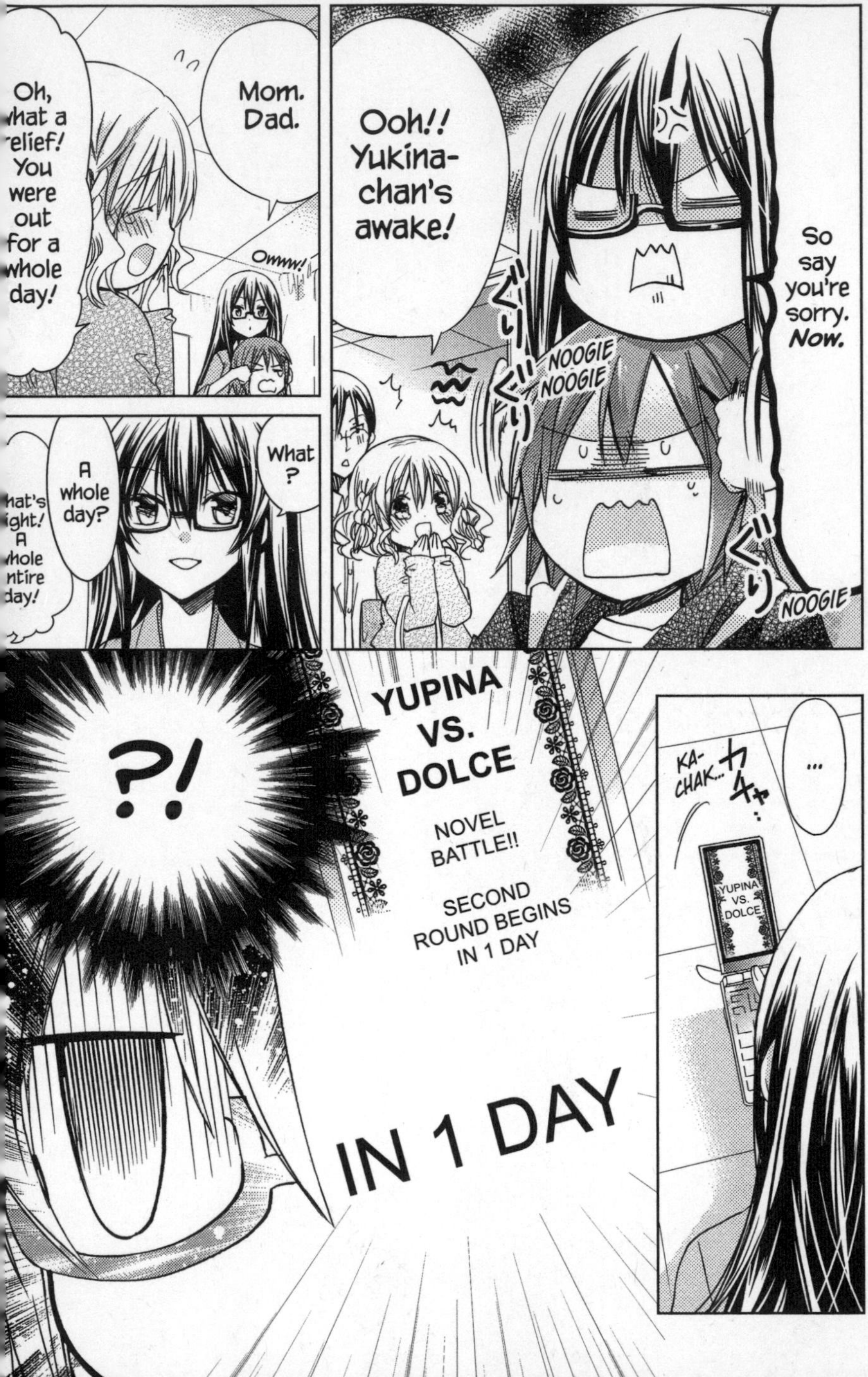
So say you're sorry. Now.
Ooh!! Yukina-chan's awake!
NOOGIE NOOGIE
NOOGIE
Mom. Dad.
Ommm!
Oh, hat a elief! You were out for a hole day!
What ?
A whole day?
hat's ight! A hole ntire day!
...
KA-CHAK...
YUPINA VS. DOLCE
?!
YUPINA VS. DOLCE
NOVEL BATTLE!!
SECOND ROUND BEGINS IN 1 DAY
IN 1 DAY

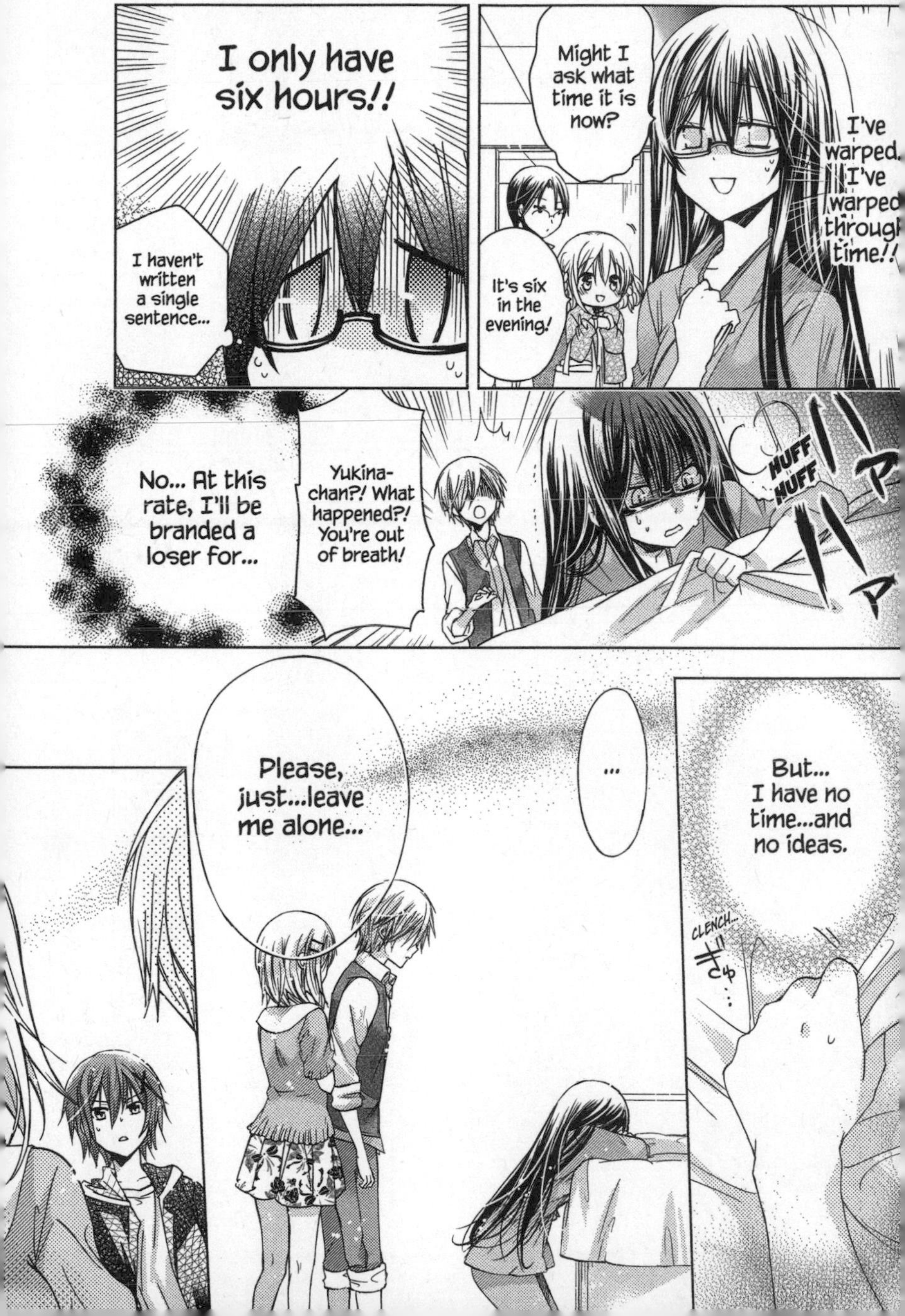
Might I ask what time it is now?
I've warped. I've warped throug time!!
It's six in the evening!
I only have six hours!!
I haven't written a single sentence...
HUFF HUFF
Yukina-chan?! What happened?! You're out of breath!
No... At this rate, I'll be branded a loser for...
But... I have no time...and no ideas.
CLENCH...
...
Please, just...leave me alone...

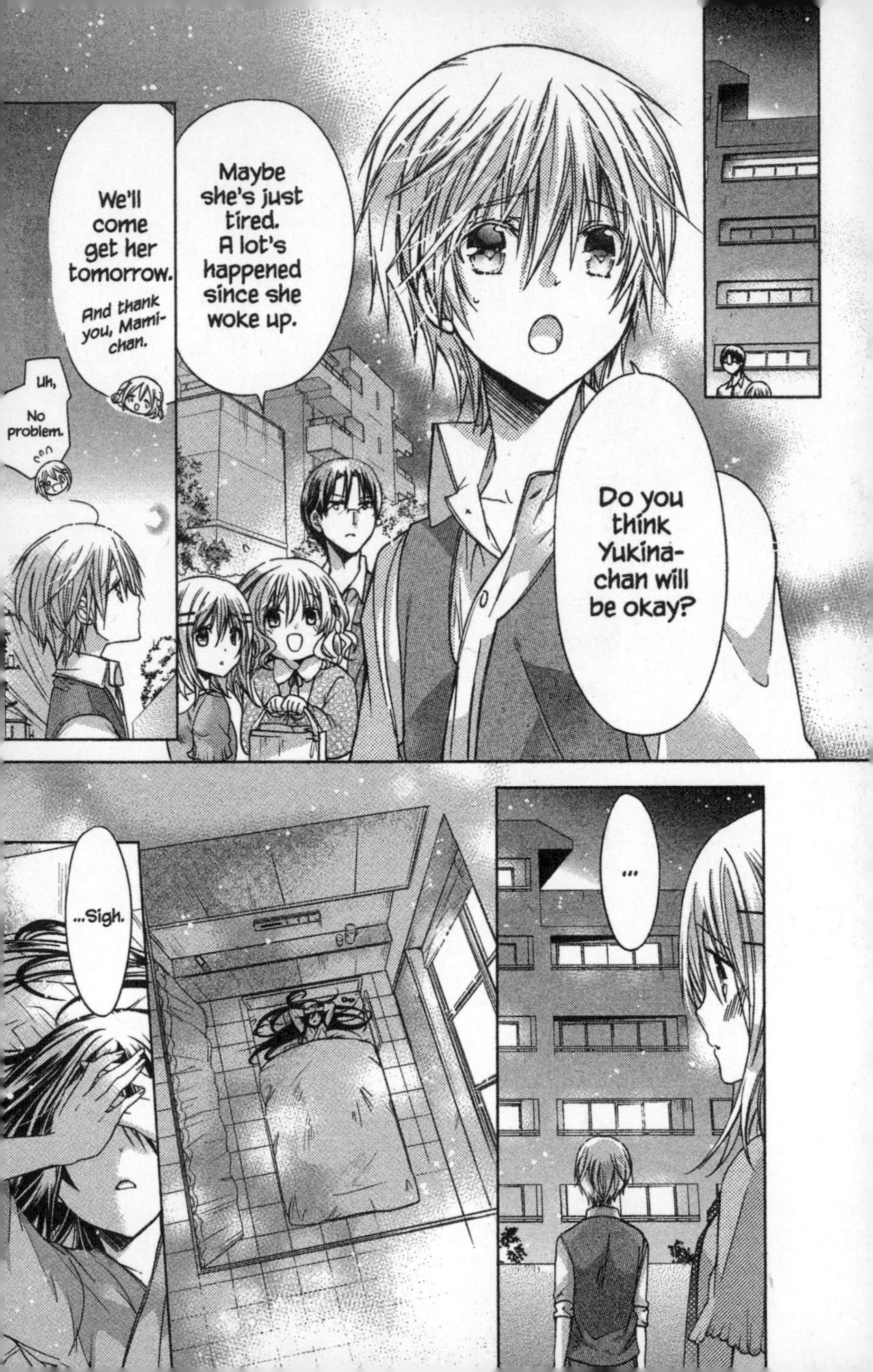
Do you think Yukina-chan will be okay?
Maybe she's just tired. A lot's happened since she woke up.
We'll come get her tomorrow.
And thank you, Mami-chan.
Uh,
No problem.
...
...Sigh.

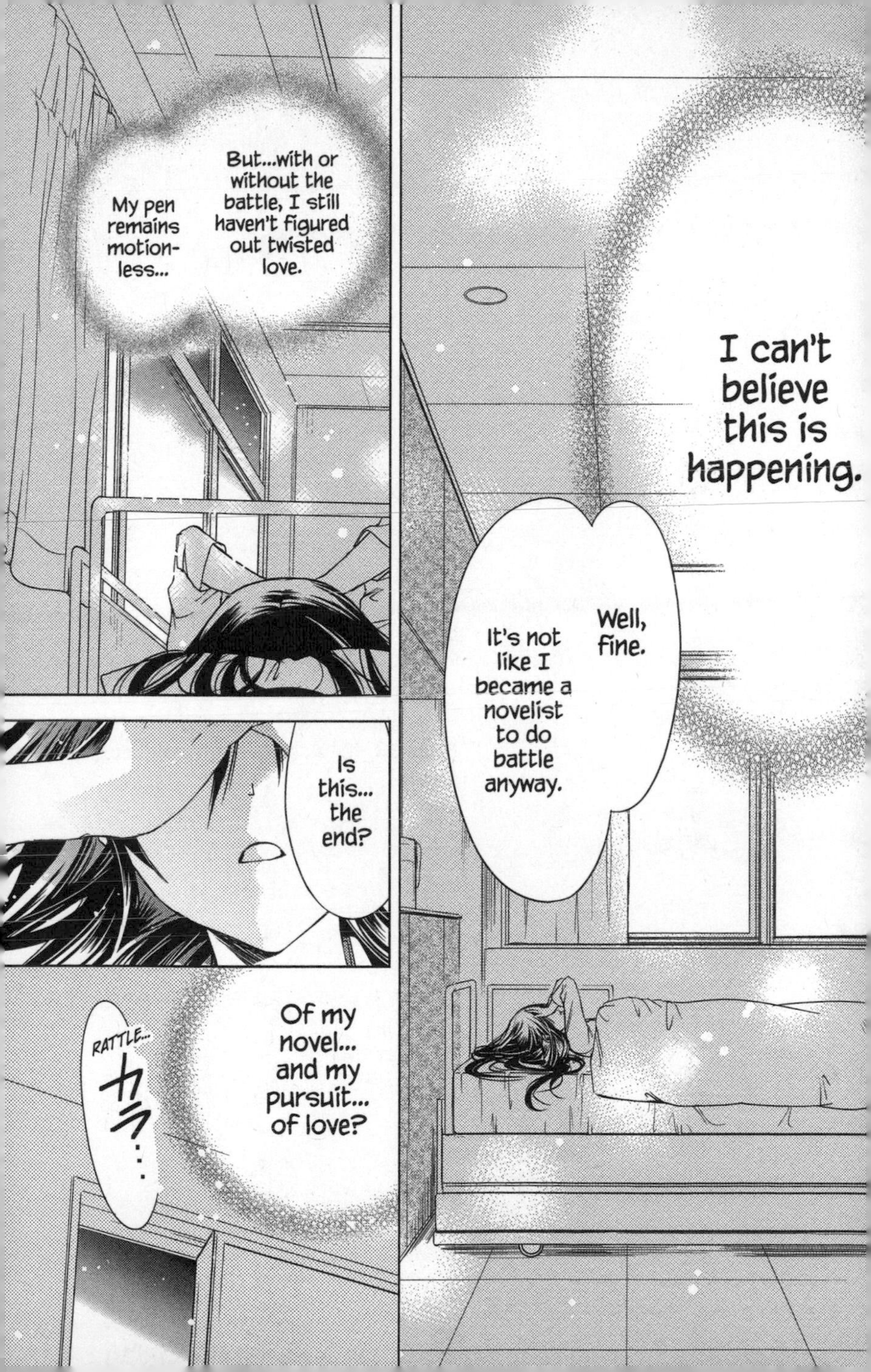
I can't believe this is happening.
Well, fine.
It's not like I became a novelist to do battle anyway.
But...with or without the battle, I still haven't figured out twisted love.
My pen remains motion-less...
Is this... the end?
Of my novel... and my pursuit... of love?
RATTLE...
カラ…

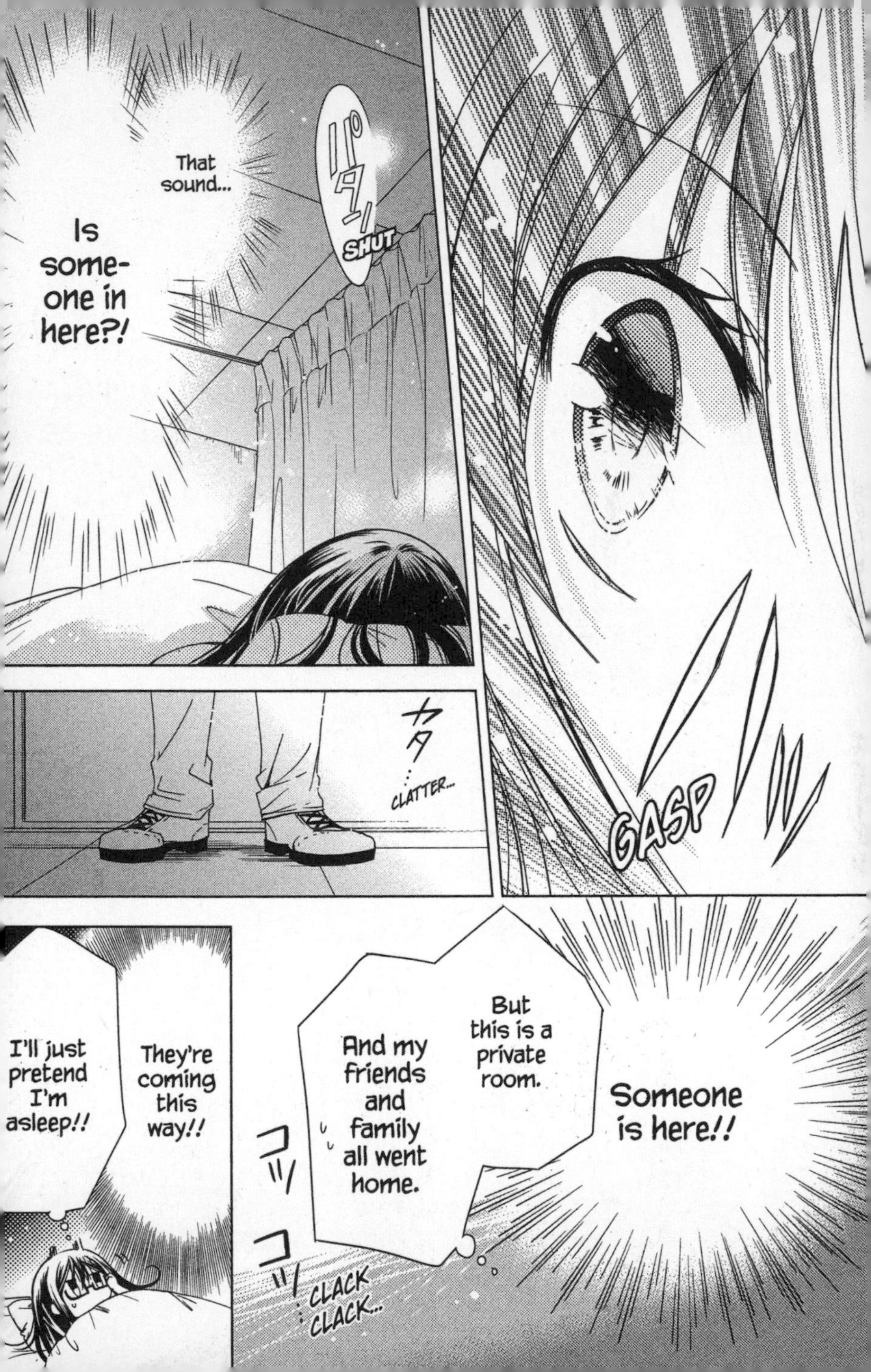
GASP
That sound...
Is someone in here?!
SHUT
CLATTER...
Someone is here!!
But this is a private room.
And my friends and family all went home.
CLACK CLACK...
They're coming this way!!
I'll just pretend I'm asleep!!

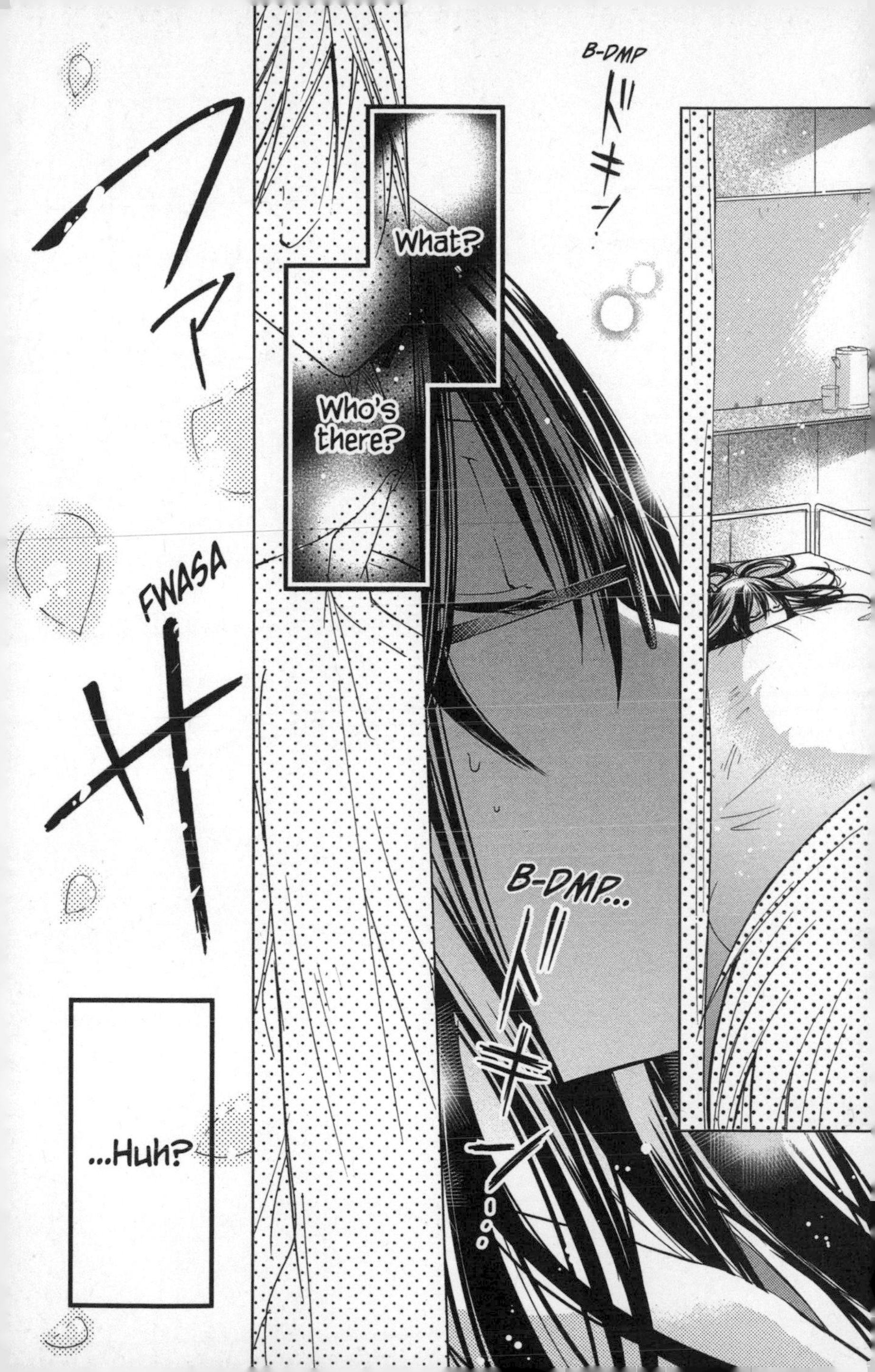
B-DMP
What?
Who's there?
B-DMP...
FWASA
...Huh?

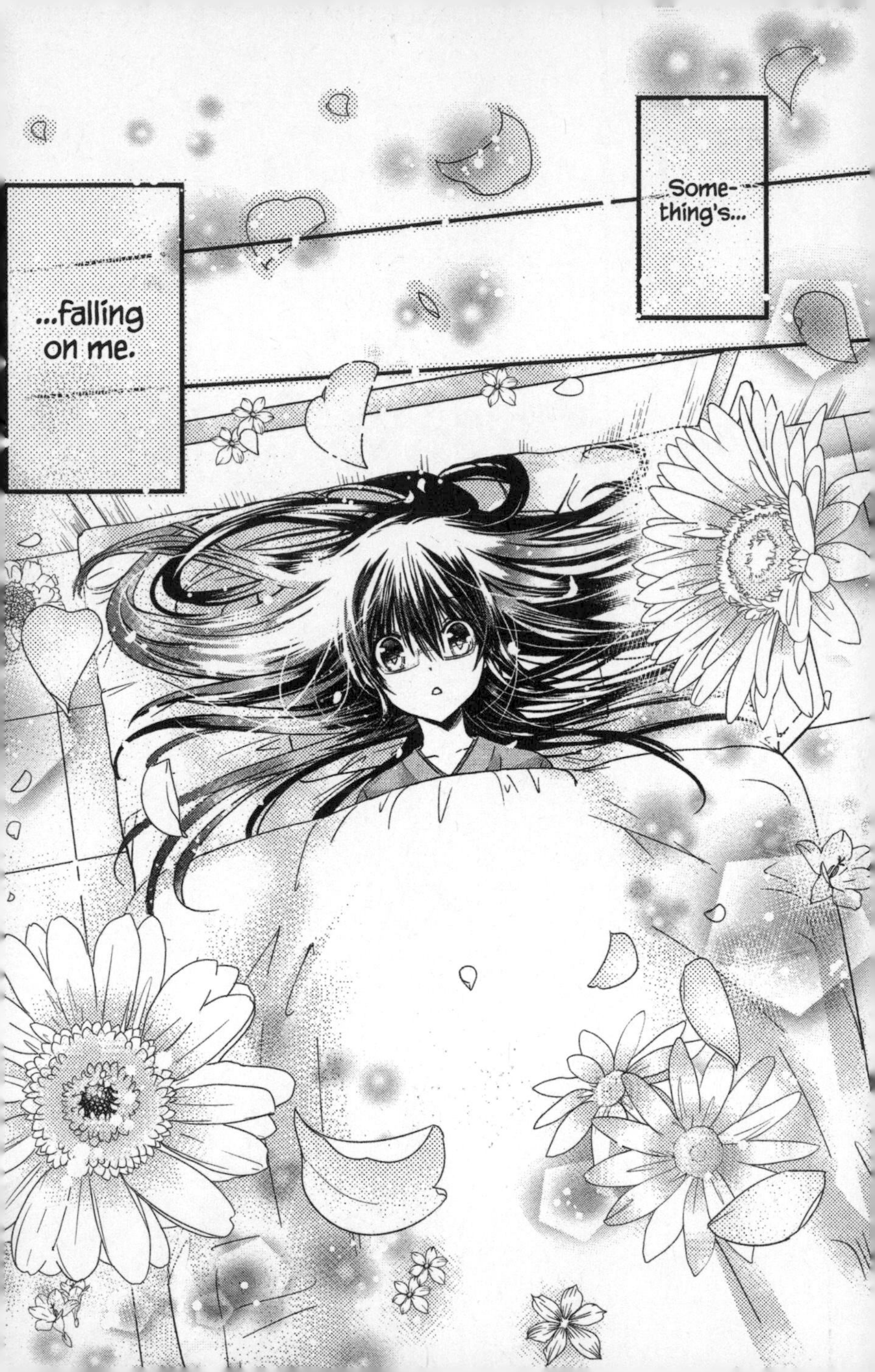
Something's...
...falling on me.

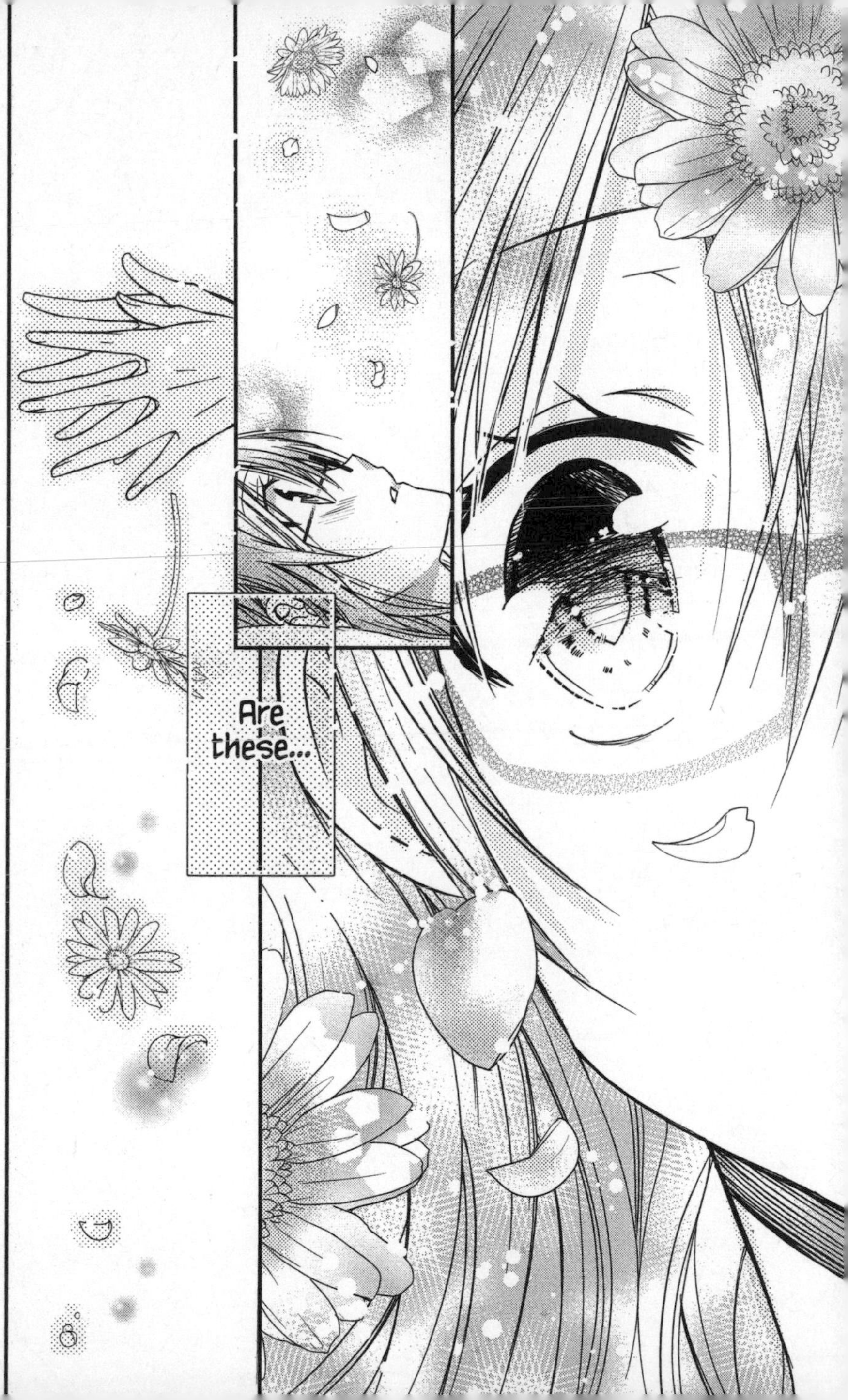
Are these...

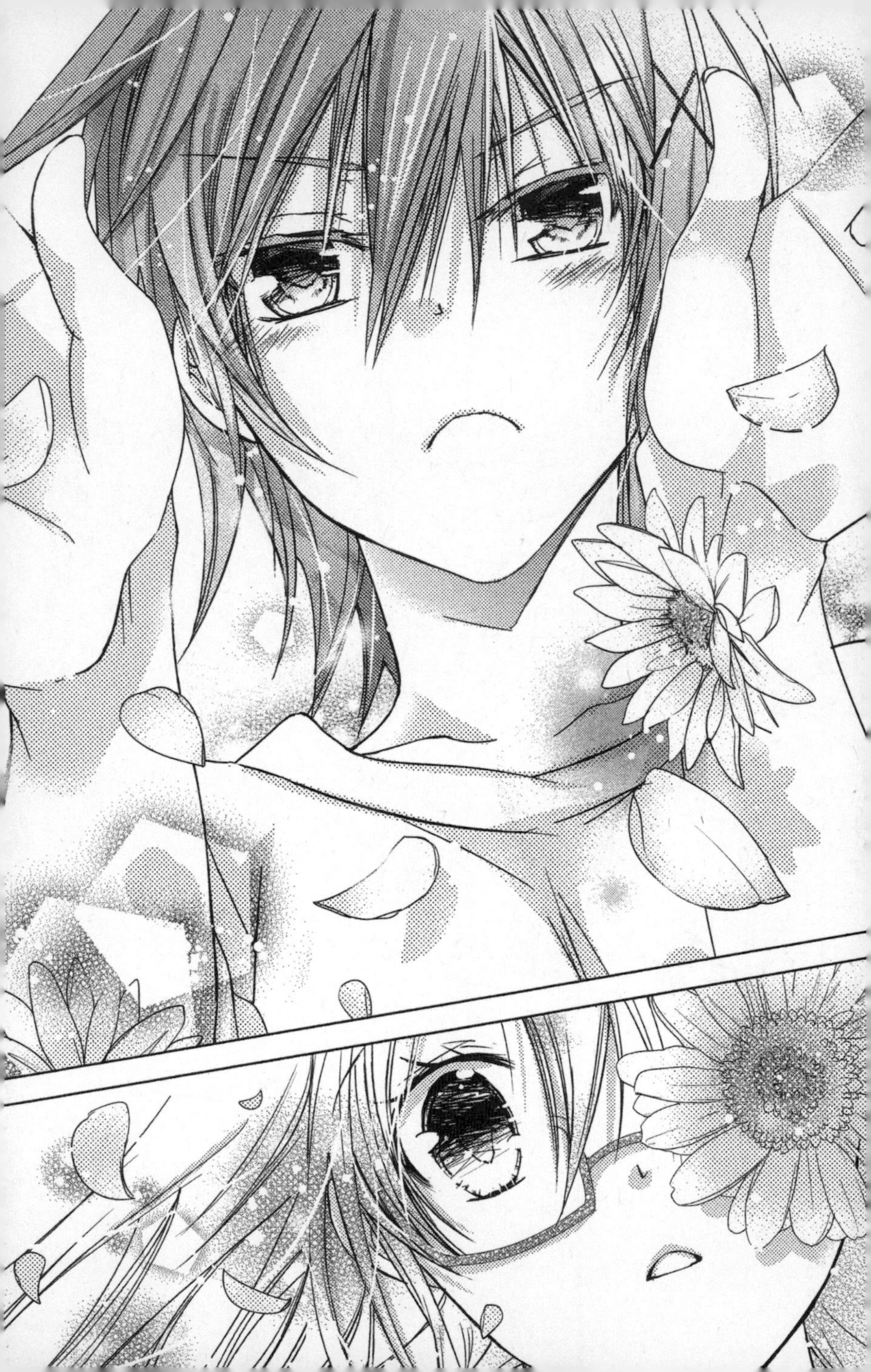

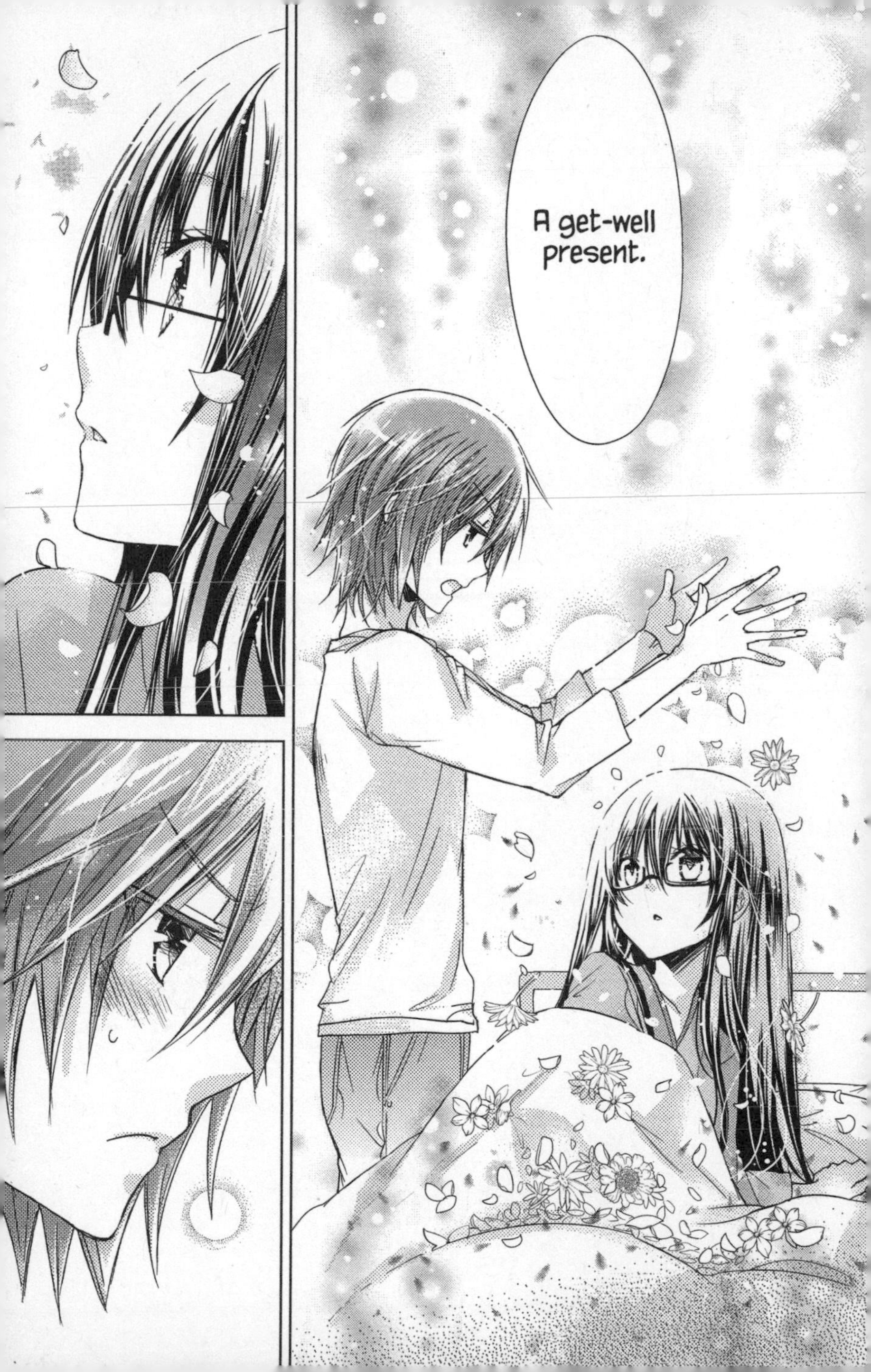
A get-well present.

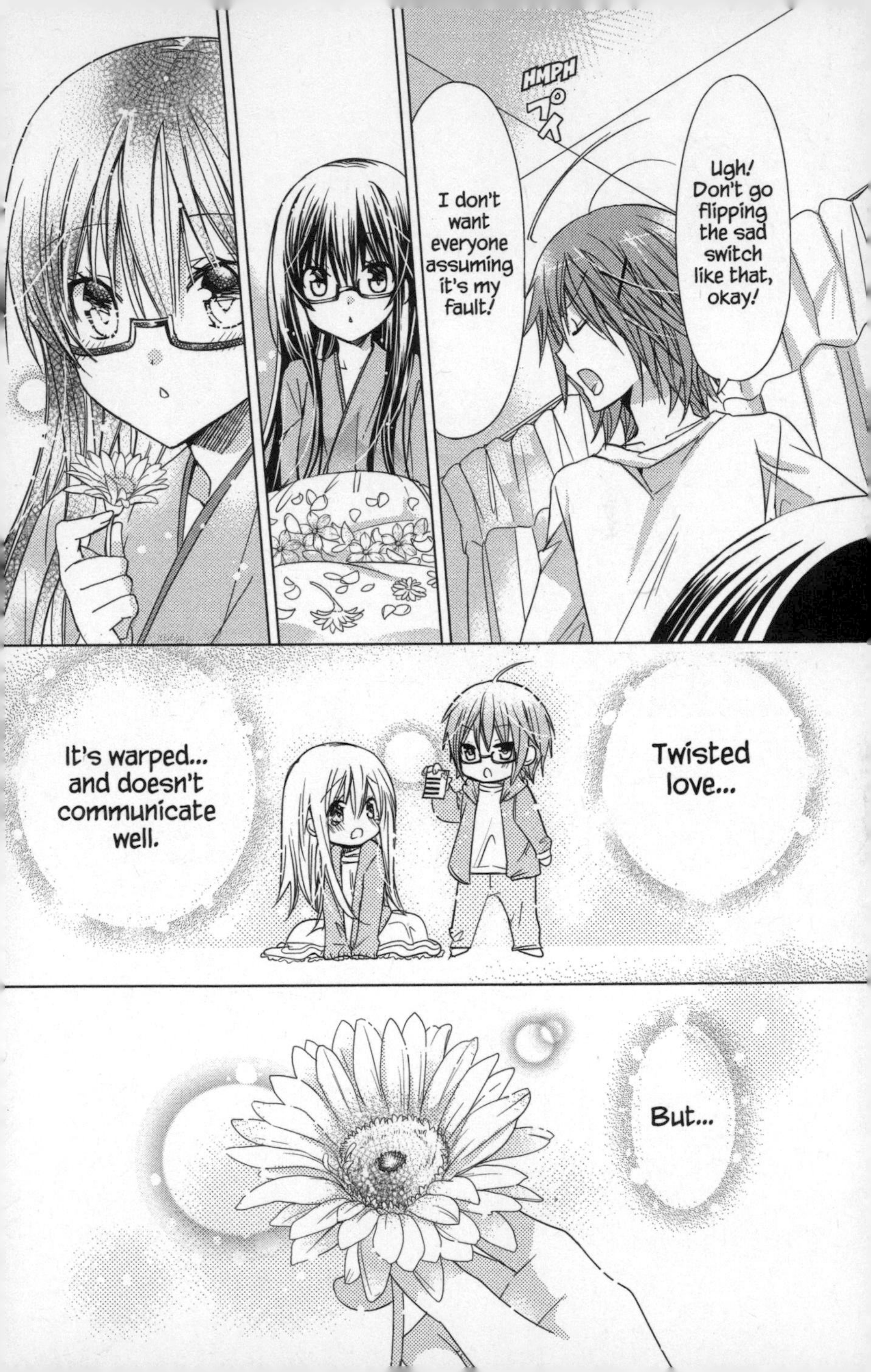
HMPH
プイ
Ugh! Don't go flipping the sad switch like that, okay!
I don't want everyone assuming it's my fault!
Twisted love...
It's warped... and doesn't communicate well.
But...

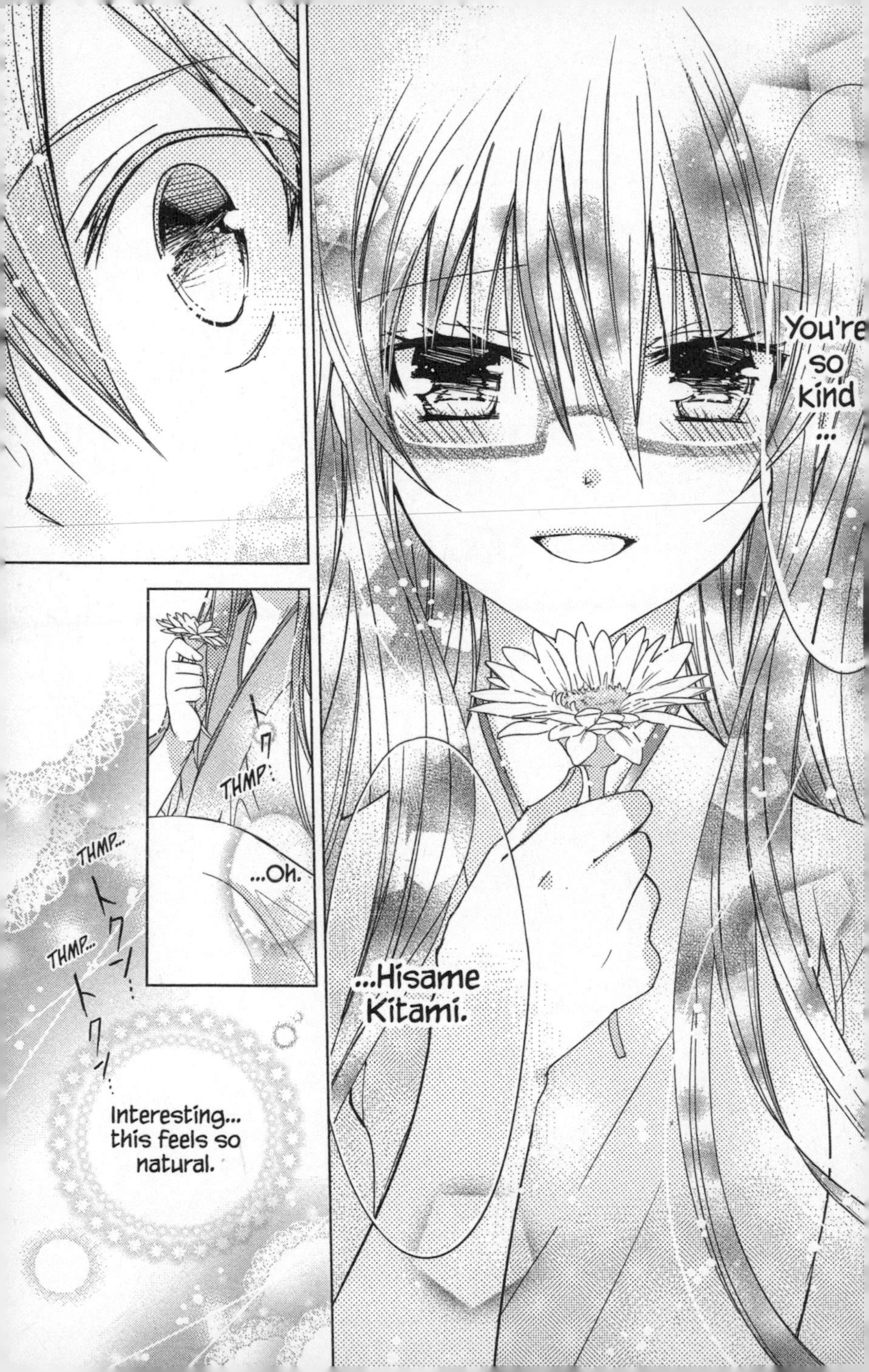
You're so kind ...
...Hisame Kitami.
THMP...
...Oh.
THMP...
THMP...
Interesting... this feels so natural.

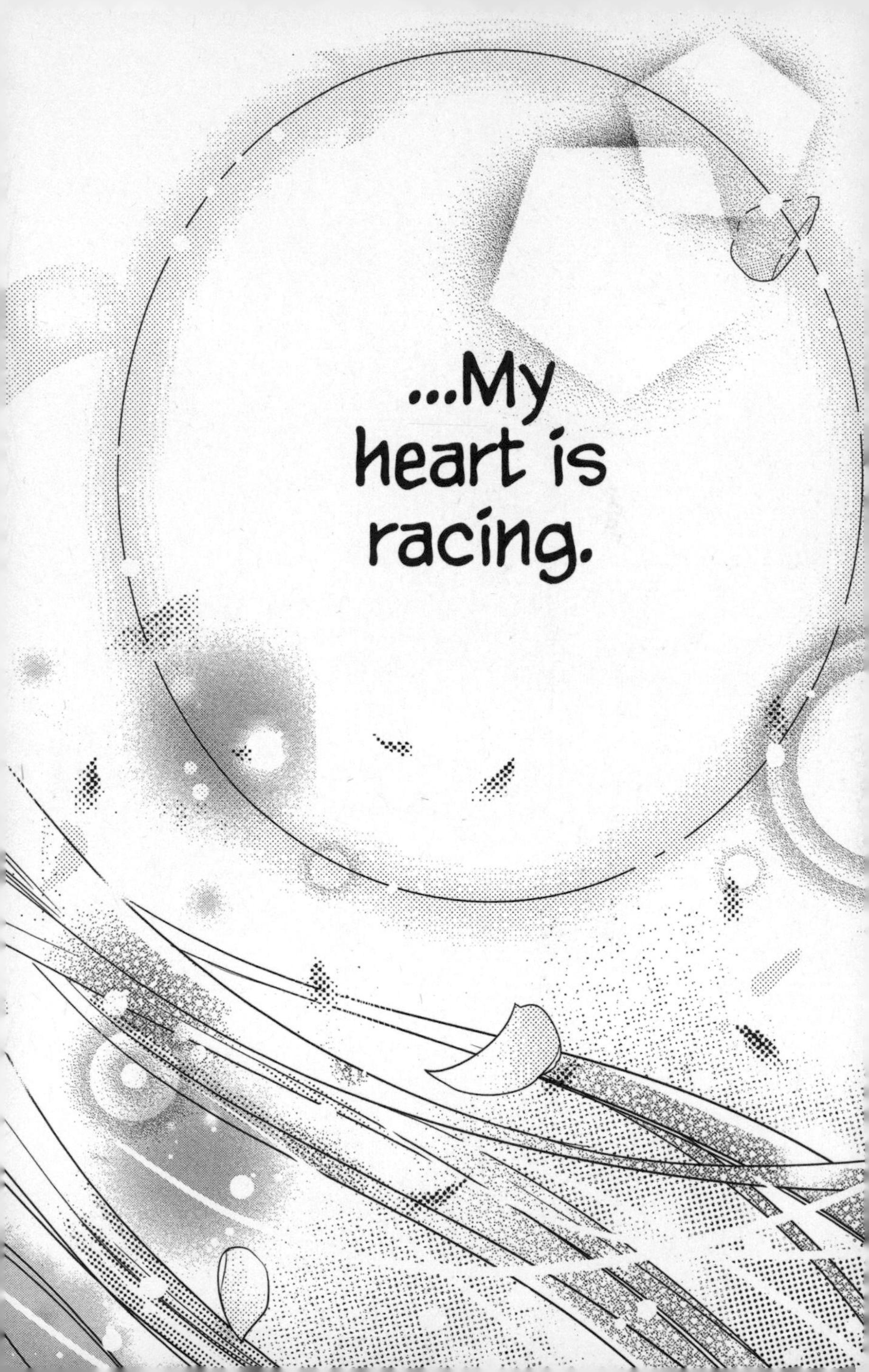
...My heart is racing.

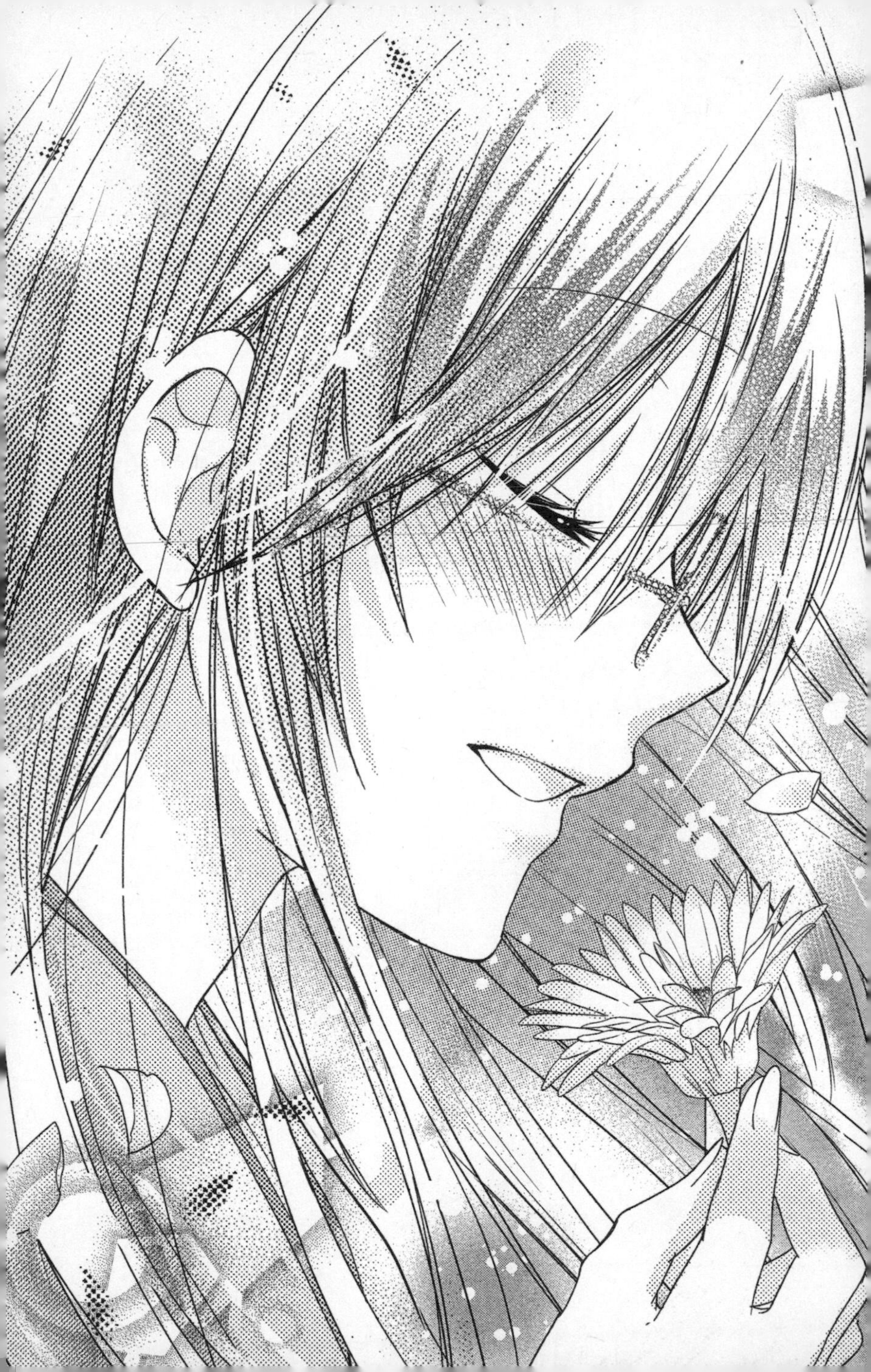

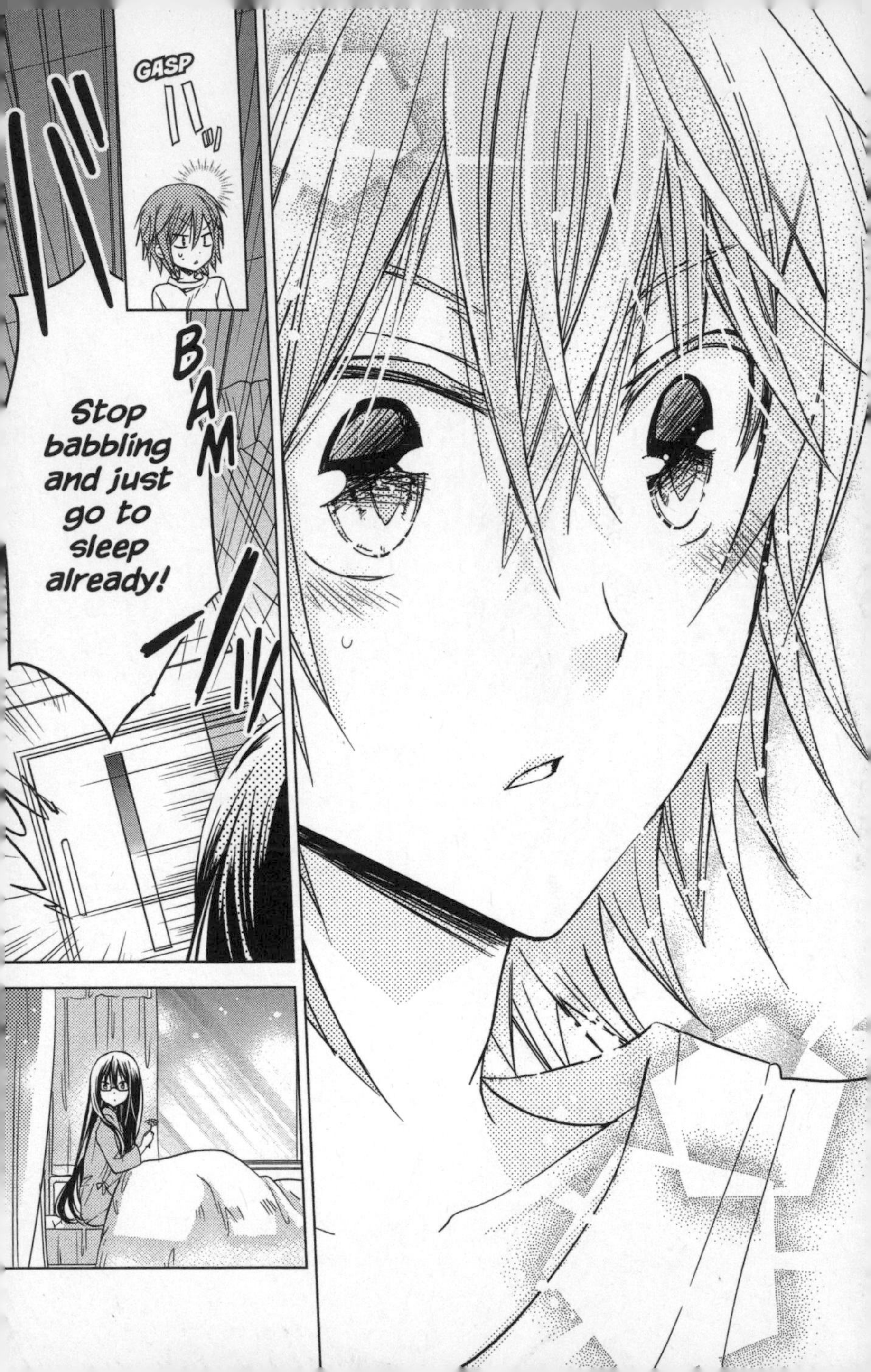
Stop babbling and just go to sleep already!
BAM
GASP

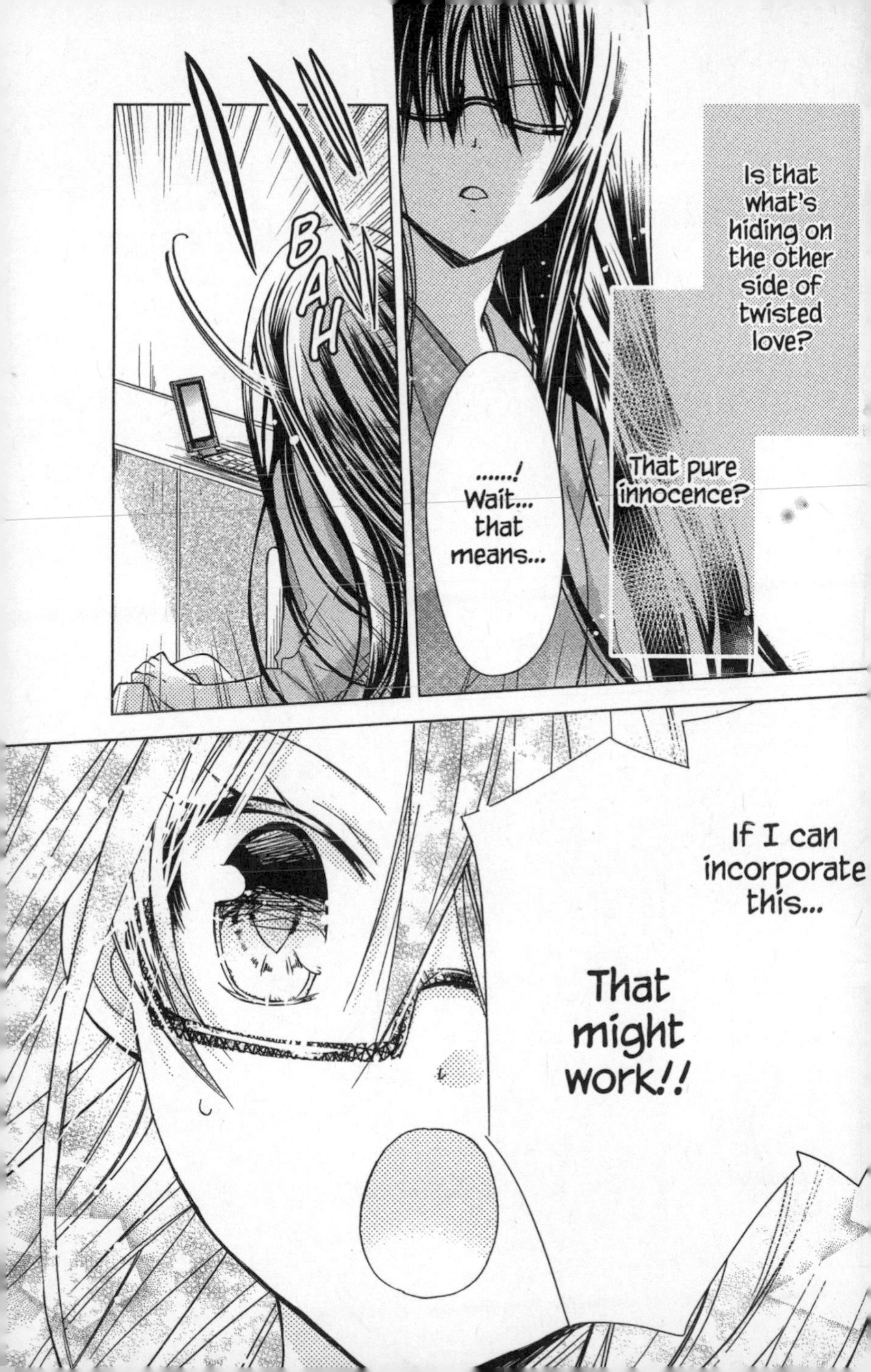
Is that what's hiding on the other side of twisted love?
That pure innocence?
......! Wait... that means...
BAH
If I can incorporate this...
That might work!!

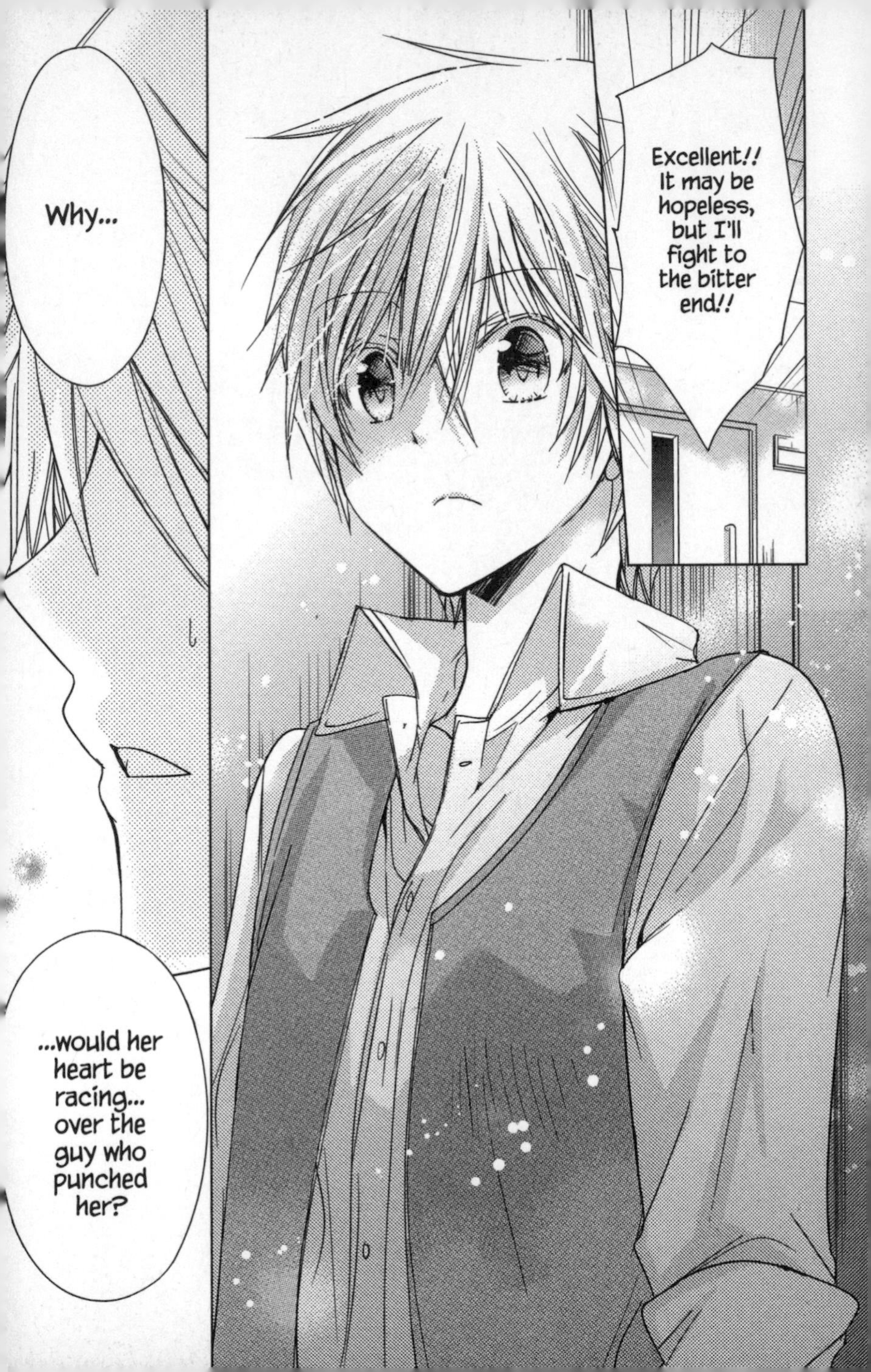
Excellent!! It may be hopeless, but I'll fight to the bitter end!!
Why...
...would her heart be racing... over the guy who punched her?

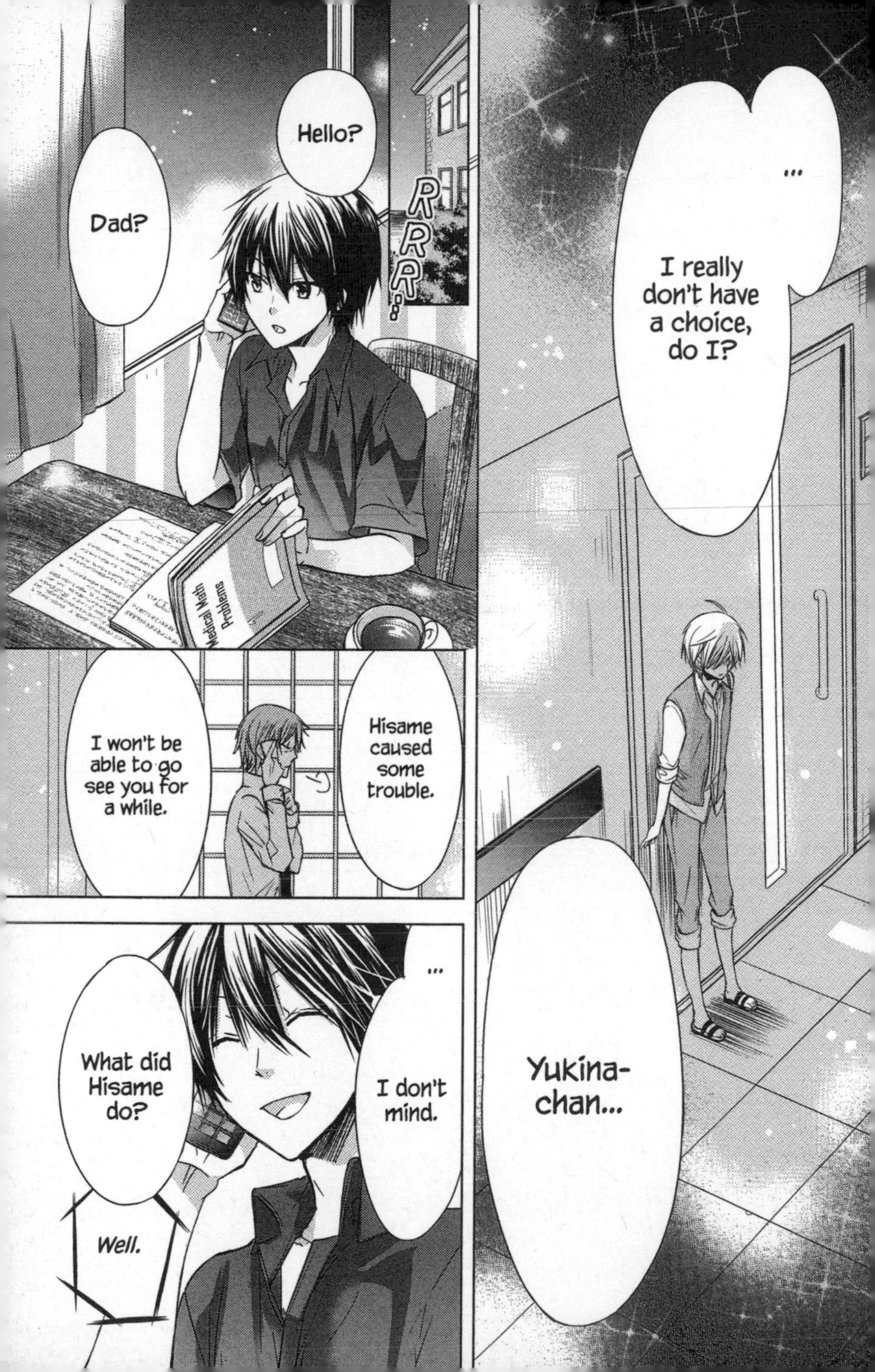
...
I really don't have a choice, do I?
Yukina-chan...
RRR
Hello?
Dad?
Medical Math Problems
Hisame caused some trouble.
I won't be able to go see you for a while.
...
I don't mind.
What did Hisame do?
Well.

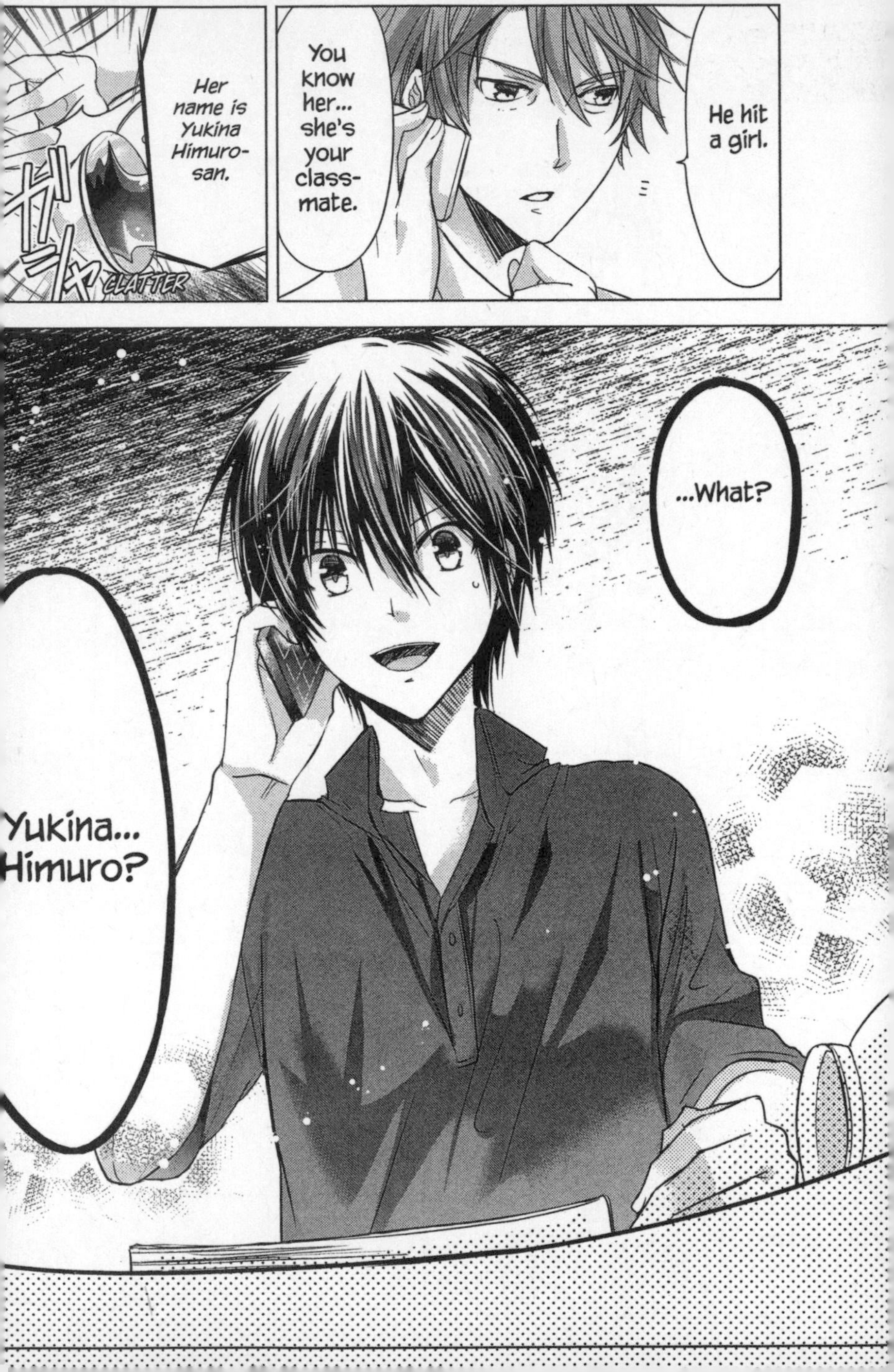
He hit a girl.
You know her... she's your classmate.
Her name is Yukina Himuro-san.
CLATTER
...What?
Yukina... Himuro?

Special Presentation

Graphic Novel Release Countdown Illustrations

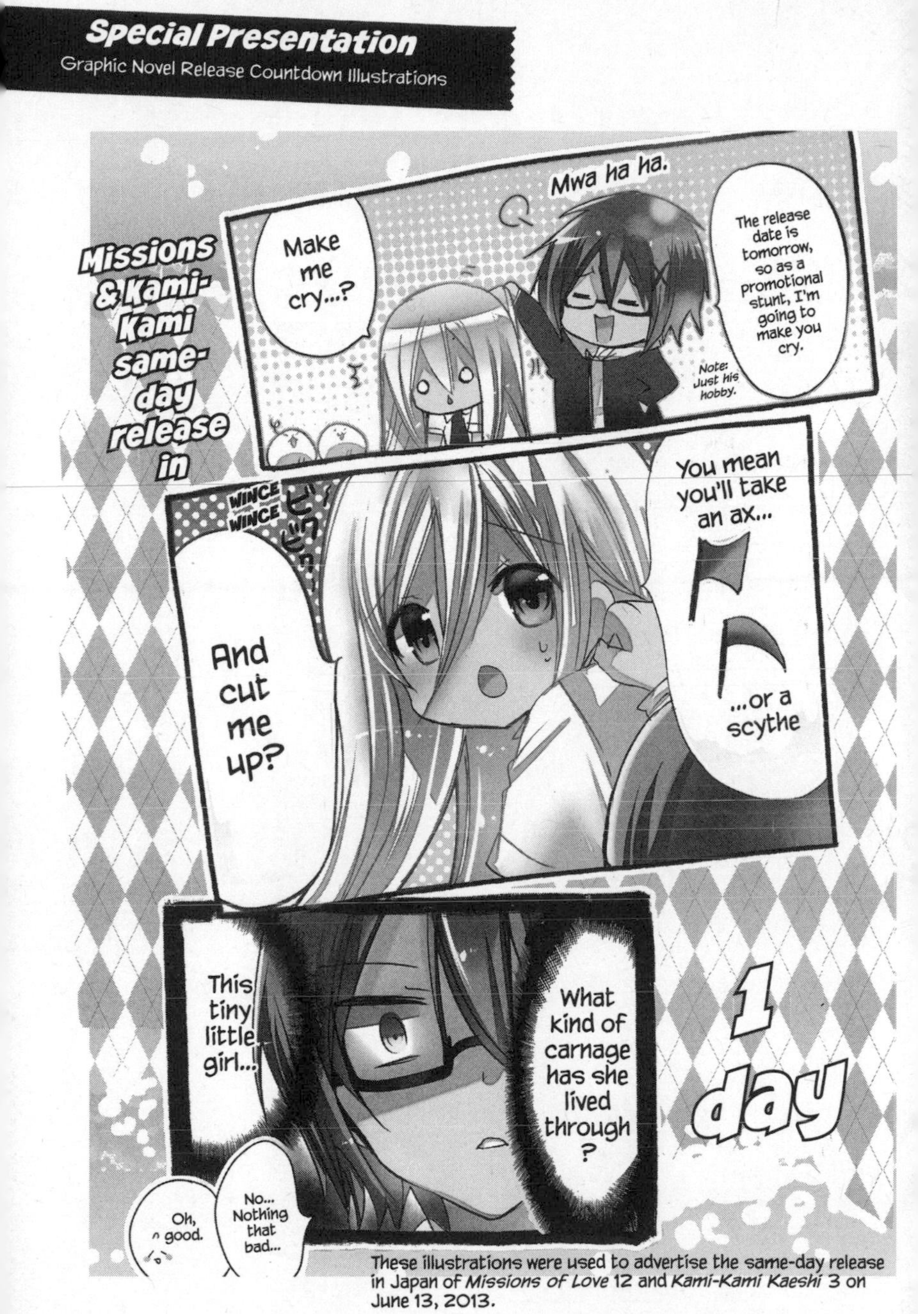
Missions & Kami-Kami same-day release in
Mwa ha ha.
The release date is tomorrow, so as a promotional stunt, I'm going to make you cry.
Note: Just his hobby.
Make me cry...?
You mean you'll take an ax...
...or a scythe
WINCE WINCE
And cut me up?
What kind of carnage has she lived through?
This tiny little girl...!
No... Nothing that bad...
Oh, good.
1 day

These illustrations were used to advertise the same-day release in Japan of *Missions of Love* 12 and *Kami-Kami Kaeshi* 3 on June 13, 2013.

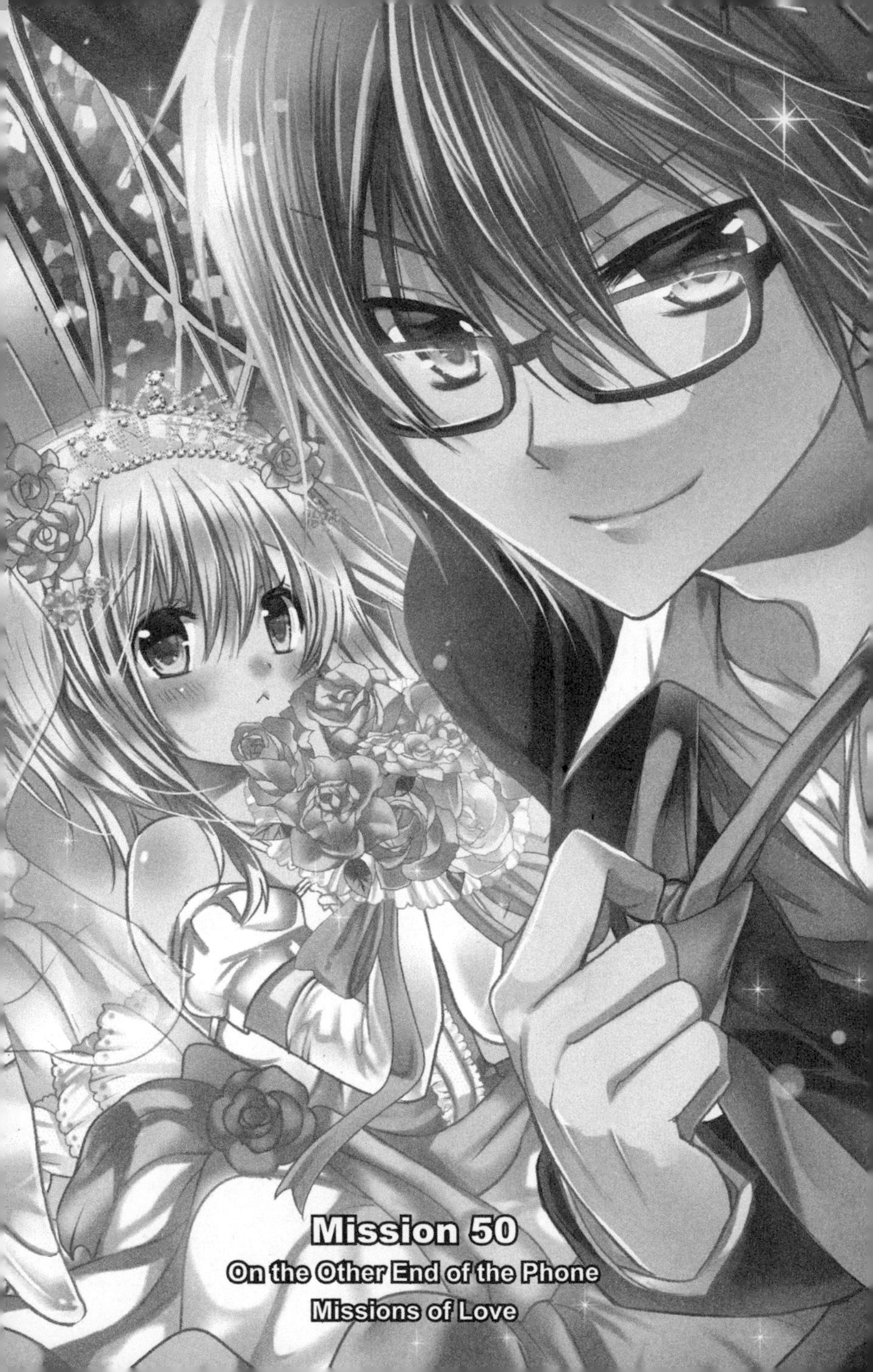

Mission 50

On the Other End of the Phone

Missions of Love

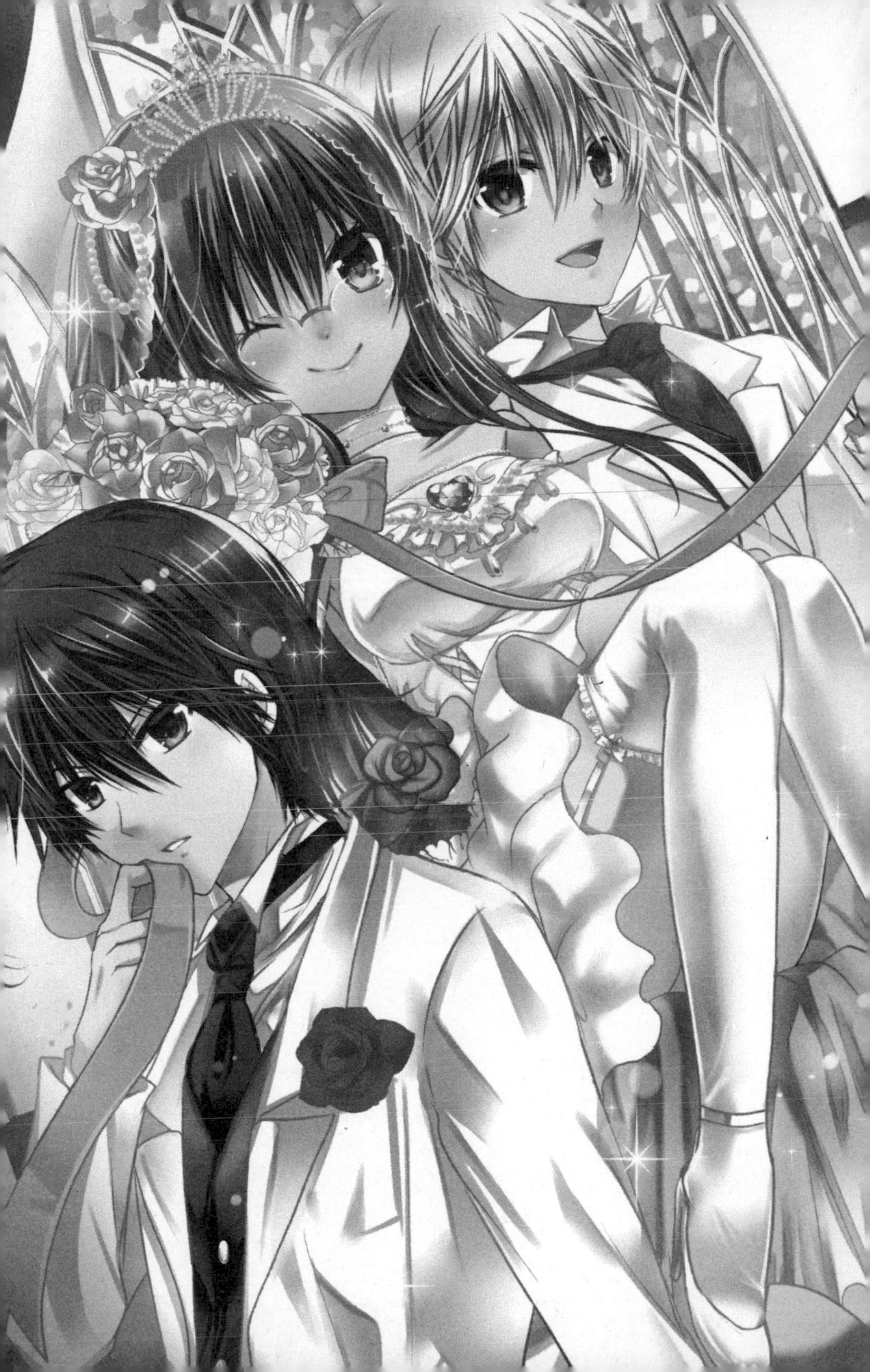

Special Presentation

Graphic Novel Release Countdown Illustrations

Missions 12 and Kami-Kami 3 on sale now!

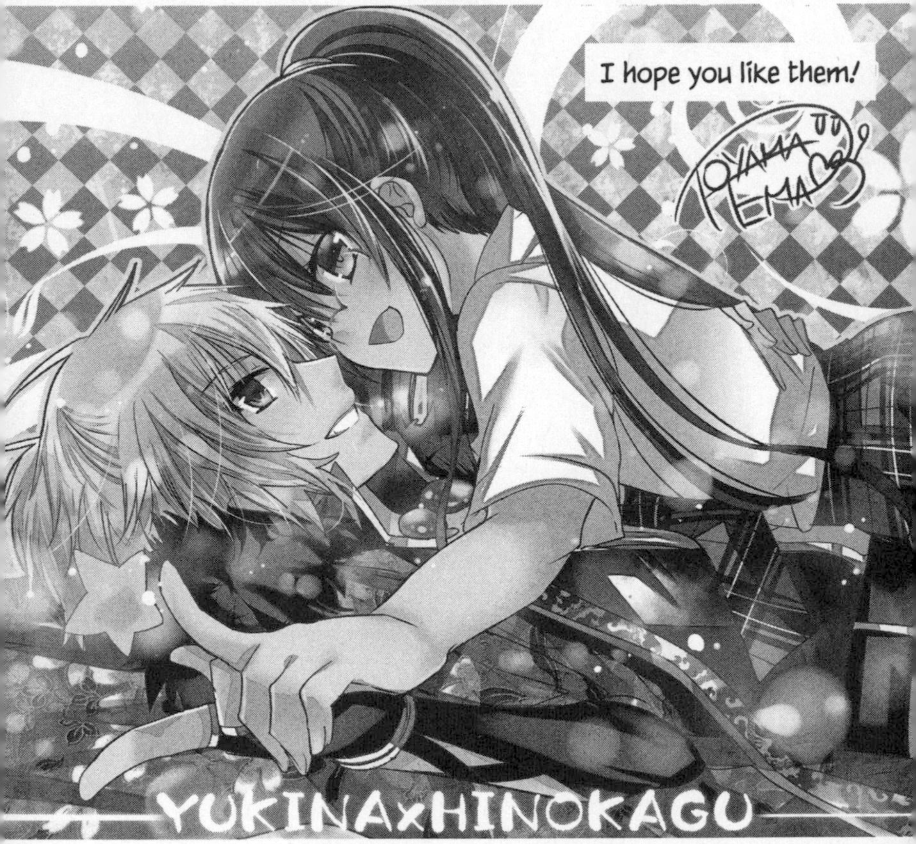
I hope you like them!
YUKINAxHINOKAGU

These illustrations were used to advertise the same-day release in Japan of *Missions of Love* 12 and *Kami-Kami Kaeshi* 3 on June 13, 2013.

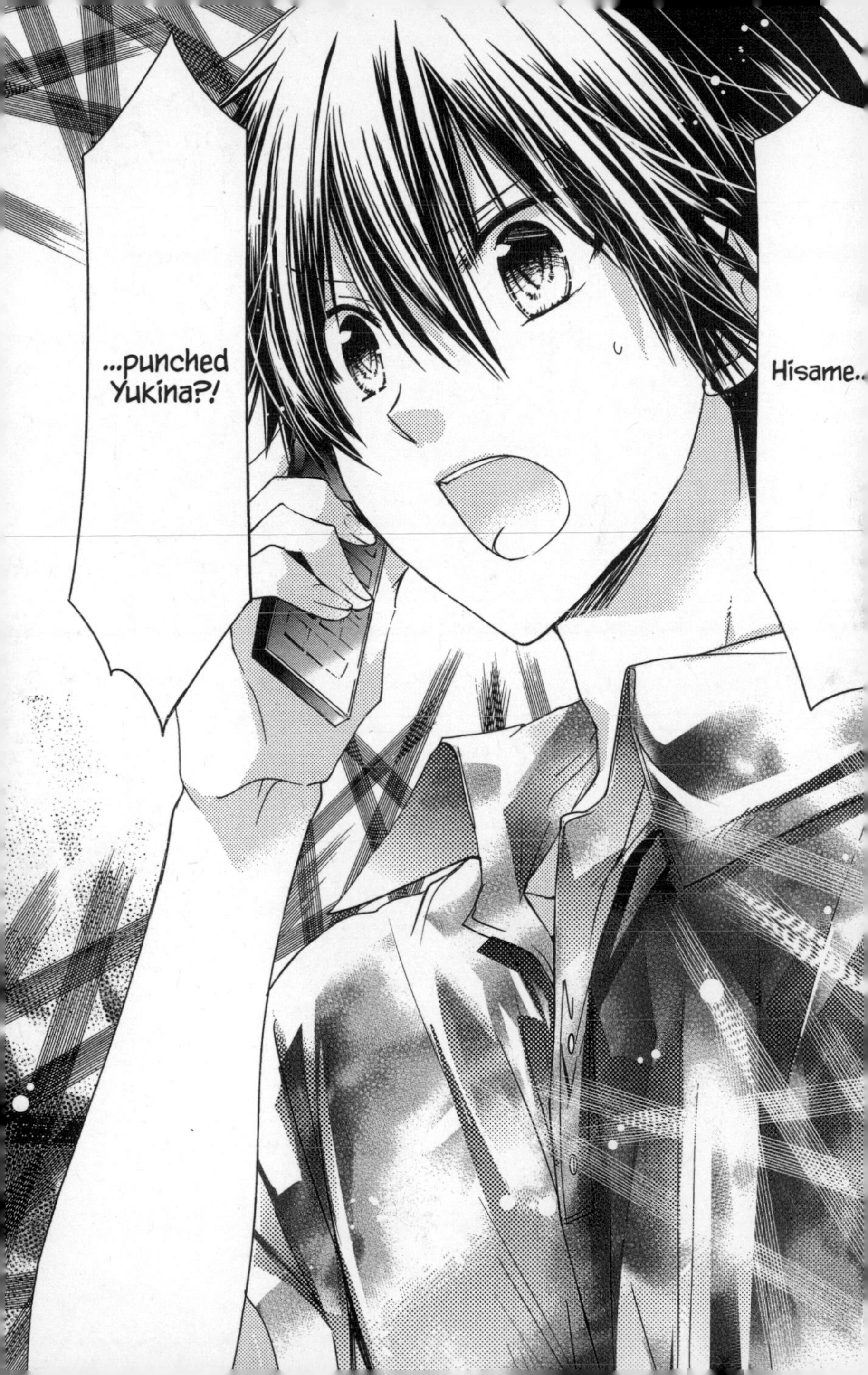
Hisame..
...punched Yukina?!

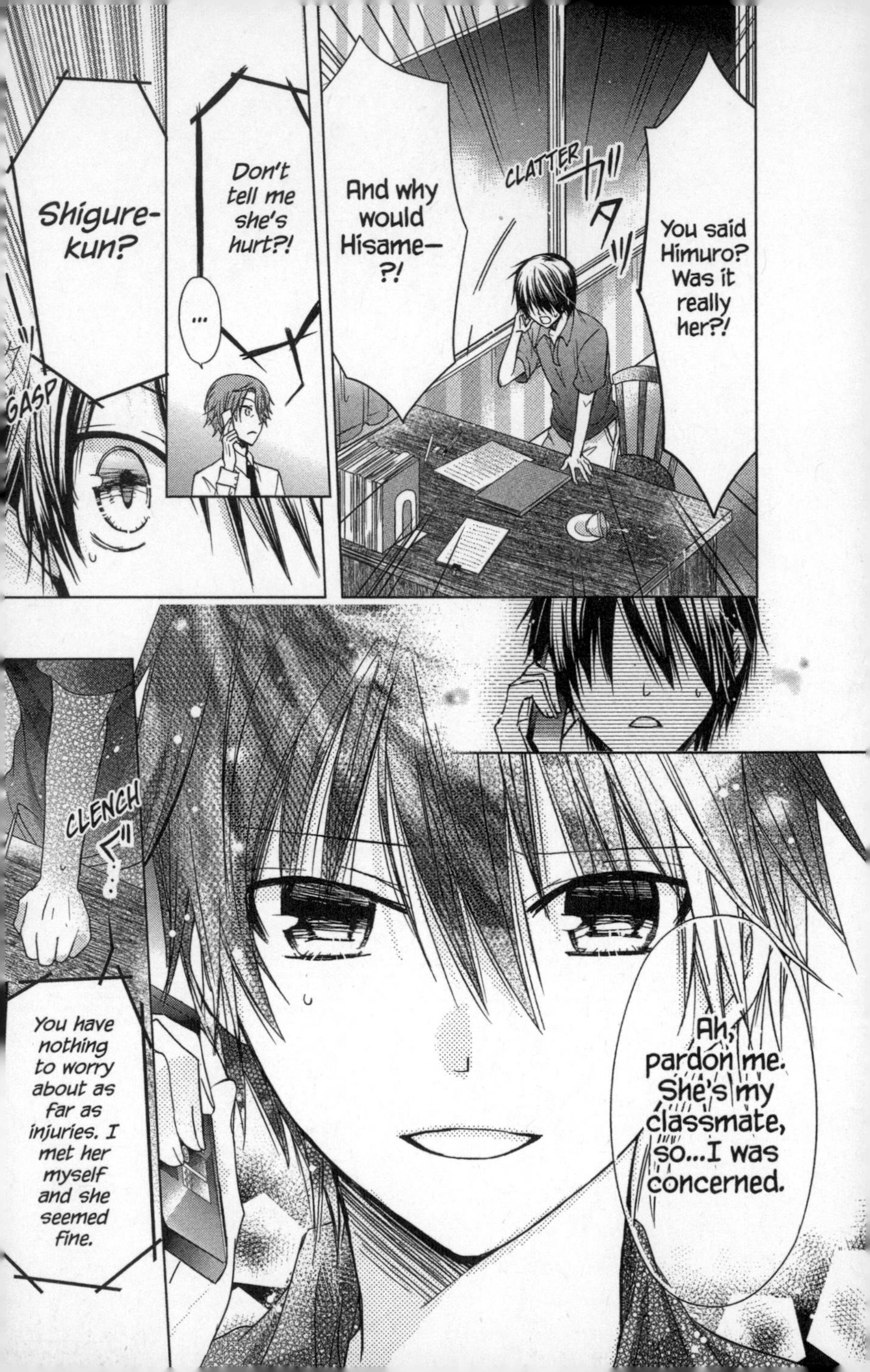
CLATTER
You said Himuro? Was it really her?!
And why would Hisame—?!
Don't tell me she's hurt?!
...
Shigure-kun?
GASP
Ah, pardon me. She's my classmate, so...I was concerned.
CLENCH
You have nothing to worry about as far as injuries. I met her myself and she seemed fine.

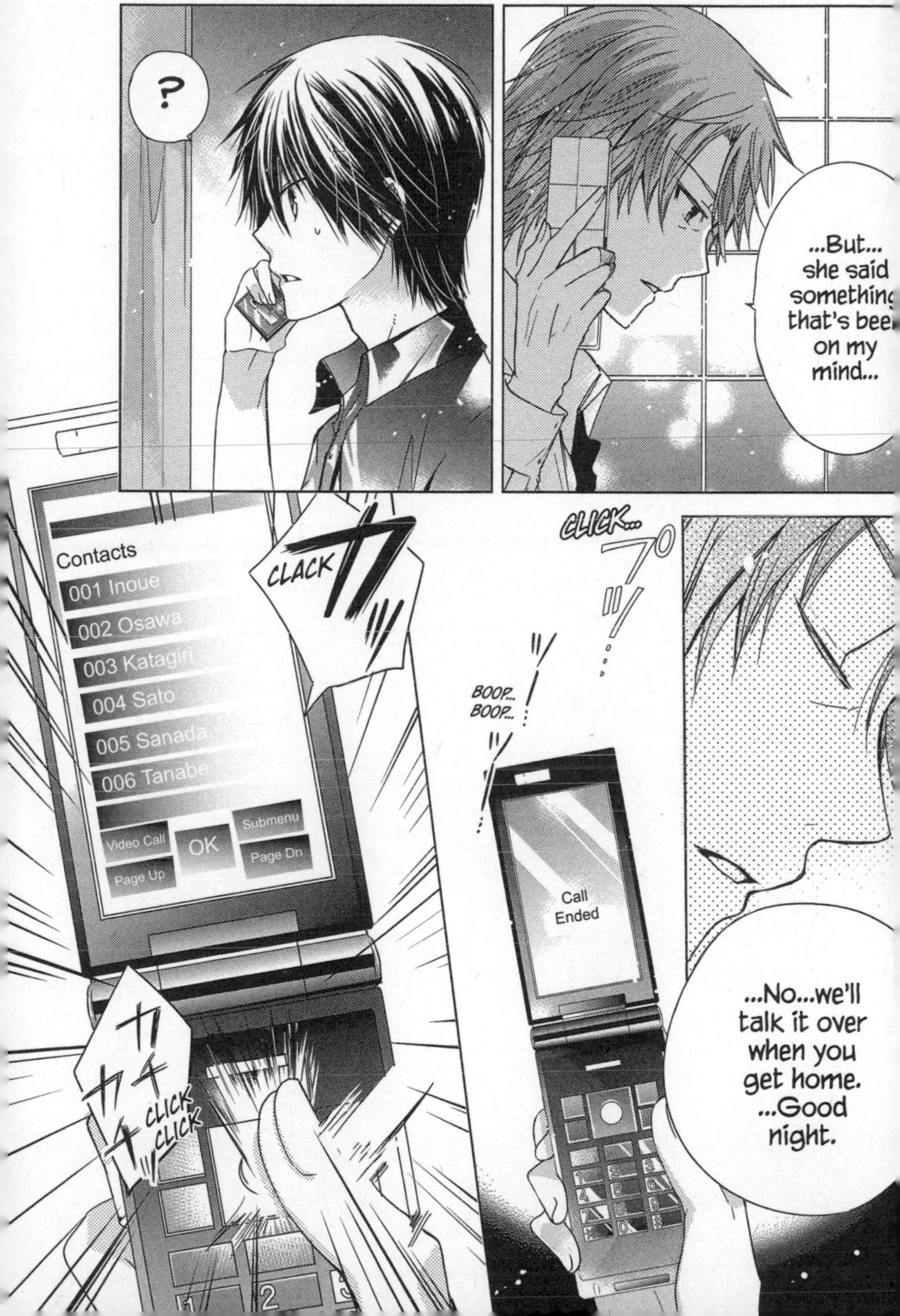
...But... she said somethin that's bee on my mind...
?
...No...we'll talk it over when you get home. ...Good night.
CLICK...
BOOP... BOOP...
Call Ended
CLACK
Contacts
001 Inoue
002 Osawa
003 Katagiri
004 Sato
005 Sanada
006 Tanabe
Video Call
OK
Submenu
Page Up
Page Dn
CLICK CLICK

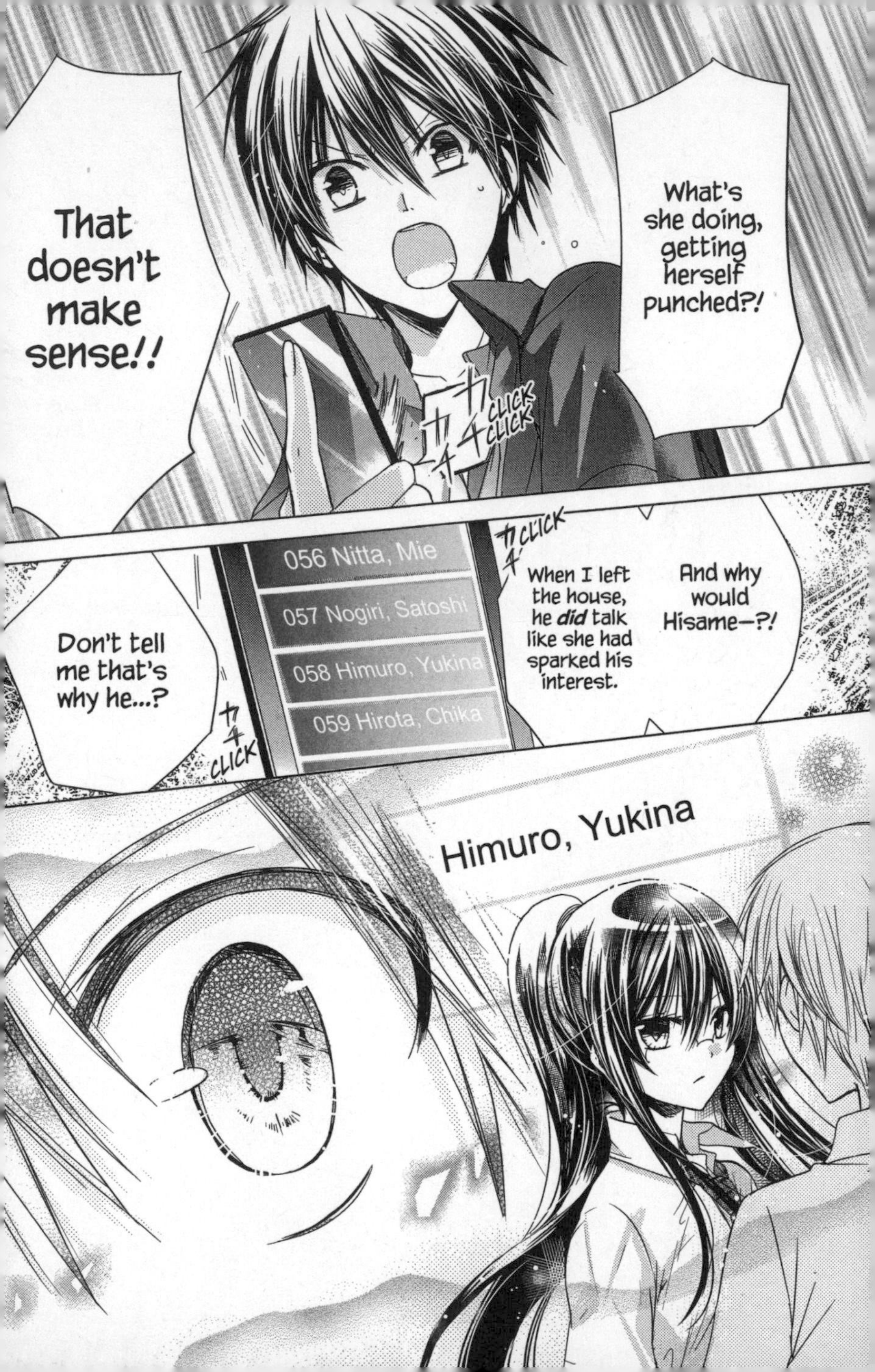
What's she doing, getting herself punched?!
That doesn't make sense!!
CLICK CLICK
And why would Hisame—?!
When I left the house, he *did* talk like she had sparked his interest.
CLICK
056 Nitta, Mie
057 Nogiri, Satoshi
058 Himuro, Yukina
059 Hirota, Chika
Don't tell me that's why he...?
CLICK
Himuro, Yukina

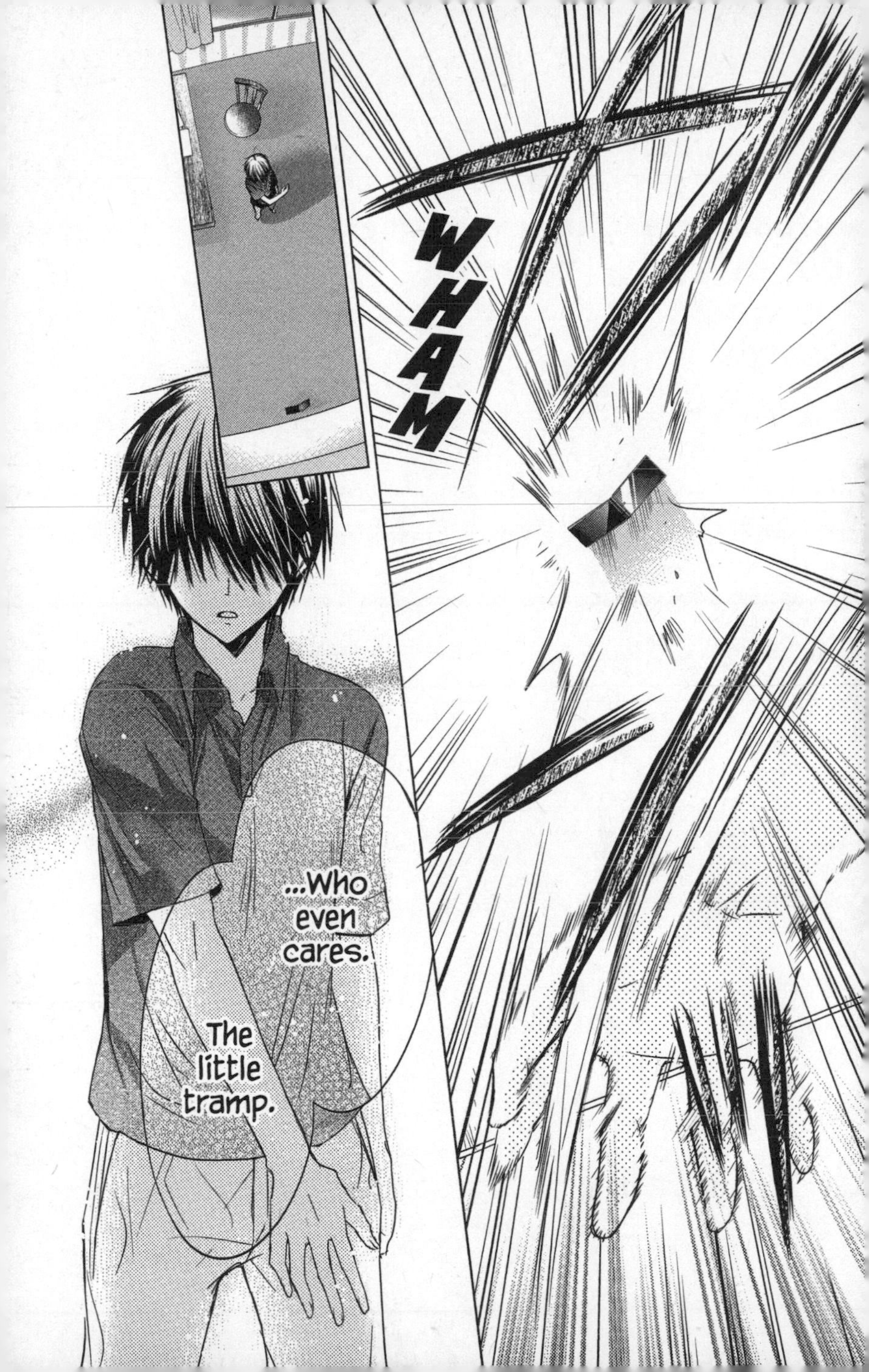
WHAM
...Who even cares.
The little tramp.

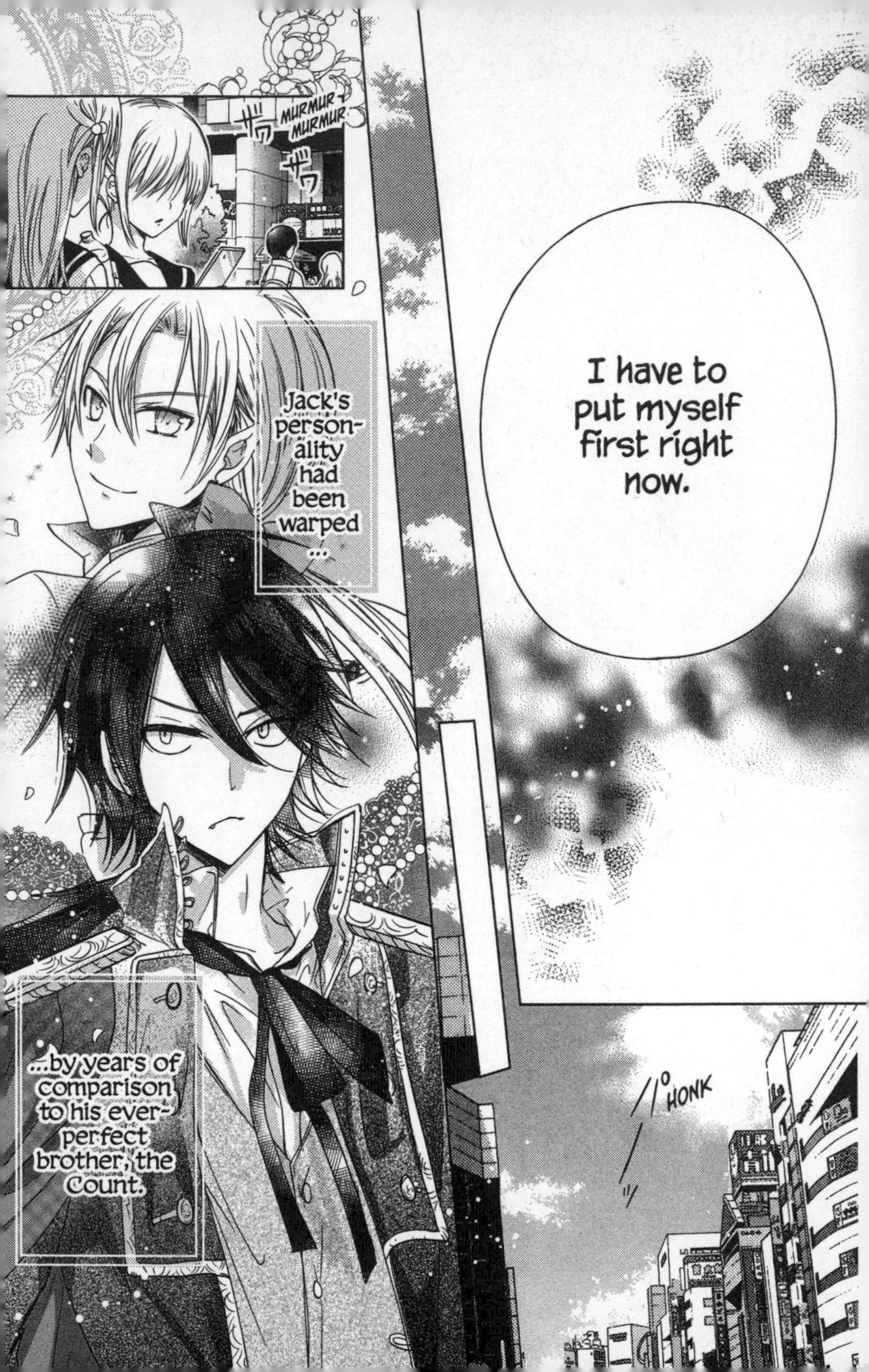

I have to put myself first right now.
HONK
MURMUR MURMUR
ザワ
ザワ
Jack's personality had been warped...
...by years of comparison to his ever-perfect brother, the Count.

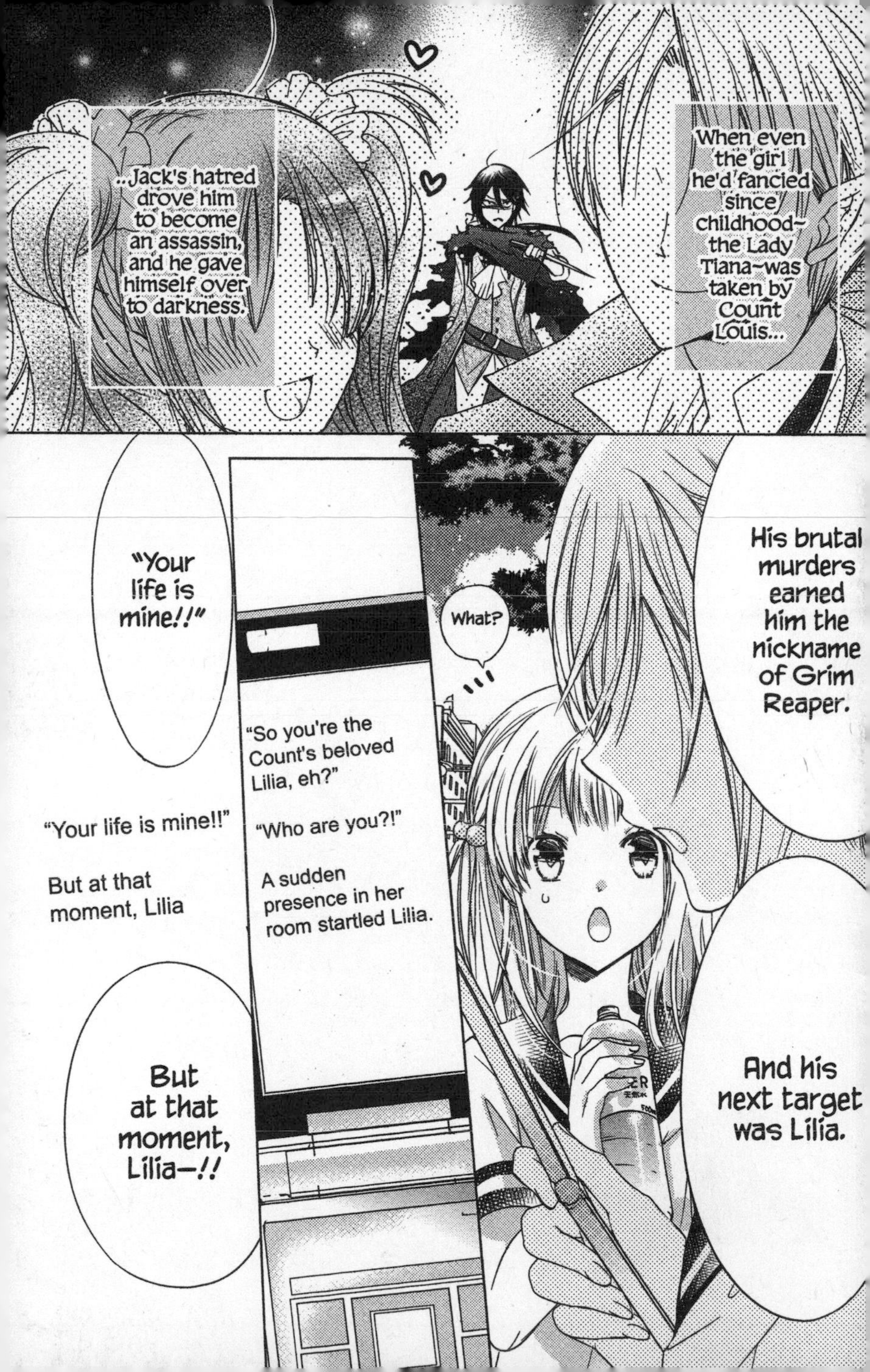
When even the girl he'd fancied since childhood~the Lady Tiana~was taken by Count Louis...
..Jack's hatred drove him to become an assassin, and he gave himself over to darkness.
His brutal murders earned him the nickname of Grim Reaper.
What?
And his next target was Lilia.
"So you're the Count's beloved Lilia, eh?"
"Who are you?!"
A sudden presence in her room startled Lilia.
"Your life is mine!!"
"Your life is mine!!"
But at that moment, Lilia
But at that moment, Lilia—!!

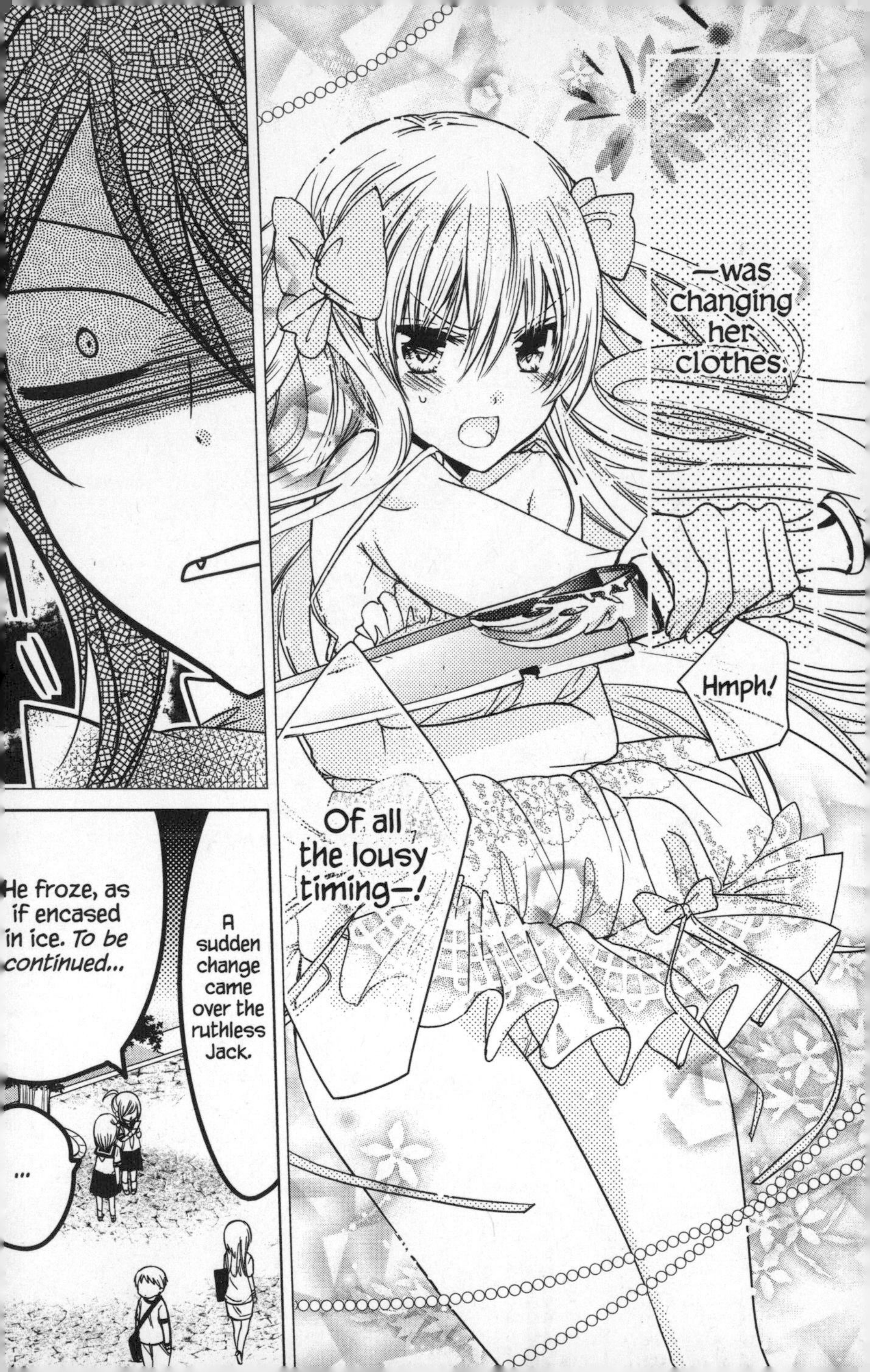
—was changing her clothes.
Hmph!
Of all the lousy timing—!
A sudden change came over the ruthless Jack.
He froze, as if encased in ice. *To be continued...*
...

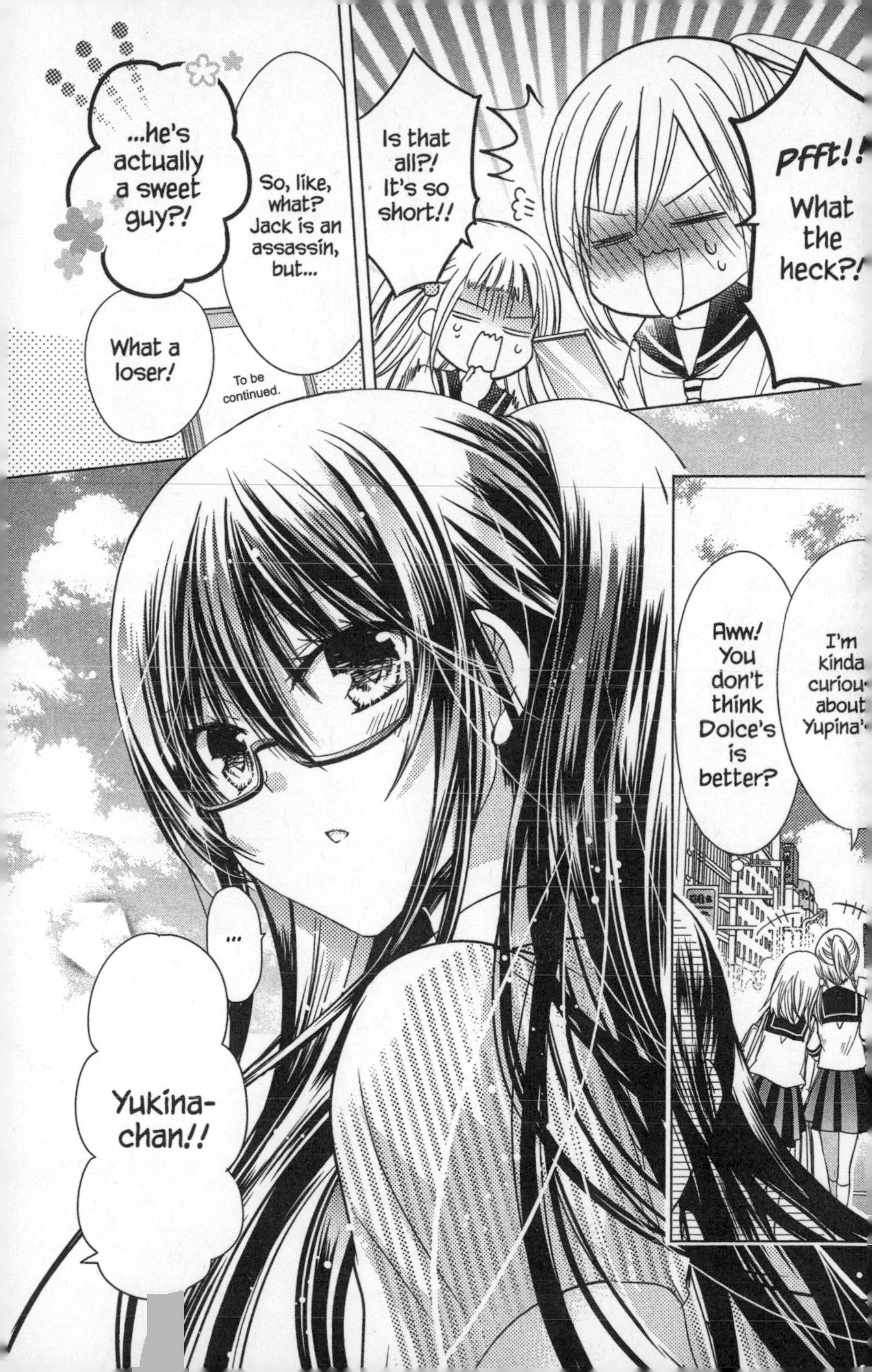
Pfft!! What the heck?!
Is that all?! It's so short!!
So, like, what? Jack is an assassin, but...
...he's actually a sweet guy?!
What a loser!
To be continued.
I'm kinda curiou about Yupina'
Aww! You don't think Dolce's is better?
...
Yukina-chan!!

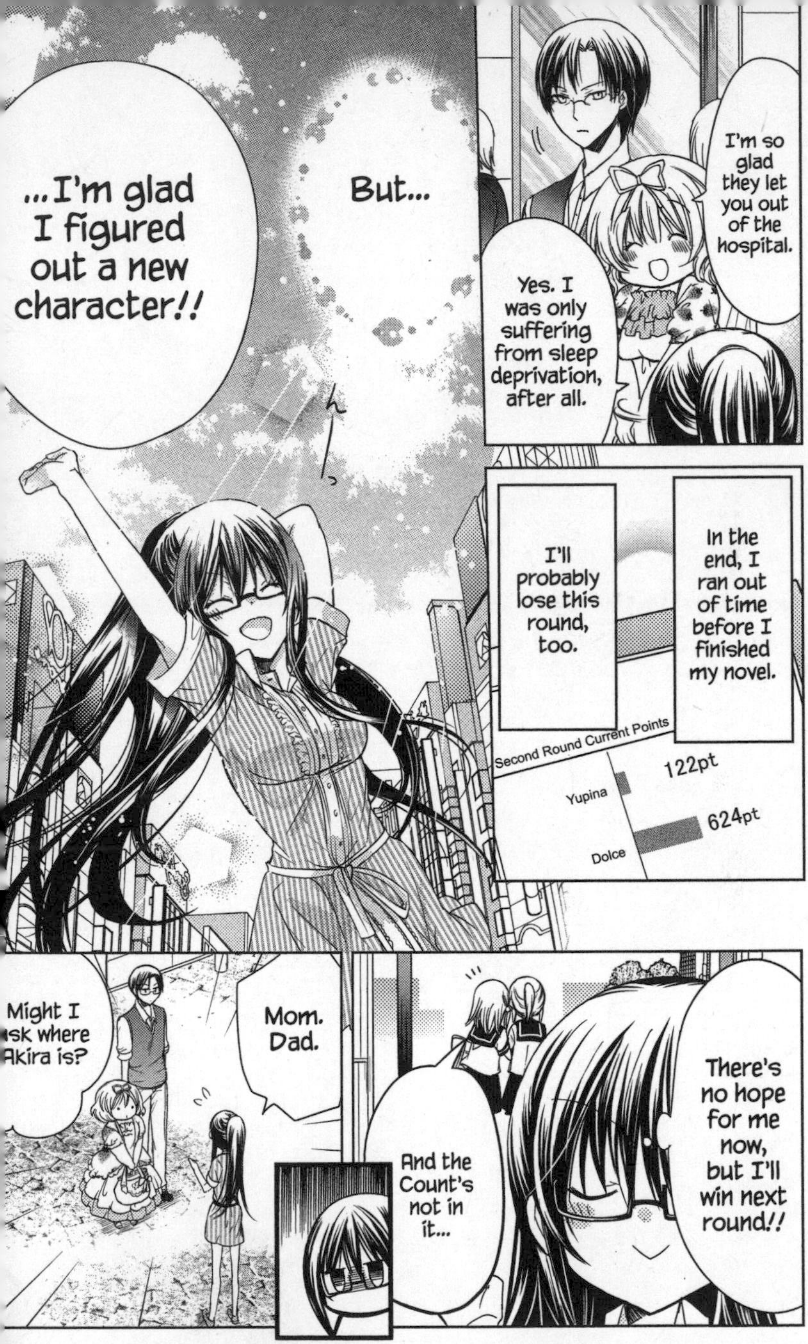
I'm so glad they let you out of the hospital.
Yes. I was only suffering from sleep deprivation, after all.
In the end, I ran out of time before I finished my novel.
I'll probably lose this round, too.
Second Round Current Points
Yupina 122pt
Dolce 624pt
But...
...I'm glad I figured out a new character!!
There's no hope for me now, but I'll win next round!!
And the Count's not in it...
Mom. Dad.
Might I ask where Akira is?

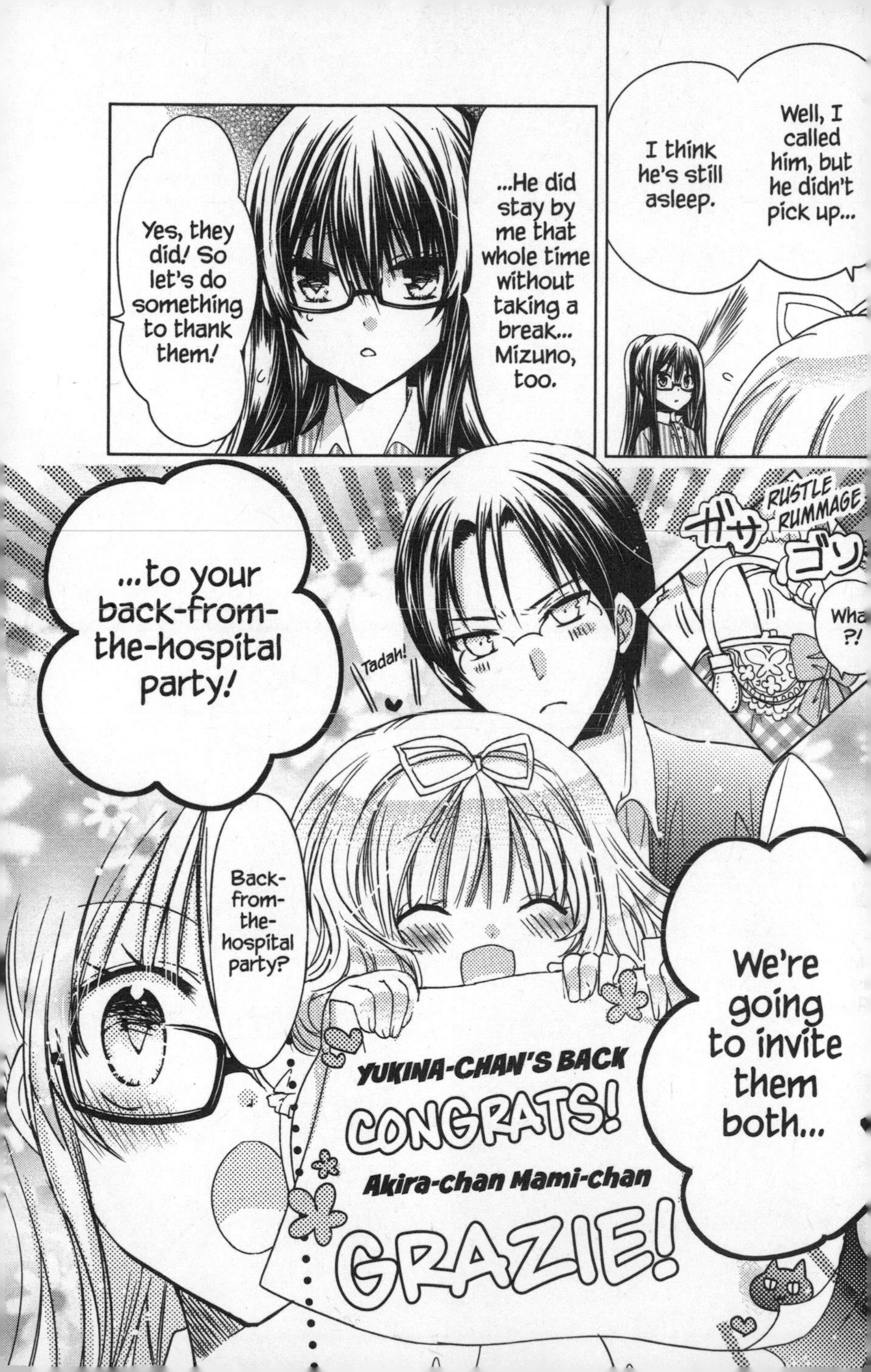
Well, I called him, but he didn't pick up...
I think he's still asleep.
...He did stay by me that whole time without taking a break... Mizuno, too.
Yes, they did! So let's do something to thank them!
ガサ RUSTLE
ゴリ RUMMAGE
Wha ?!
We're going to invite them both...
...to your back-from-the-hospital party!
Tadah!
Back-from-the-hospital party?
YUKINA-CHAN'S BACK
CONGRATS!
Akira-chan Mami-chan
GRAZIE!

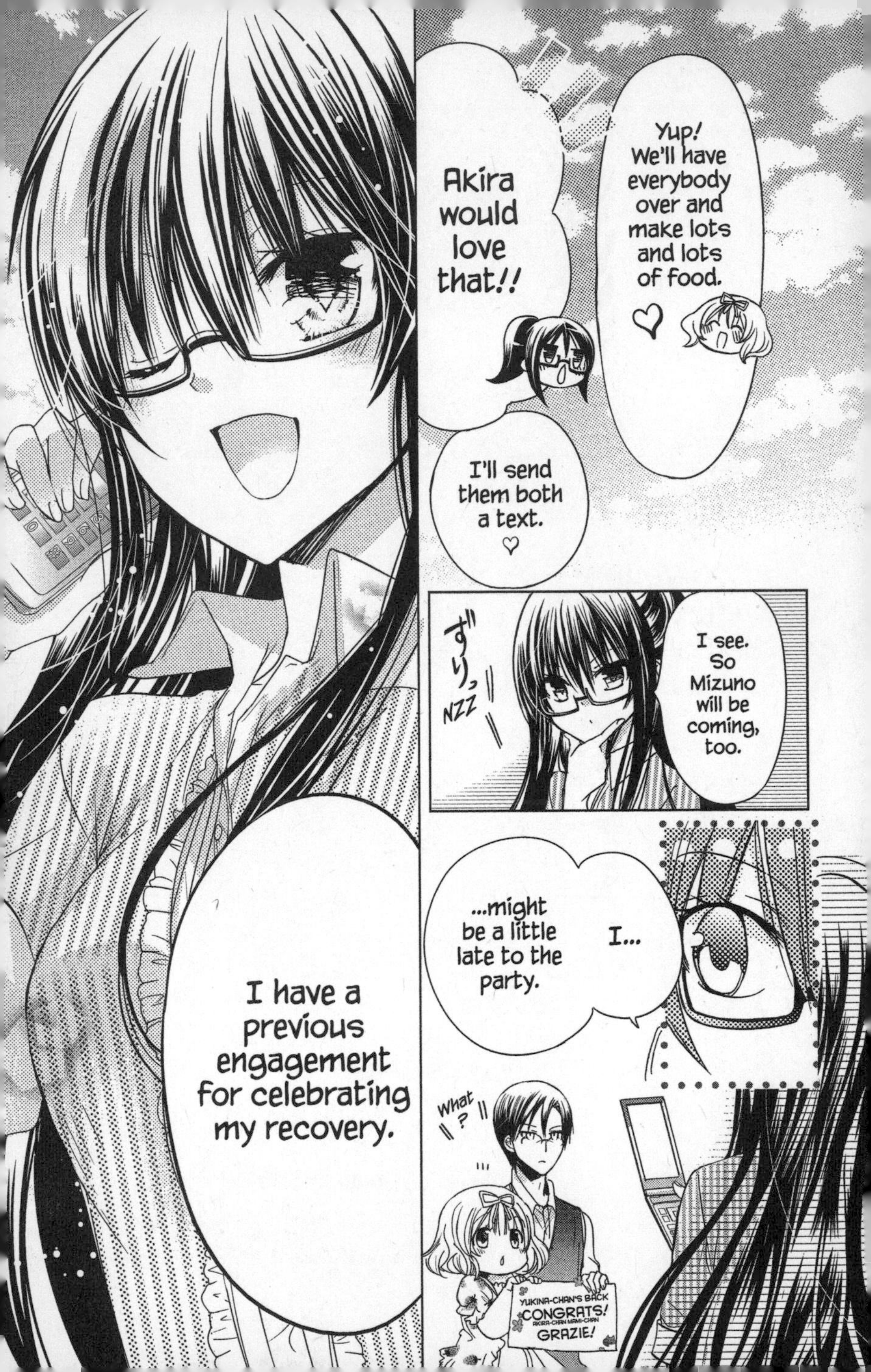
Yup! We'll have everybody over and make lots and lots of food. ♡
Akira would love that!!
I'll send them both a text. ♡
I see. So Mizuno will be coming, too.
ずりっ
NZZ
I...
...might be a little late to the party.
What?
YUKINA-CHAN'S BACK
CONGRATS!
AKIRA-CHAN MAMI-CHAN
GRAZIE!
I have a previous engagement for celebrating my recovery.

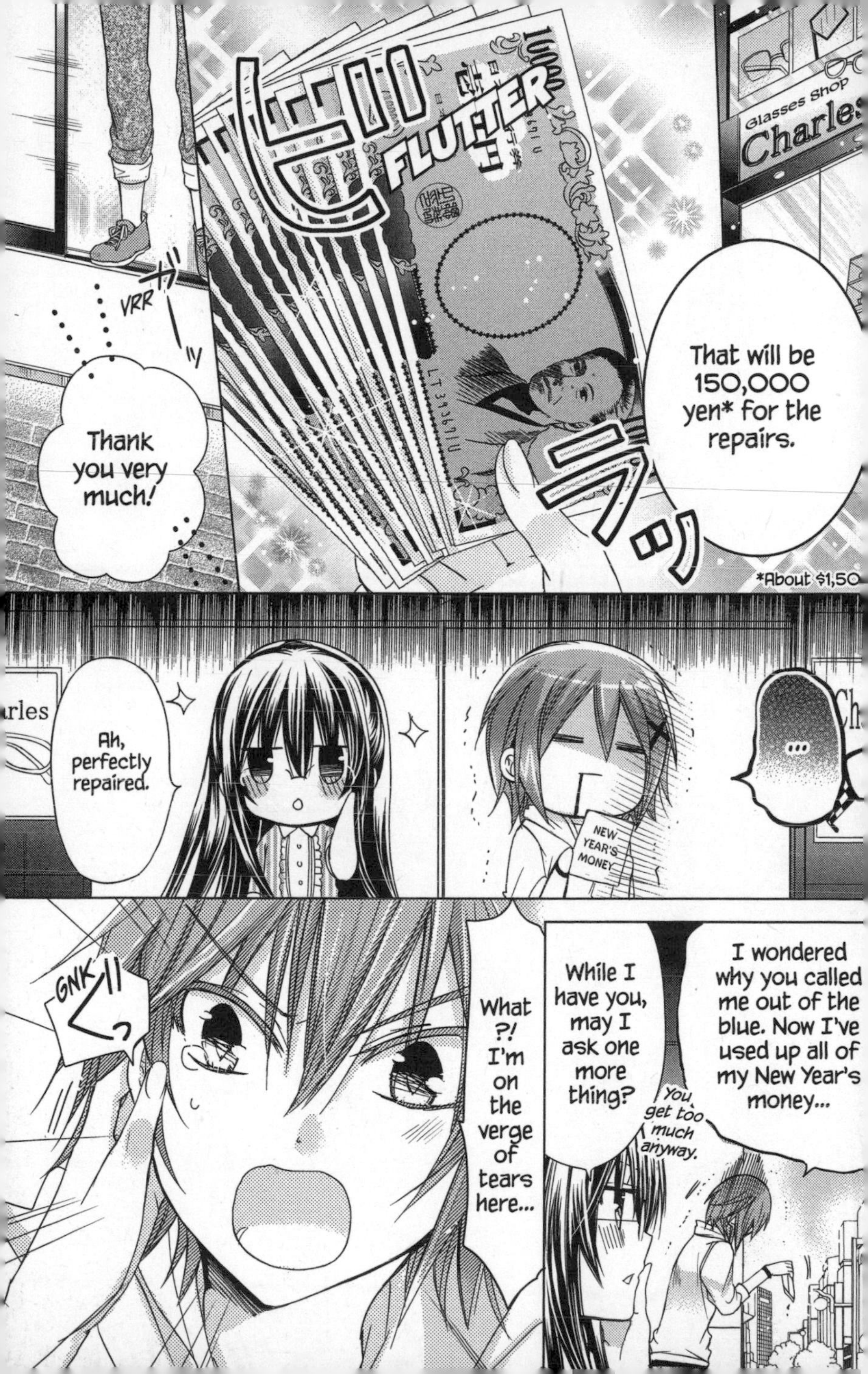
Glasses Shop
Charles
That will be 150,000 yen* for the repairs.
FLUTTER
VRR
Thank you very much!
*About $1,50
...
NEW YEAR'S MONEY
Ah, perfectly repaired.
I wondered why you called me out of the blue. Now I've used up all of my New Year's money...
You get too much anyway.
While I have you, may I ask one more thing?
What ?! I'm on the verge of tears here...
GNK

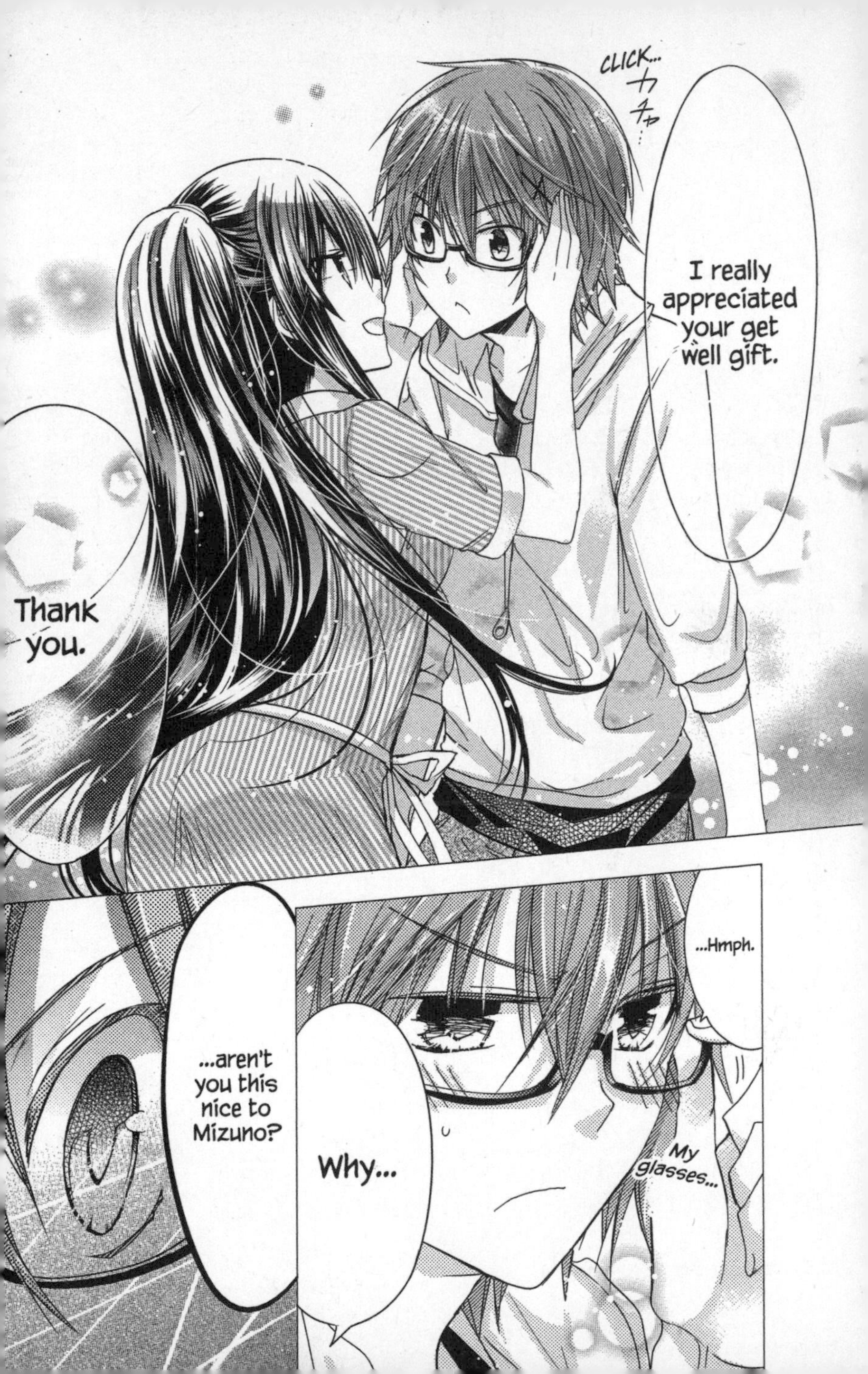
CLICK...
カチャ...
I really appreciated your get well gift.
Thank you.
...Hmph.
My glasses...
Why...
...aren't you this nice to Mizuno?

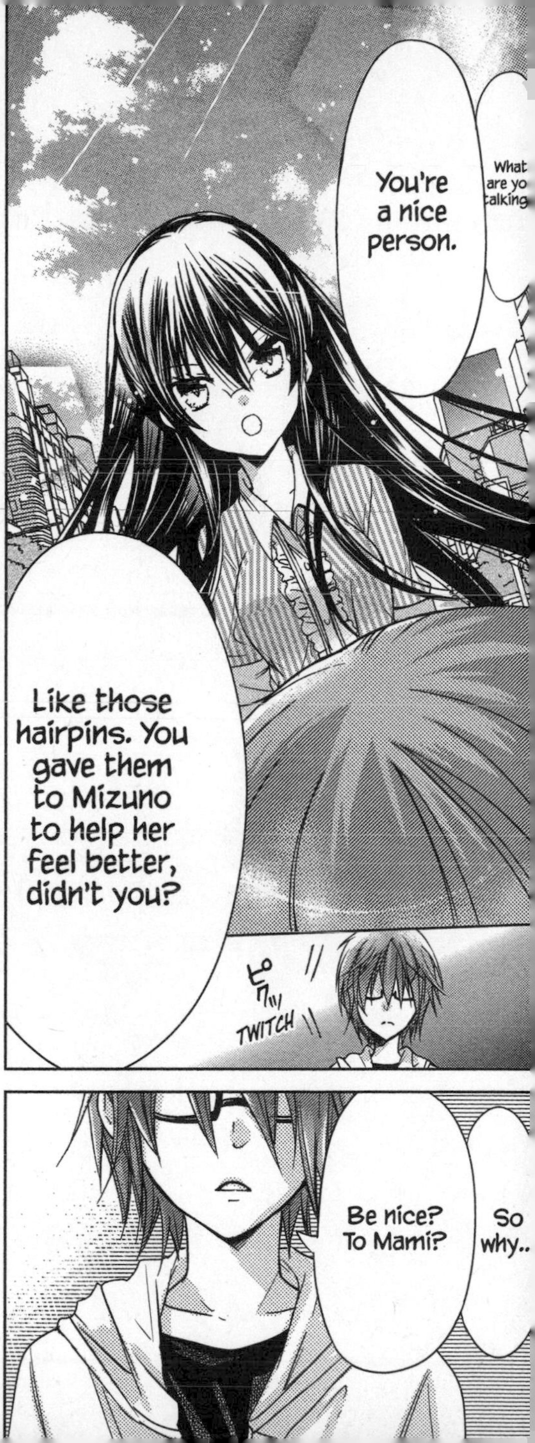
What are yo talking
You're a nice person.
Like those hairpins. You gave them to Mizuno to help her feel better, didn't you?
TWITCH
So why..
Be nice? To Mami?

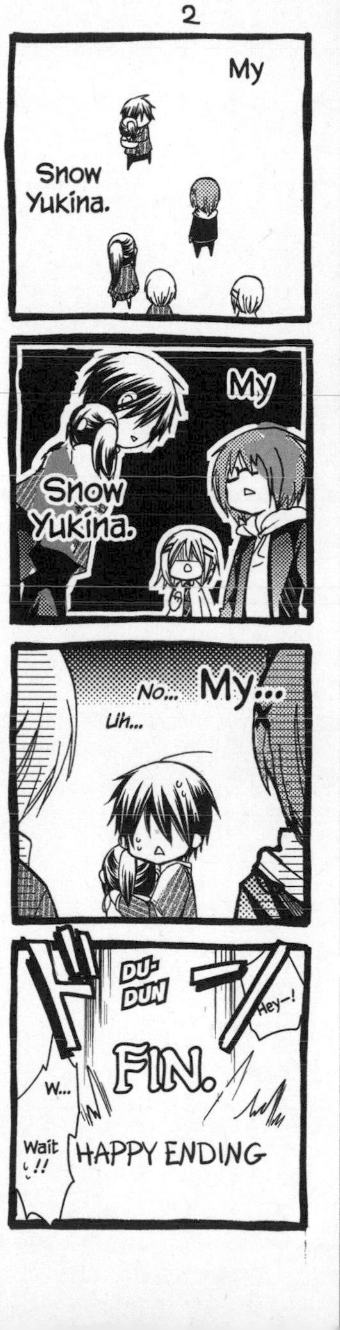
2
My
Snow Yukina.
My
Snow Yukina.
My...
No...
Uh...
DU-DUN
Hey—!
FIN.
W...
Wait!!
HAPPY ENDING

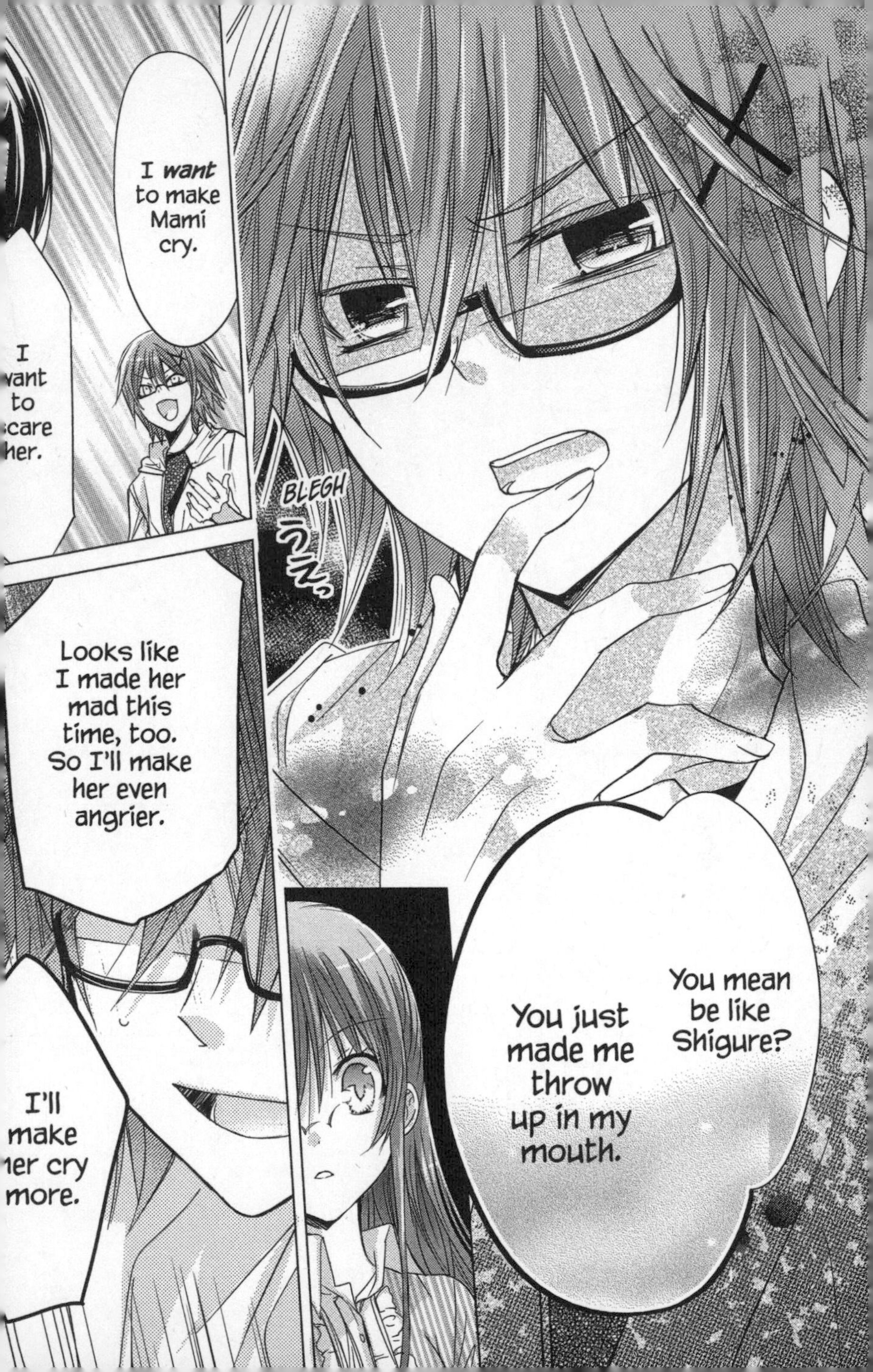
BLEGH
I want to make Mami cry.
I want to scare her.
Looks like I made her mad this time, too. So I'll make her even angrier.
You mean be like Shigure?
You just made me throw up in my mouth.
I'll make her cry more.

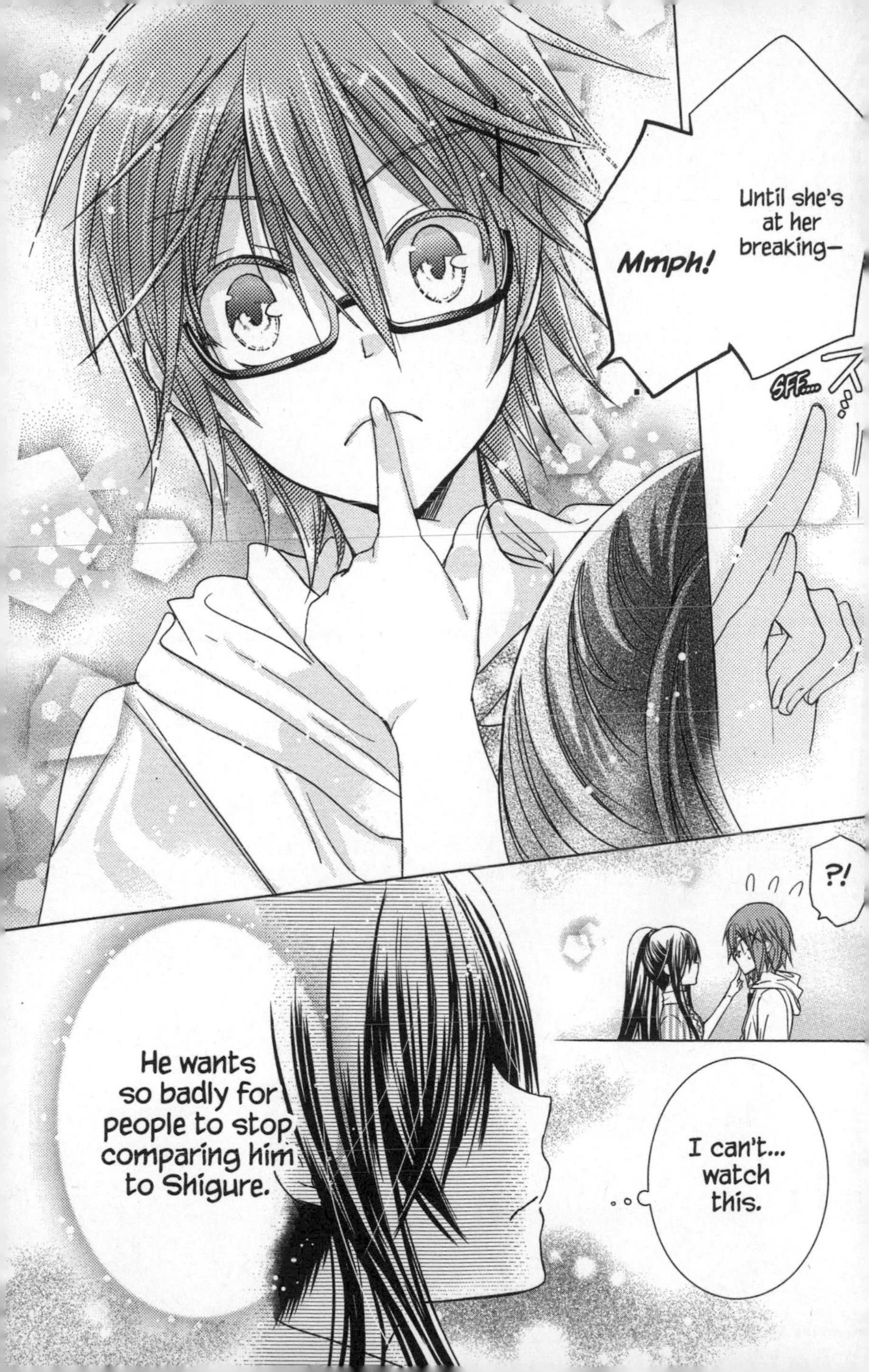

Until she's at her breaking—
Mmph!
SFF...
?!
I can't... watch this.
He wants so badly for people to stop comparing him to Shigure.

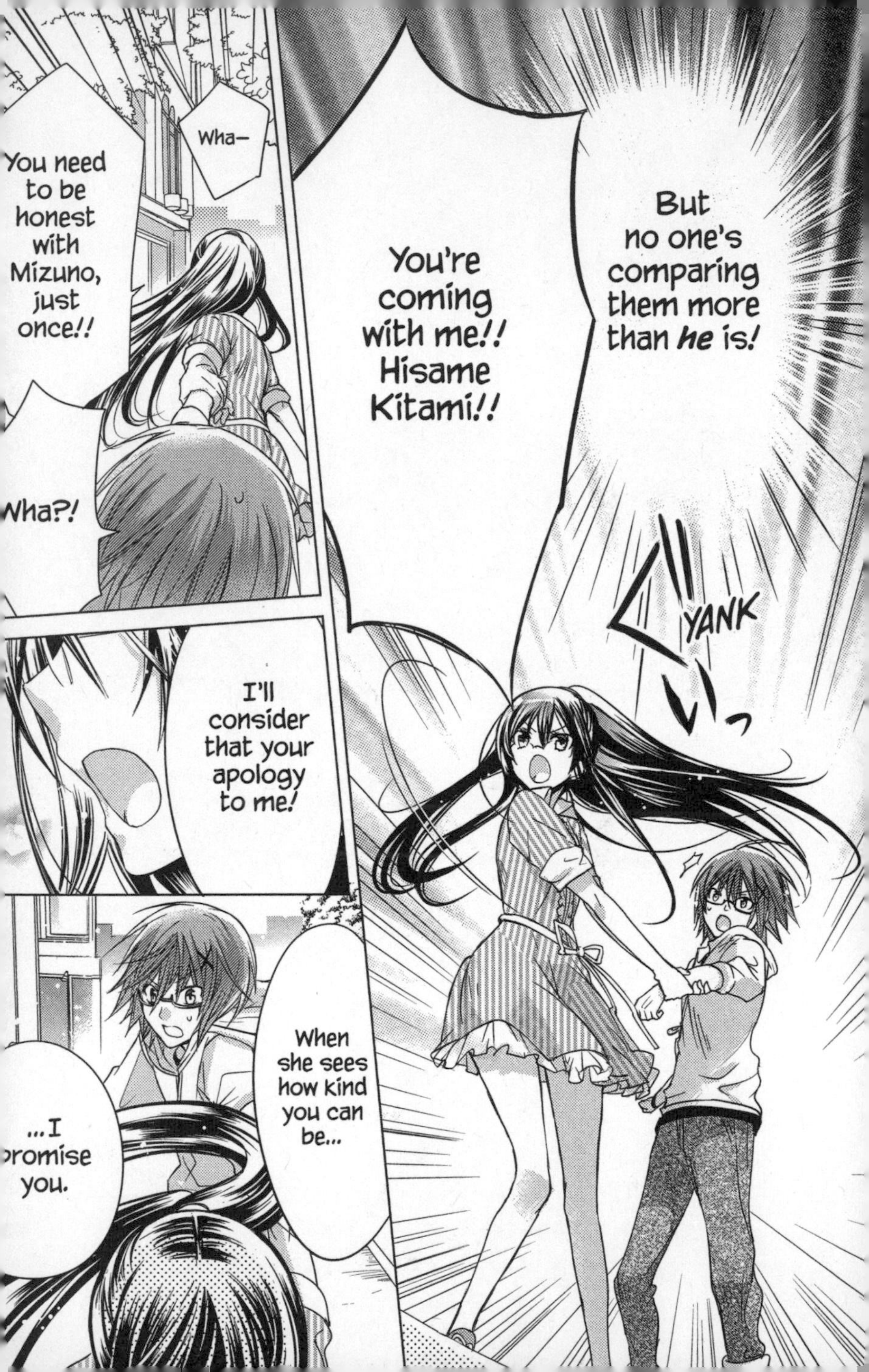
But no one's comparing them more than *he* is!
You're coming with me!! Hisame Kitami!!
YANK
Wha—
You need to be honest with Mizuno, just once!!
Wha?!
I'll consider that your apology to me!
When she sees how kind you can be...
...I promise you.

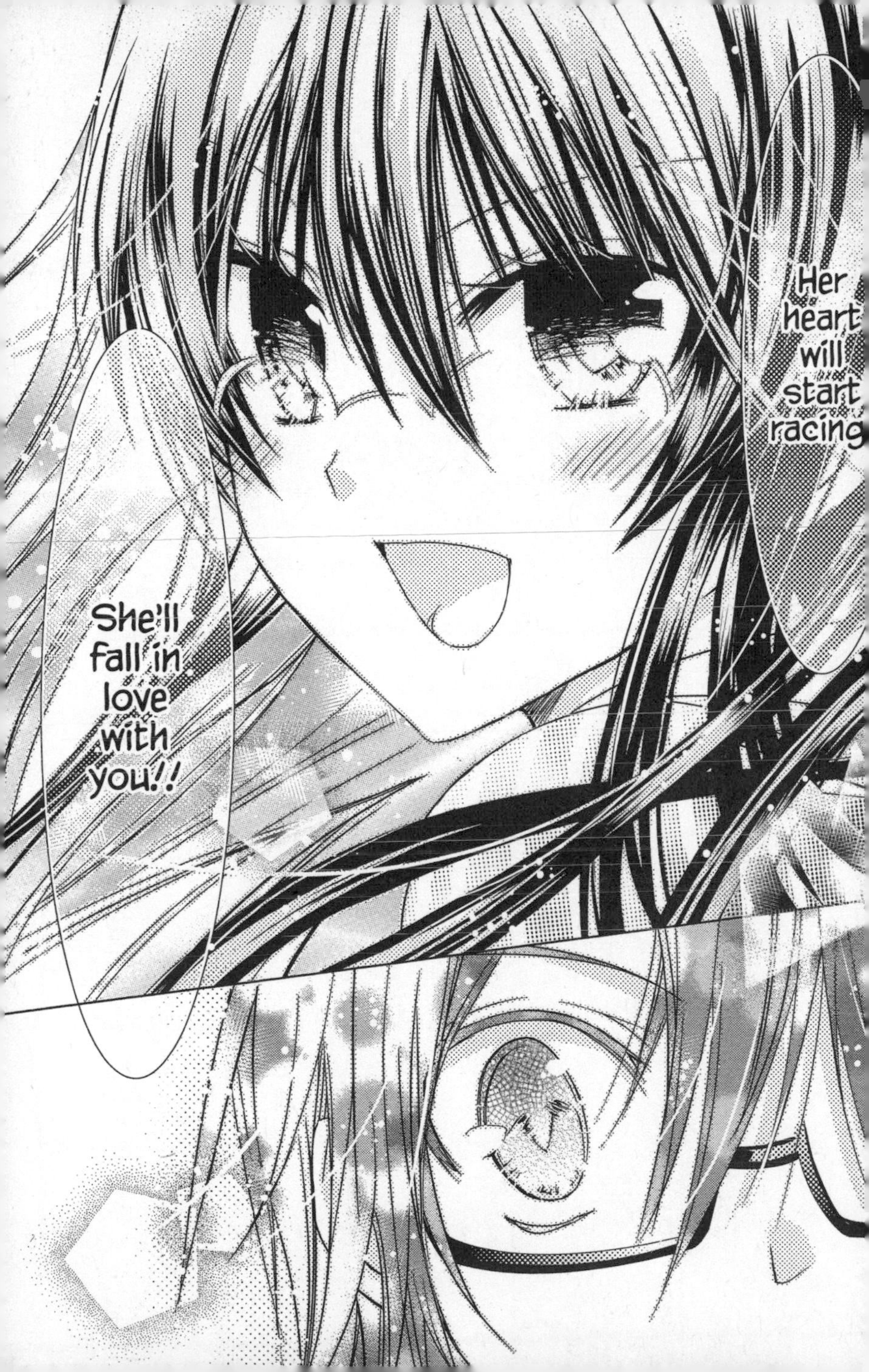
Her heart will start racing
She'll fall in love with you!!

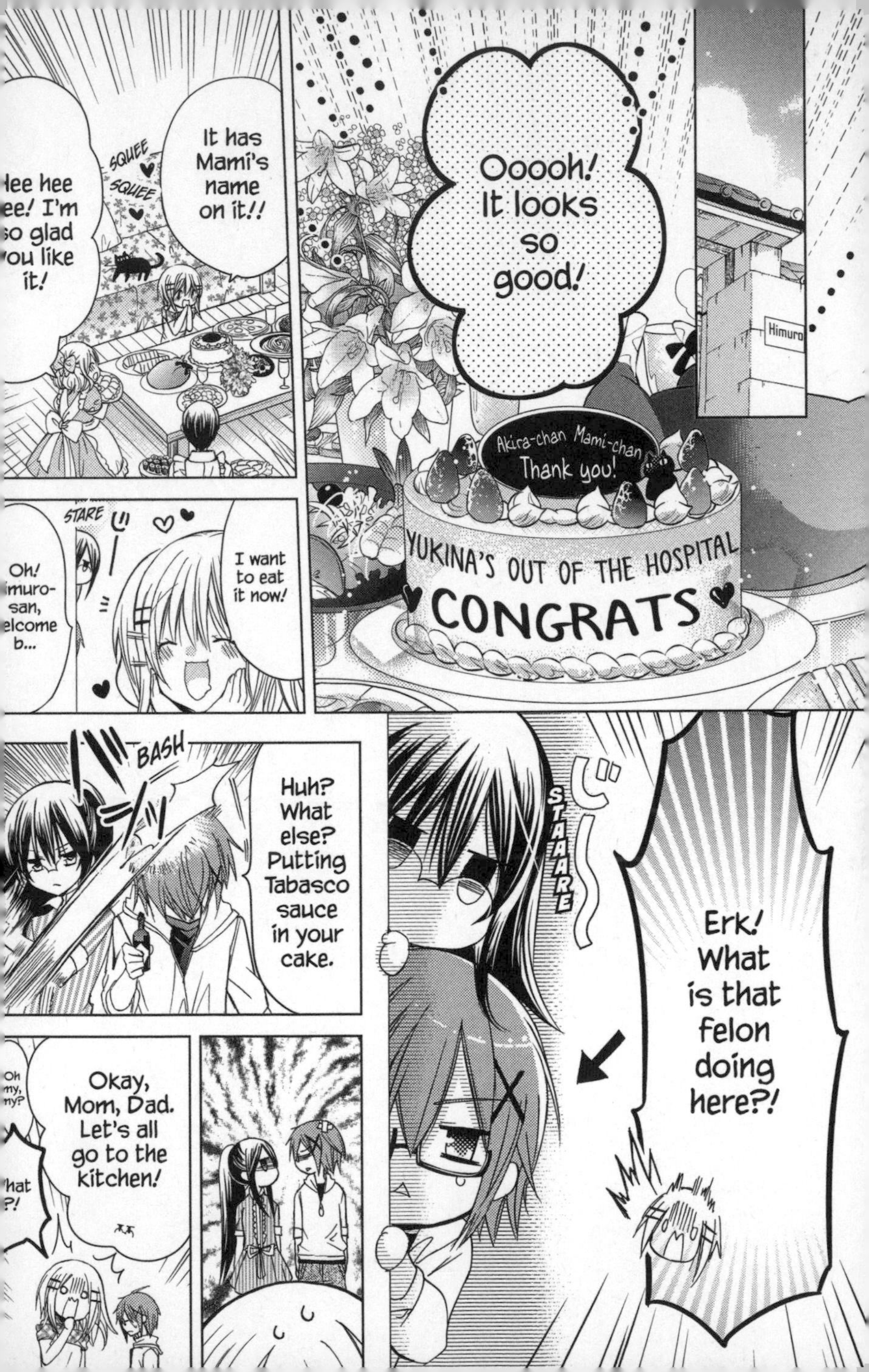

Himuro
Ooooh! It looks so good!
Akira-chan Mami-chan Thank you!
YUKINA'S OUT OF THE HOSPITAL CONGRATS
It has Mami's name on it!!
SQUEE SQUEE
Hee hee ee! I'm o glad ou like it!
I want to eat it now!
STARE
Oh! imuro-san, elcome b...
STAAARE
Erk! What is that felon doing here?!
BASH
Huh? What else? Putting Tabasco sauce in your cake.
Okay, Mom, Dad. Let's all go to the kitchen!
Oh my, ny?
hat ?!

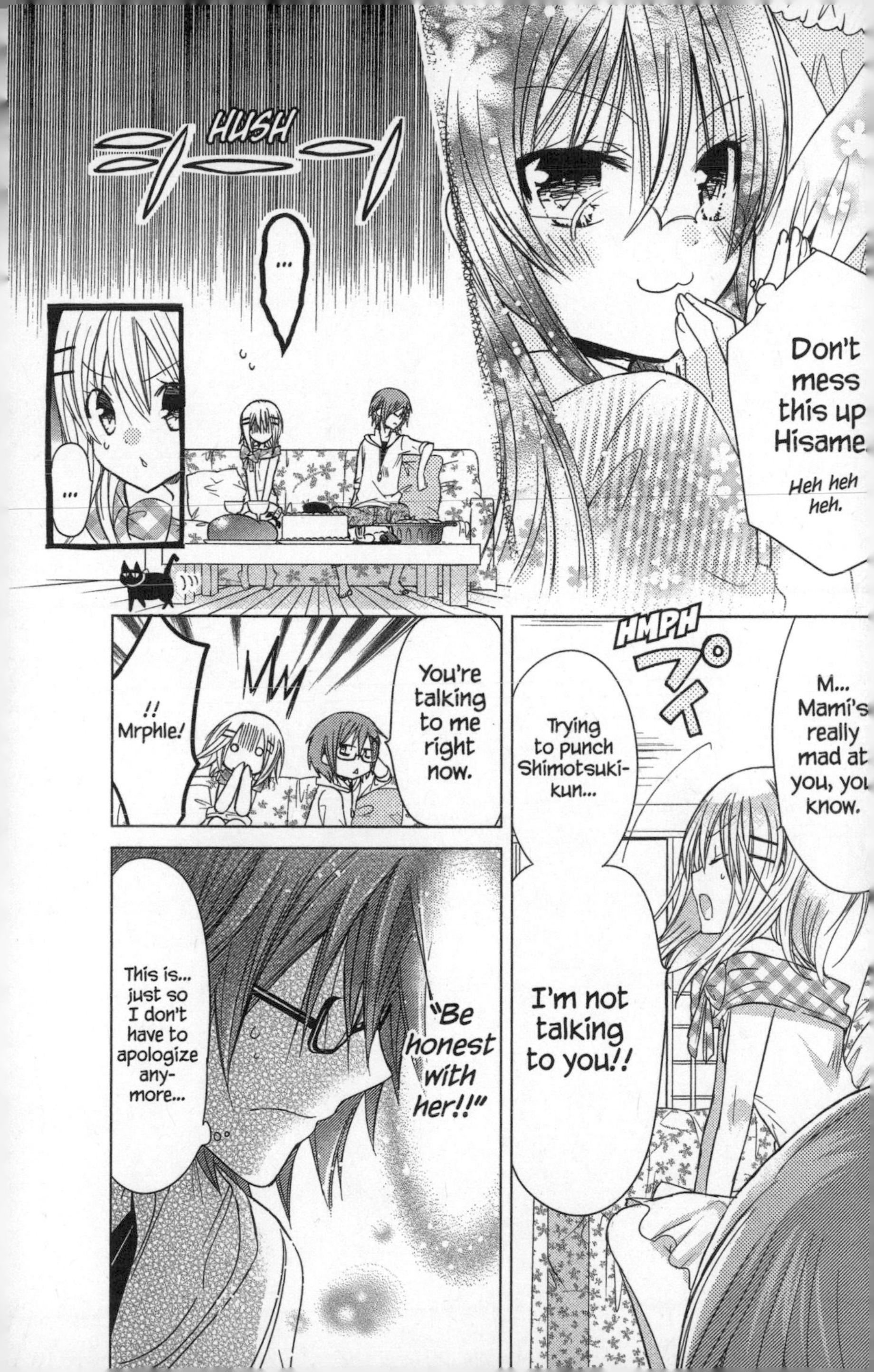
Don't mess this up Hisame.
Heh heh heh.
HUSH
...
...
HMPH
M... Mami's really mad at you, you know.
Trying to punch Shimotsuki-kun...
I'm not talking to you!!
You're talking to me right now.
!! Mrphle!
"Be honest with her!!"
This is... just so I don't have to apologize any-more...

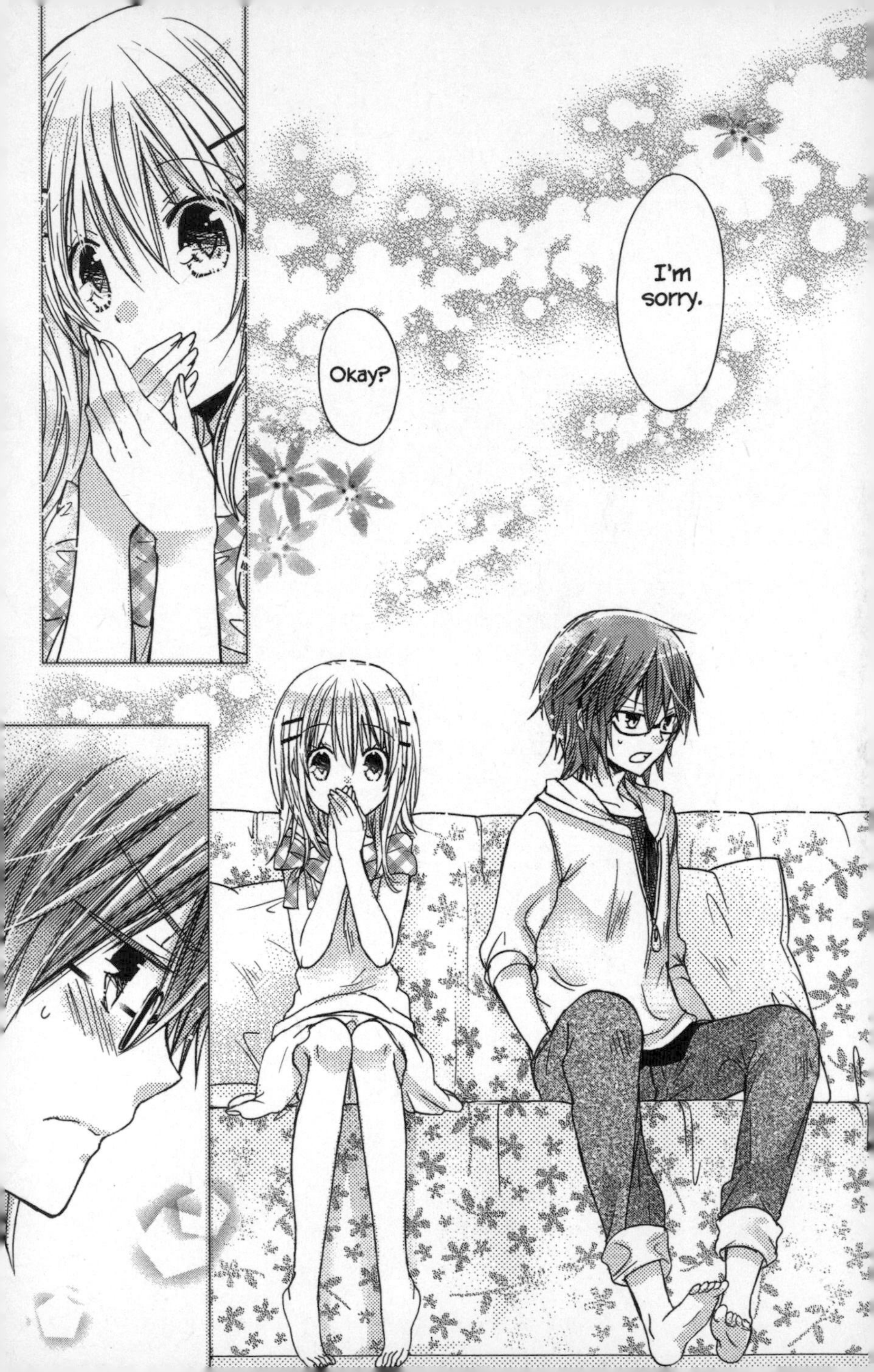
I'm sorry.
Okay?

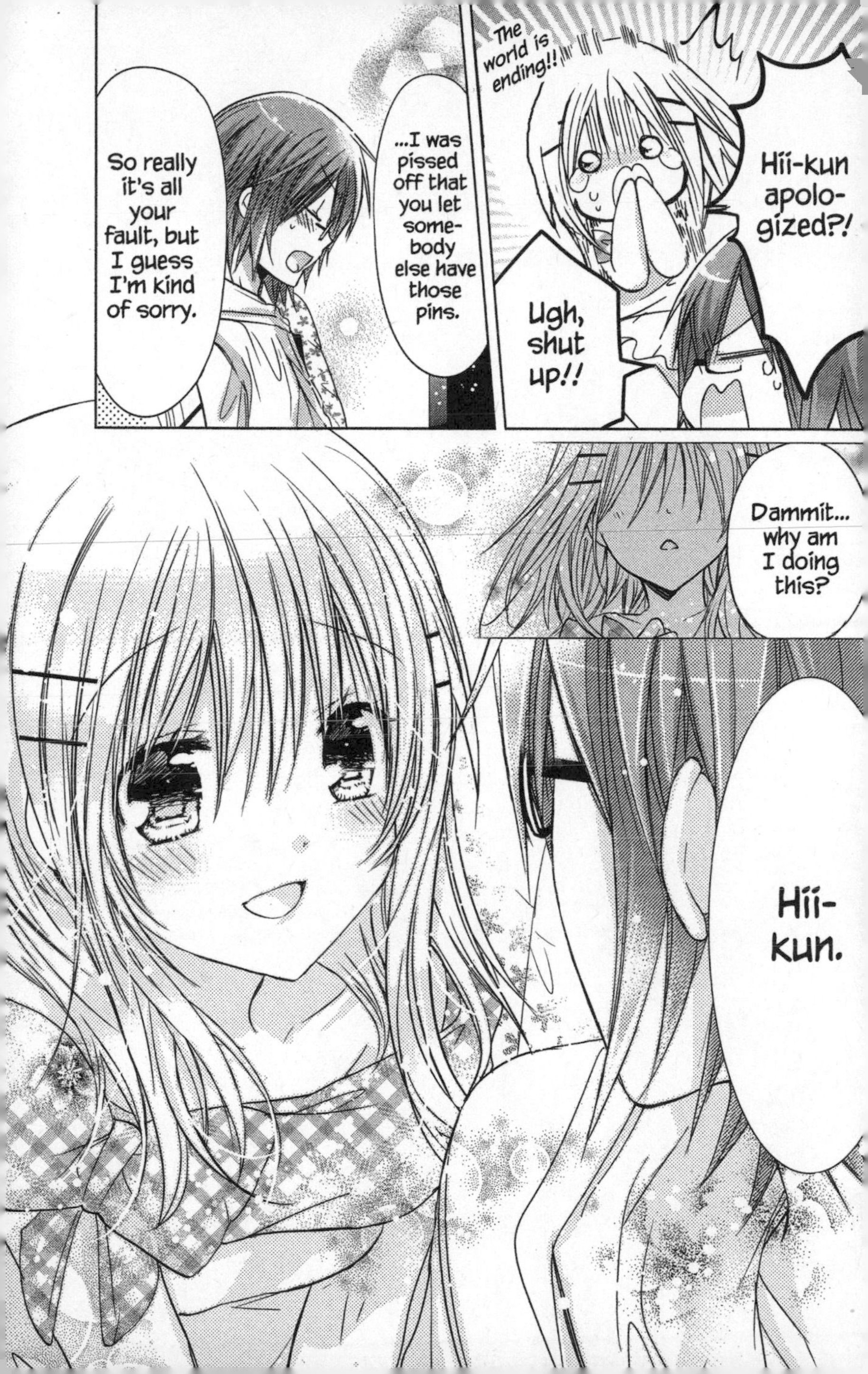
The world is ending!!
Hii-kun apologized?!
Ugh, shut up!!
...I was pissed off that you let somebody else have those pins.
So really it's all your fault, but I guess I'm kind of sorry.
Dammit... why am I doing this?
Hii-kun.

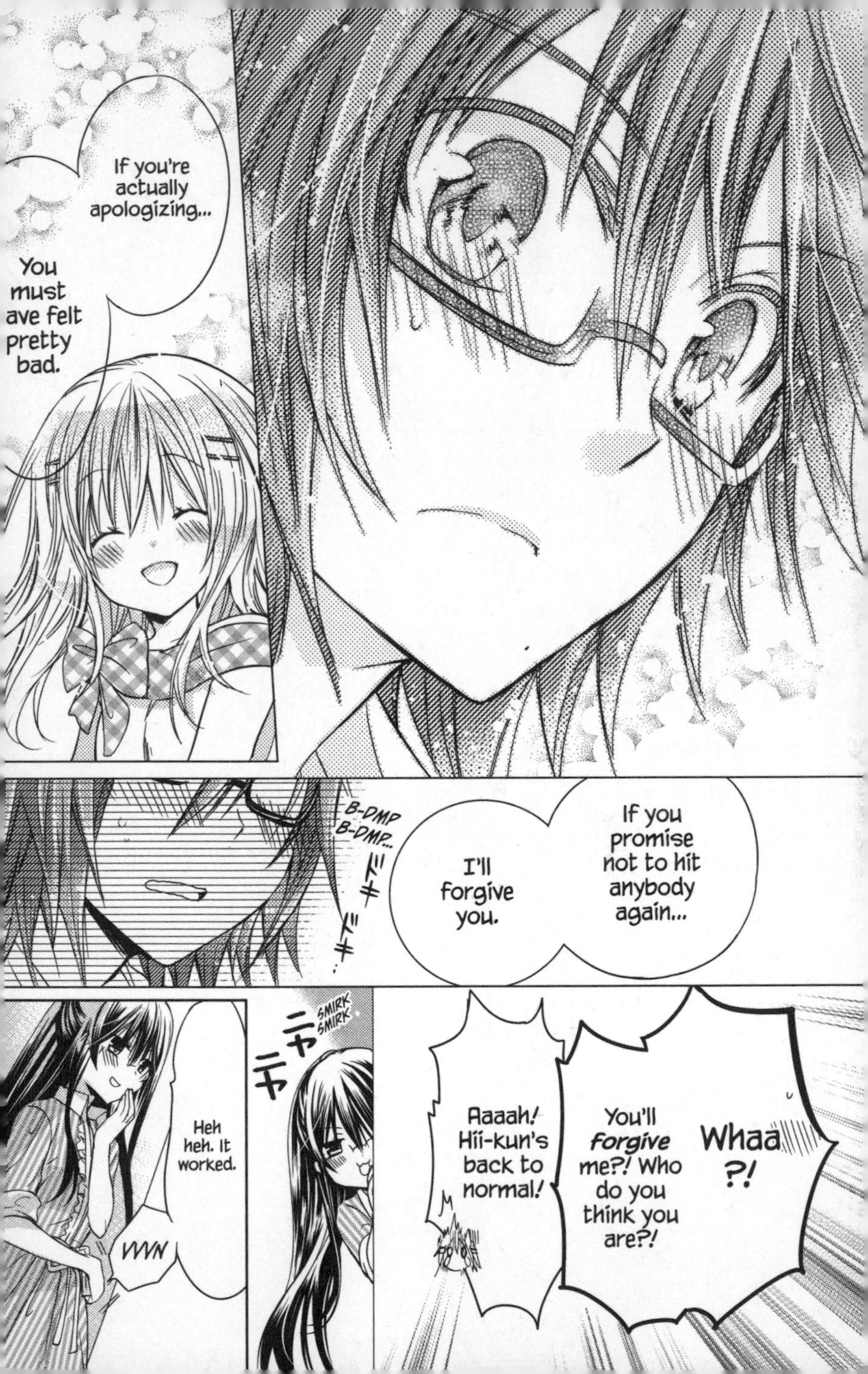
If you're actually apologizing...
You must ave felt pretty bad.
If you promise not to hit anybody again...
I'll forgive you.
B-DMP B-DMP...
ドキ ドキ
Whaa ?!
You'll *forgive* me?! Who do you think you are?!
Aaaah! Hii-kun's back to normal!
SMIRK SMIRK
ニヤ ニヤ
Heh heh. It worked.
VVVN

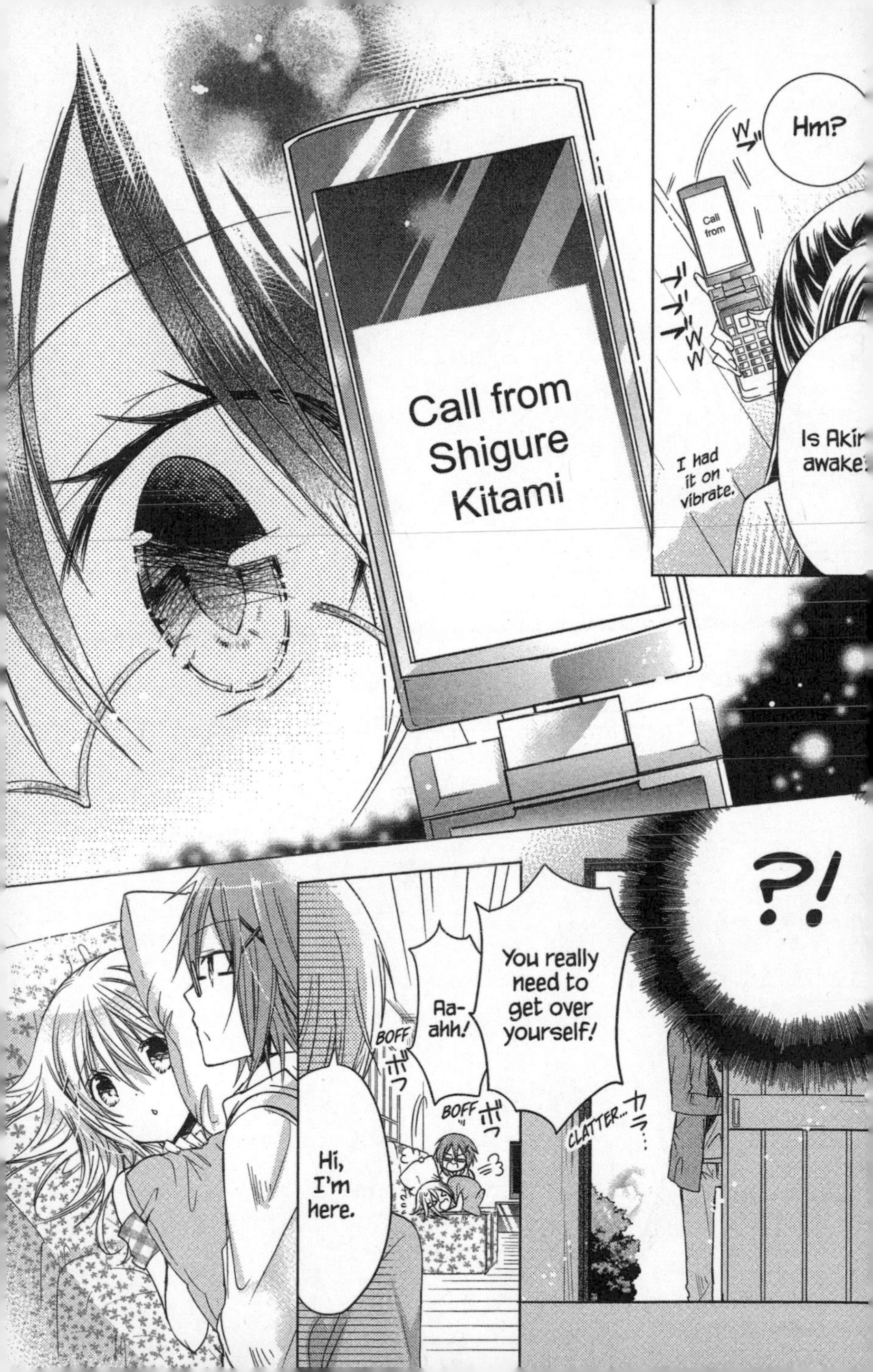
Hm?
W
Call from
W W
Is Akir awake
I had it on vibrate.
Call from Shigure Kitami
?!
CLATTER... カラ…
You really need to get over yourself!
Aa-ahh!
BOFF ボフ
BOFF ボフ
Hi, I'm here.

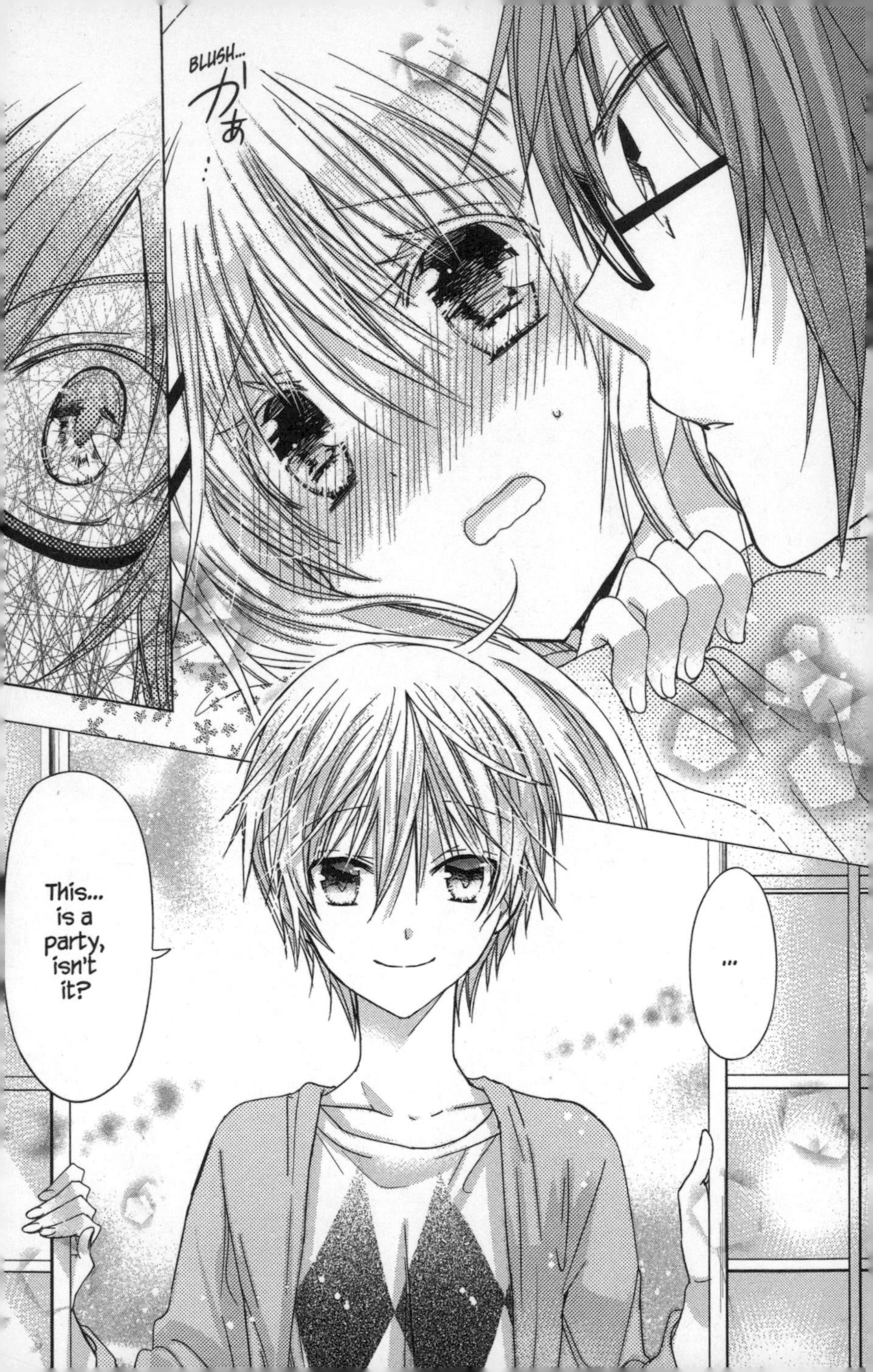
BLUSH...
かぁ…
...
This... is a party, isn't it?

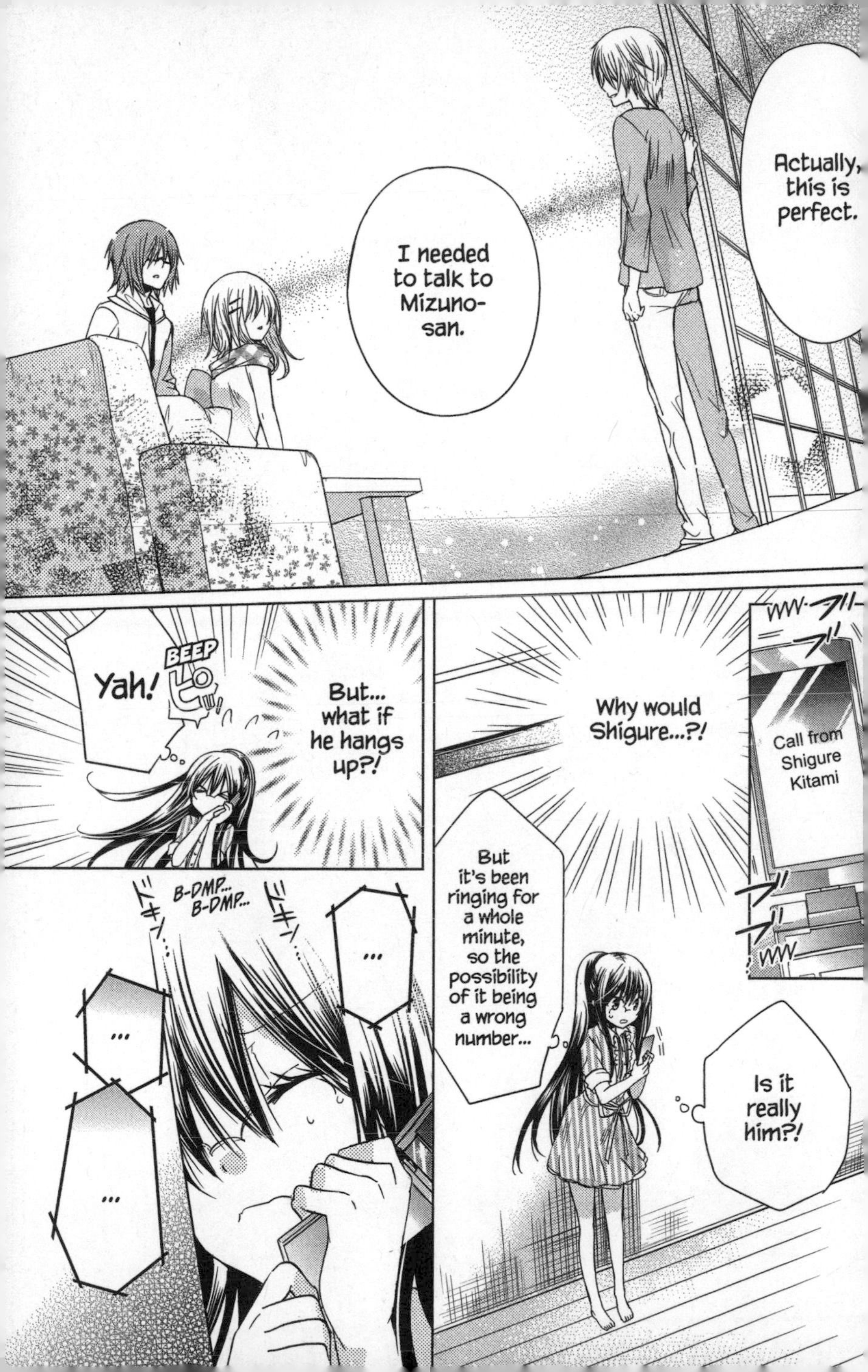

Actually, this is perfect.
I needed to talk to Mizuno-san.
WWV-
Call from Shigure Kitami
WWV
Why would Shigure...?!
But... what if he hangs up?!
BEEP
Yah!
Is it really him?!
But it's been ringing for a whole minute, so the possibility of it being a wrong number...
...
B-DMP... B-DMP...
...
...

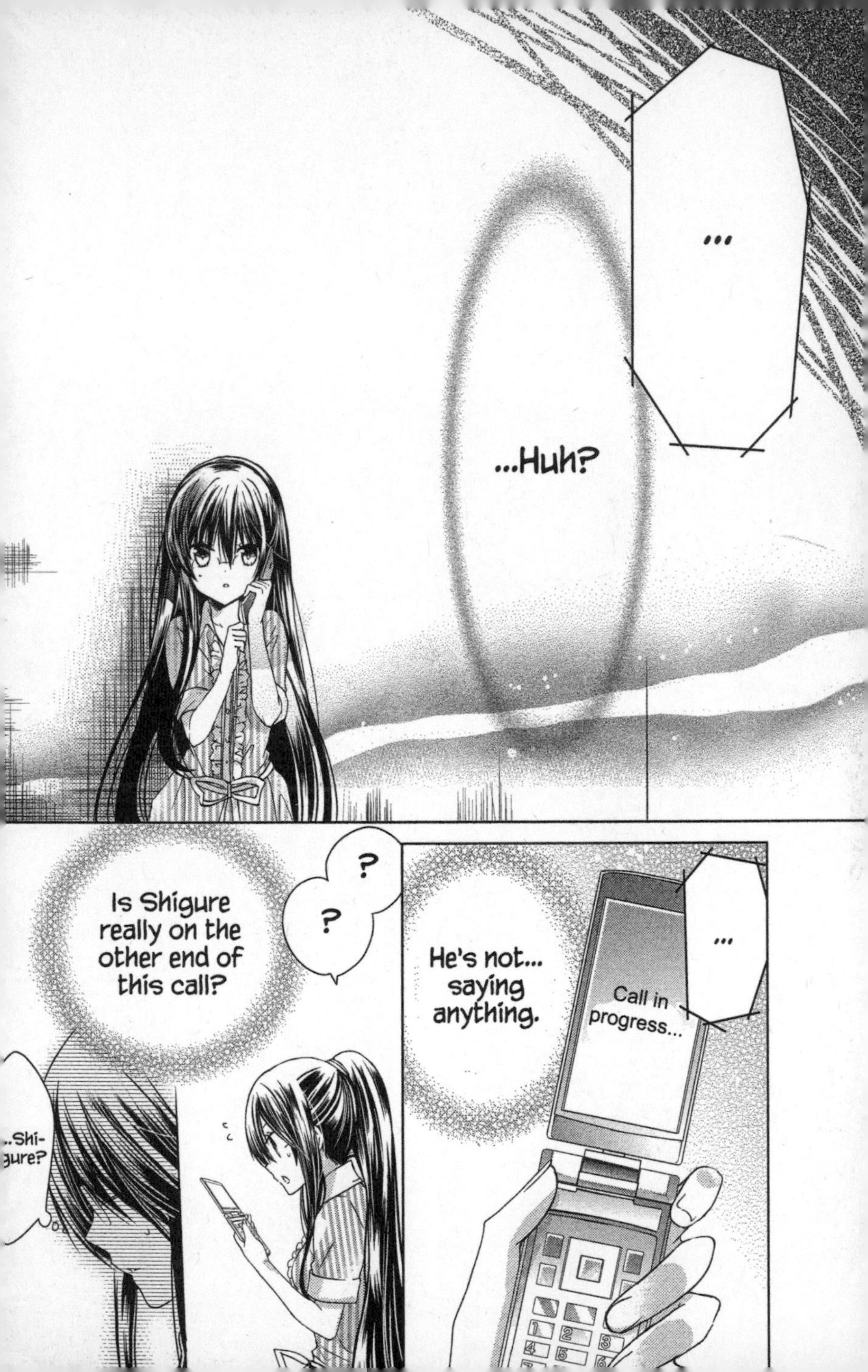
...
...Huh?
...
He's not... saying anything.
Call in progress...
? ?
Is Shigure really on the other end of this call?
...Shi-gure?

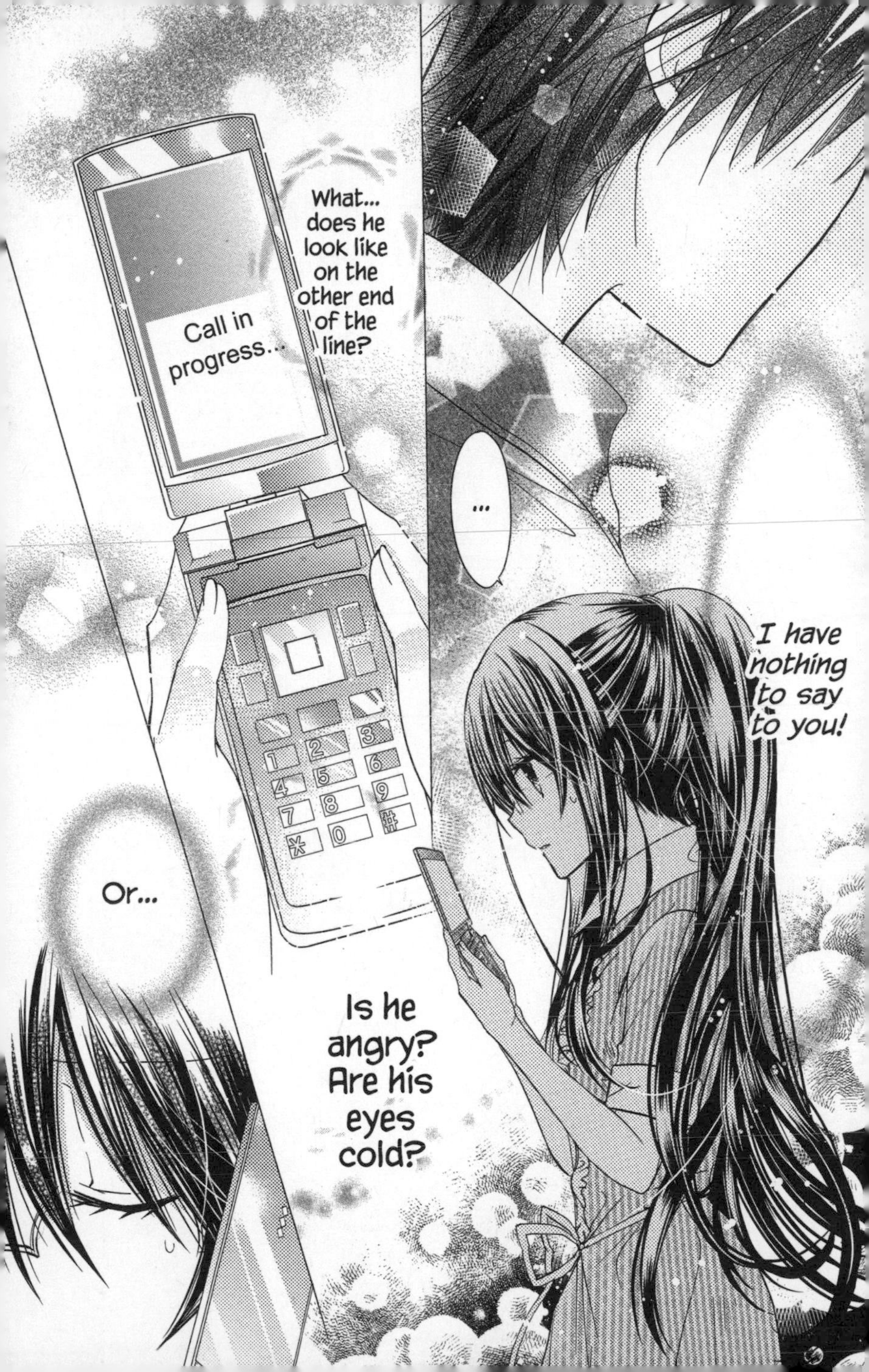
...
I have nothing to say to you!
Call in progress...
What... does he look like on the other end of the line?
Or...
Is he angry? Are his eyes cold?

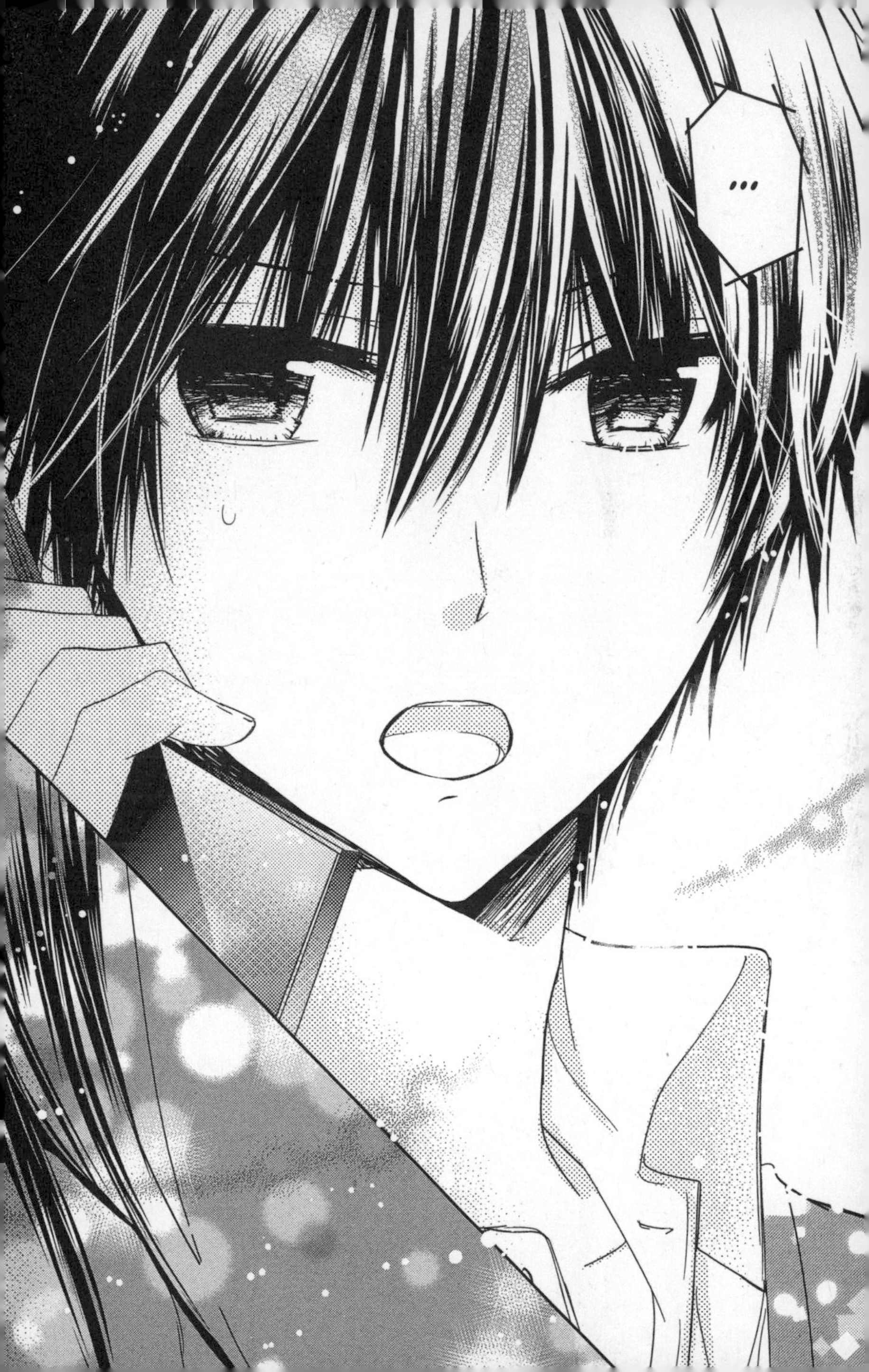
...

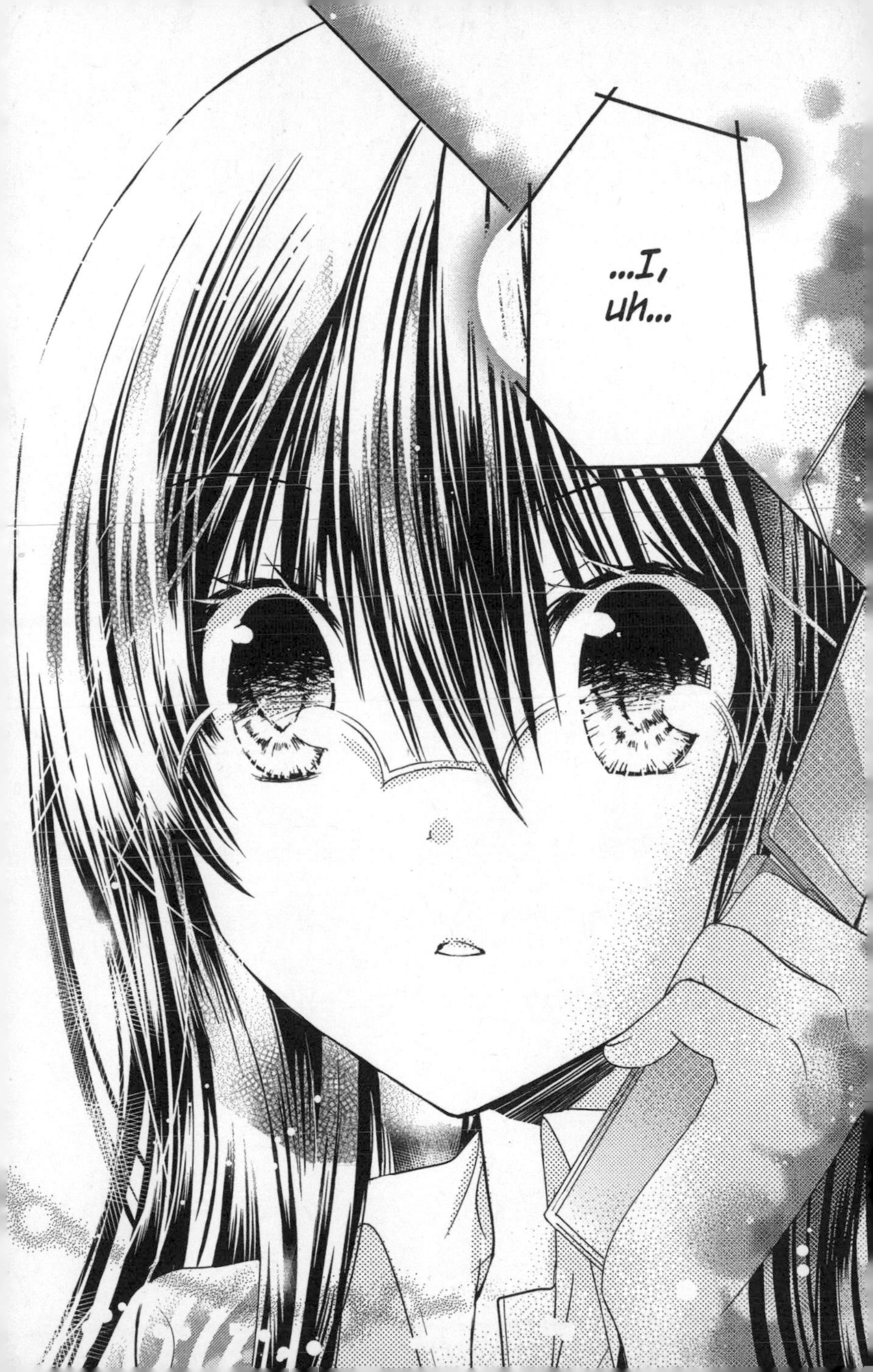
...I, uh...

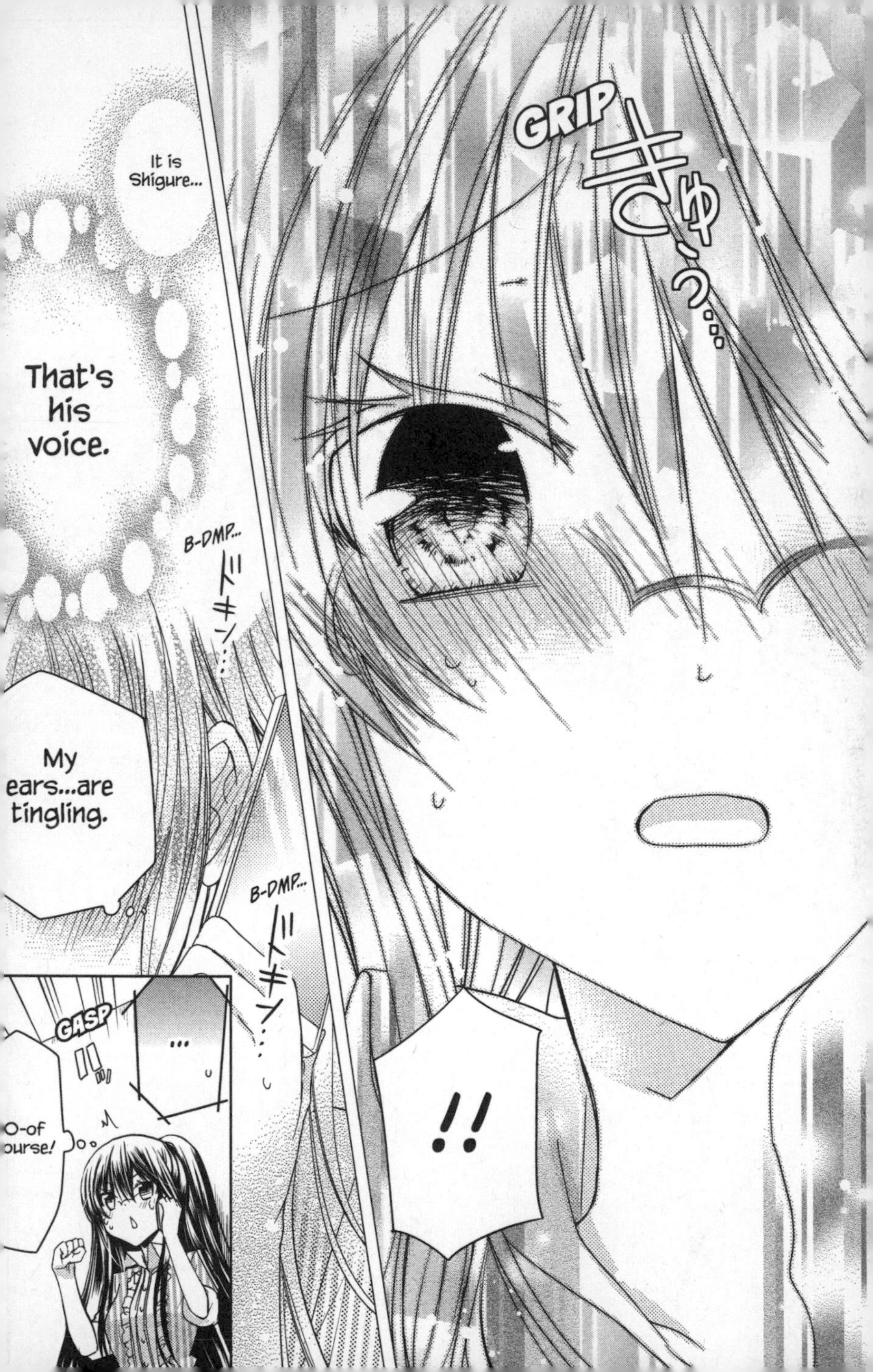
GRIP
きゅう…
B-DMP…
ドキン…
B-DMP…
ドキン…
!!
It is Shigure...
That's his voice.
My ears...are tingling.
...
GASP
O-of ourse!

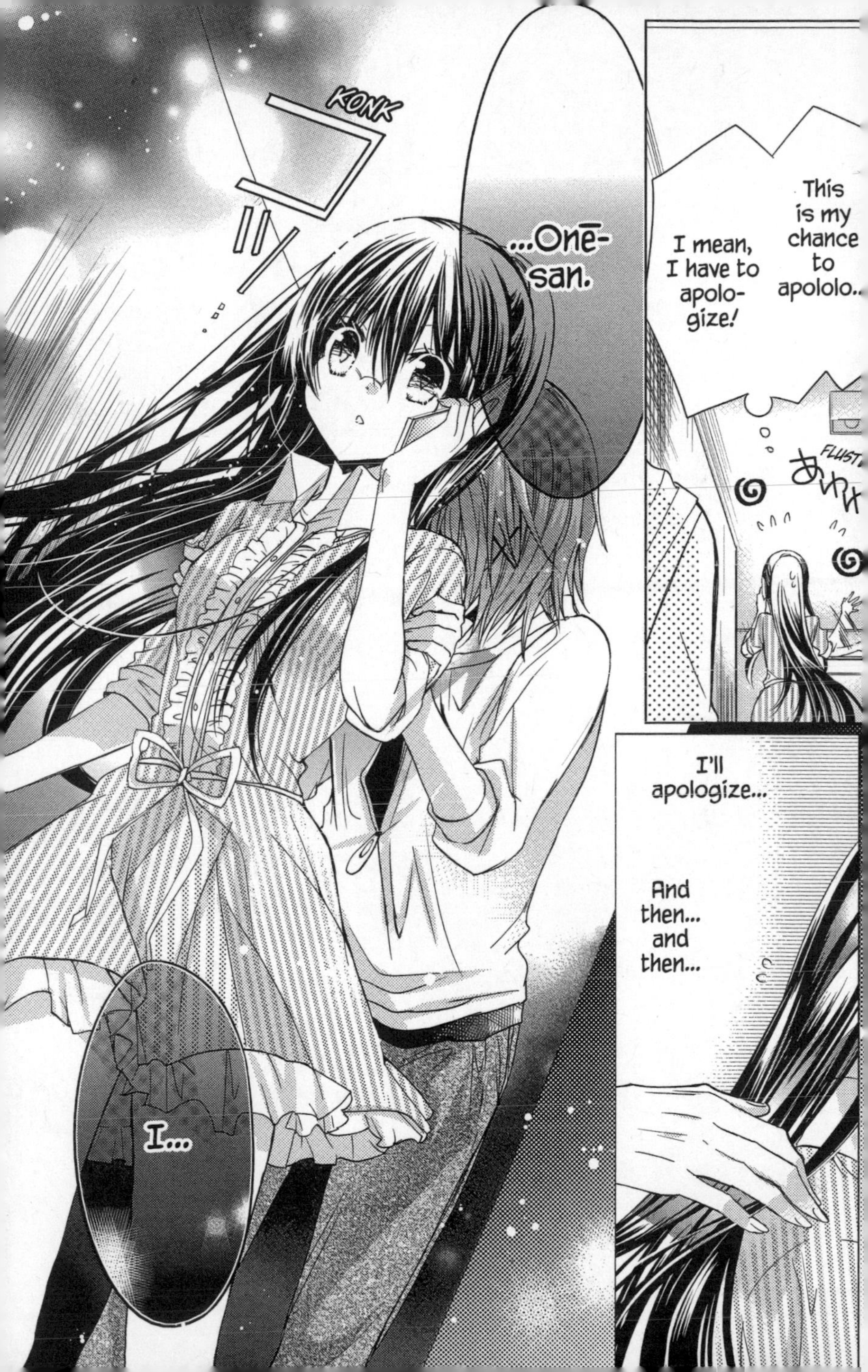
This is my chance to apololo..
I mean, I have to apologize!
FLUST.
I'll apologize...
And then... and then...
...Onē-san.
KONK
I...

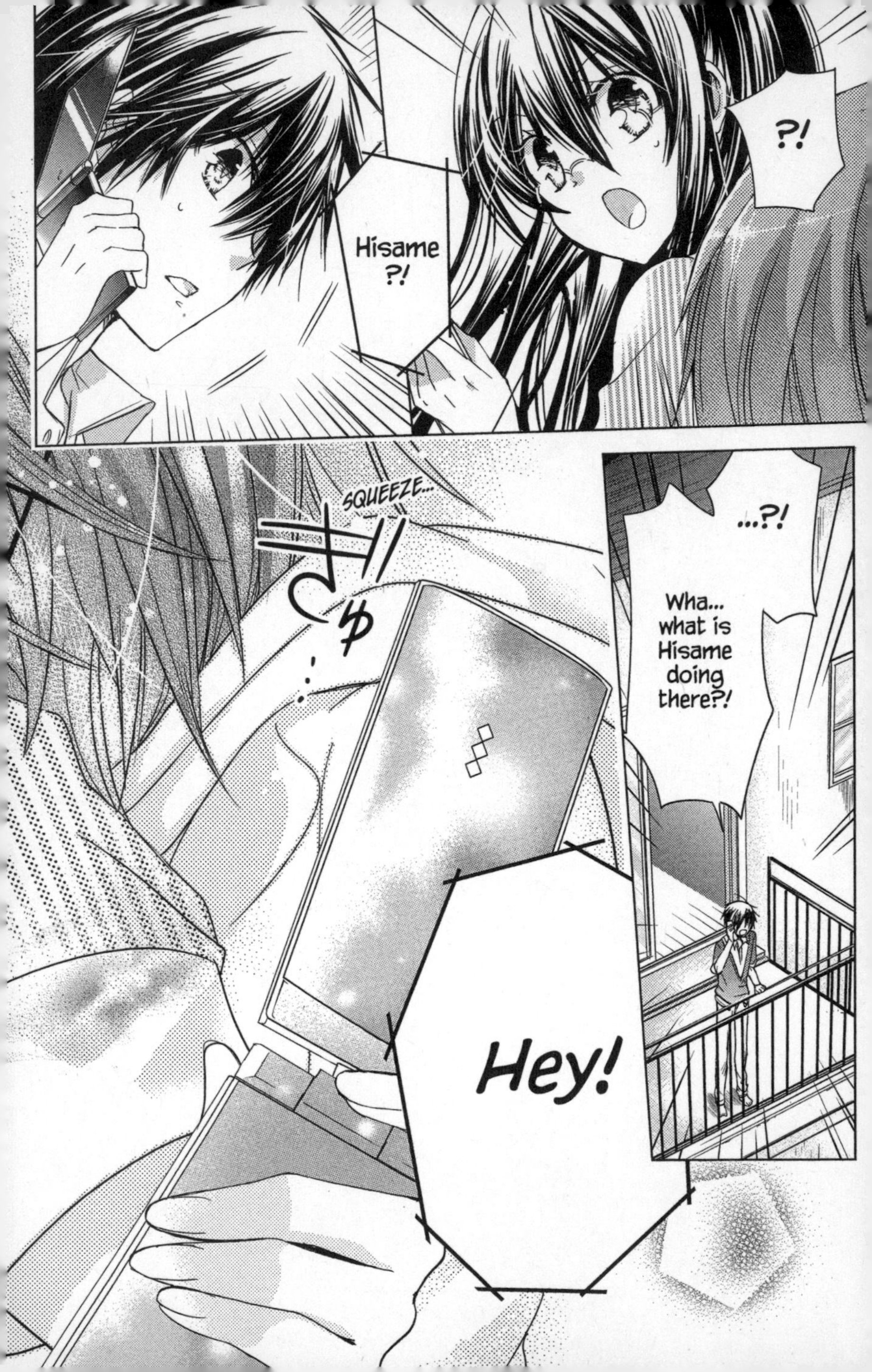
?!
Hisame ?!
...?!
Wha... what is Hisame doing there?!
SQUEEZE...
Hey!

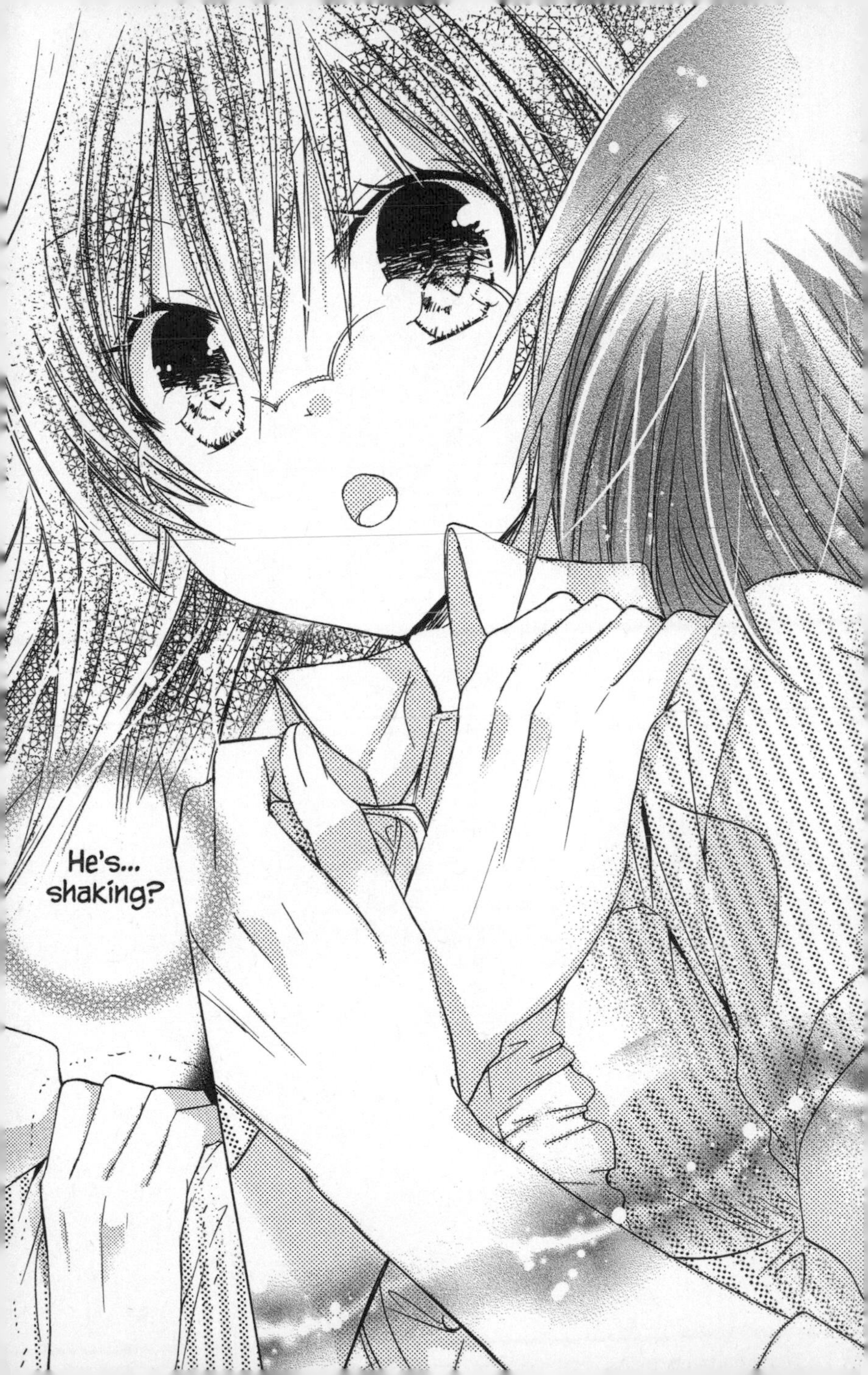
He's... shaking?

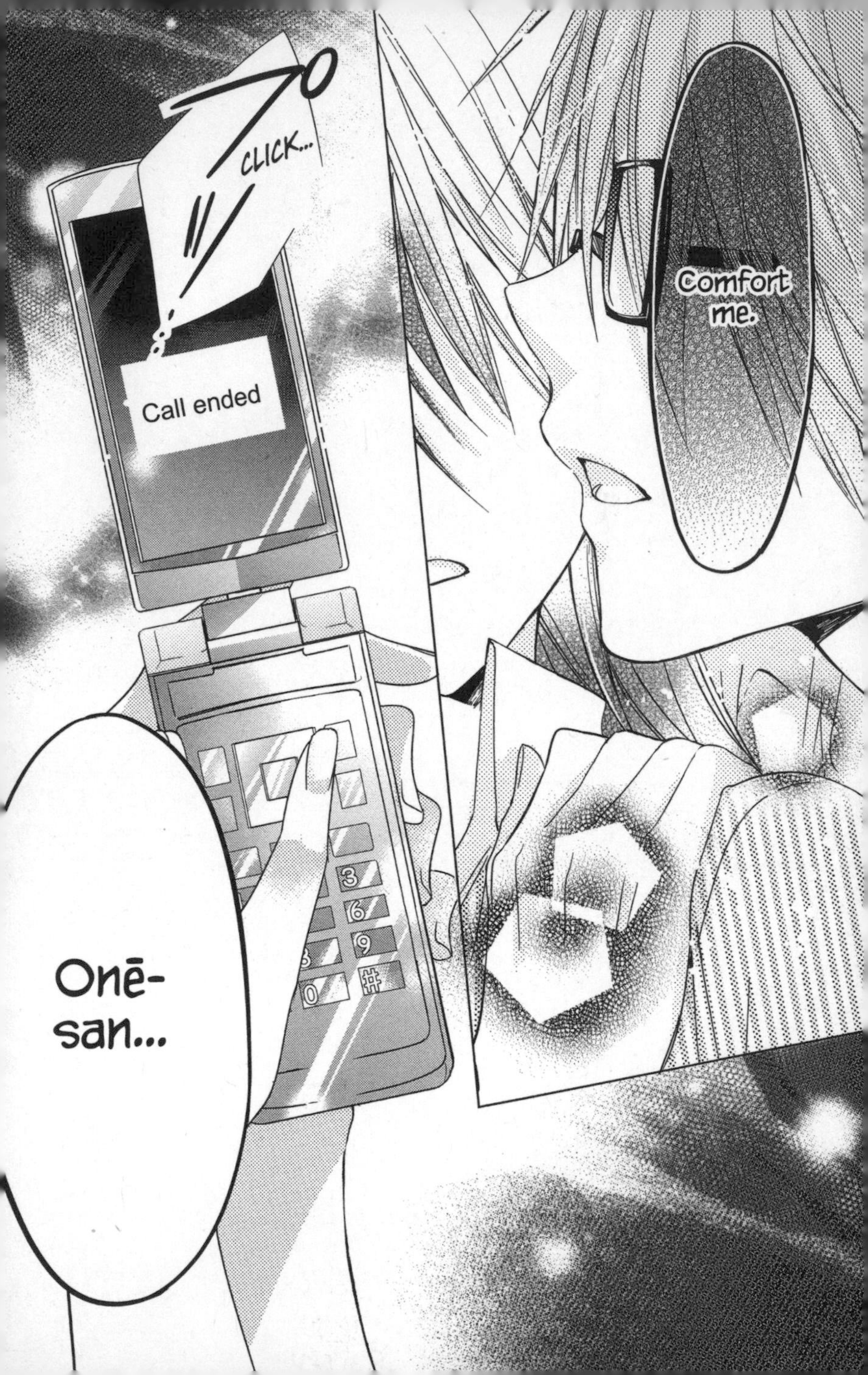
Comfort me.
CLICK...
Call ended
Onē-san...

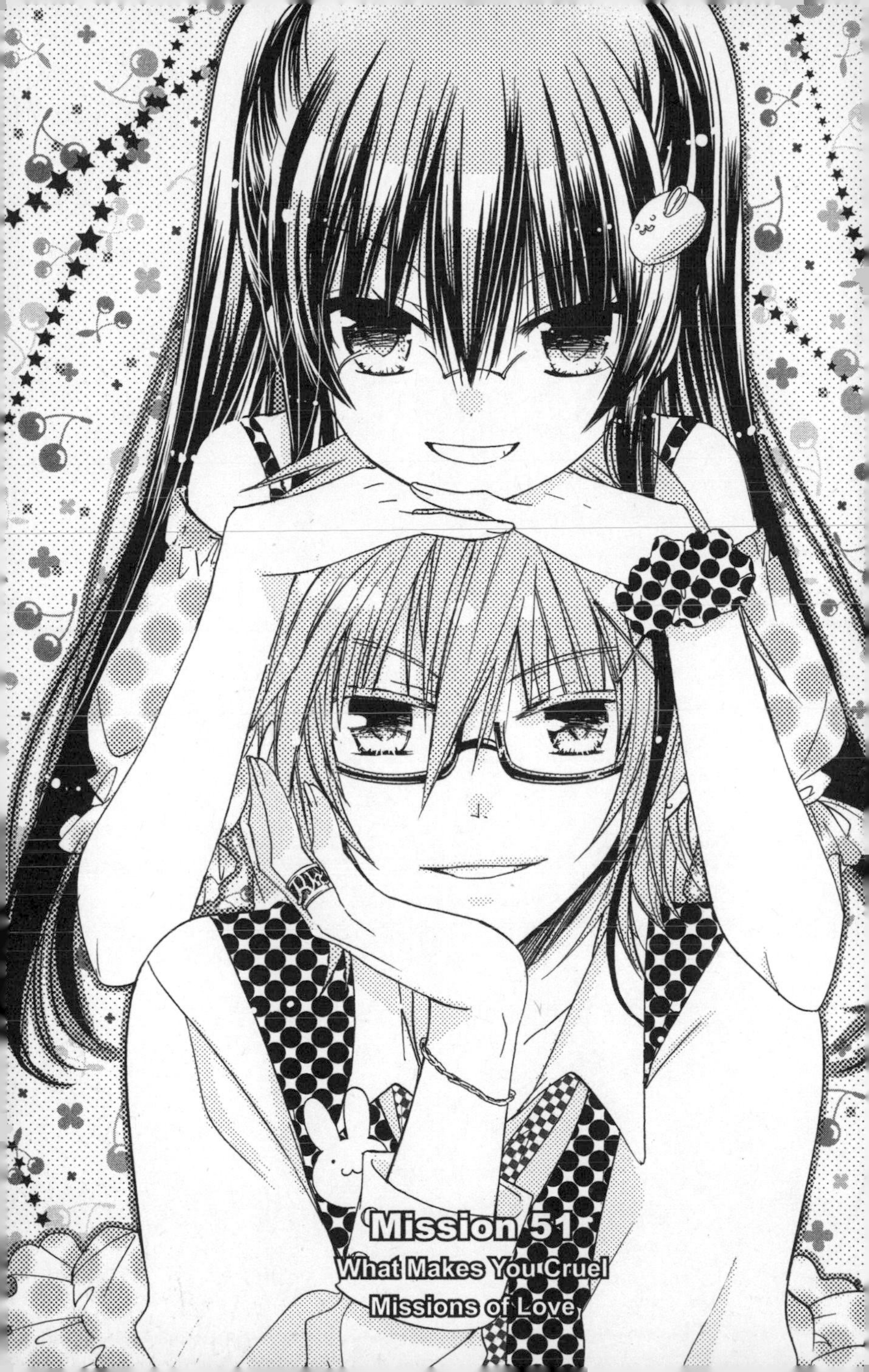
Mission 51
What Makes You Cruel
Missions of Love

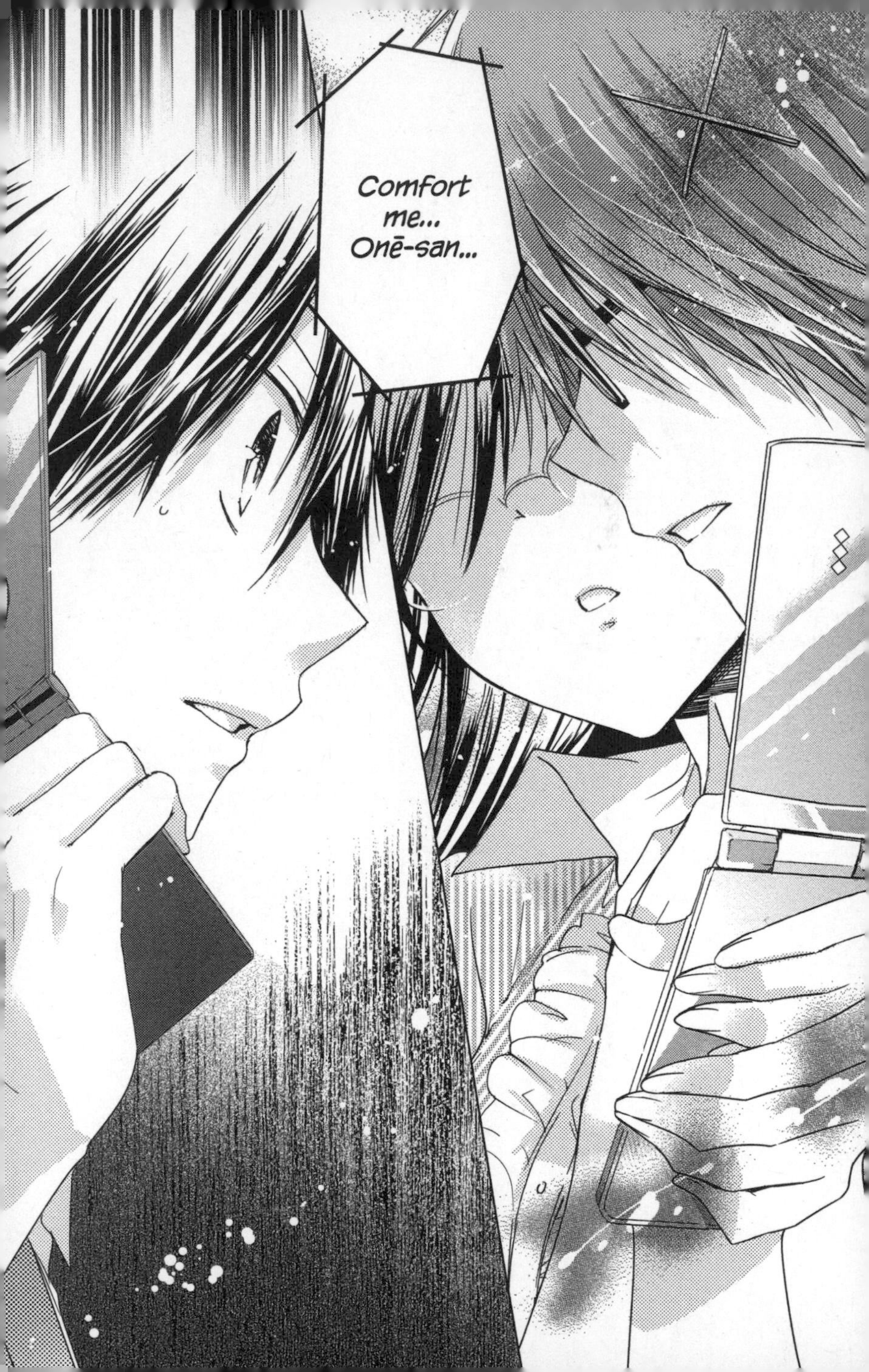
Comfort me... Onē-san...

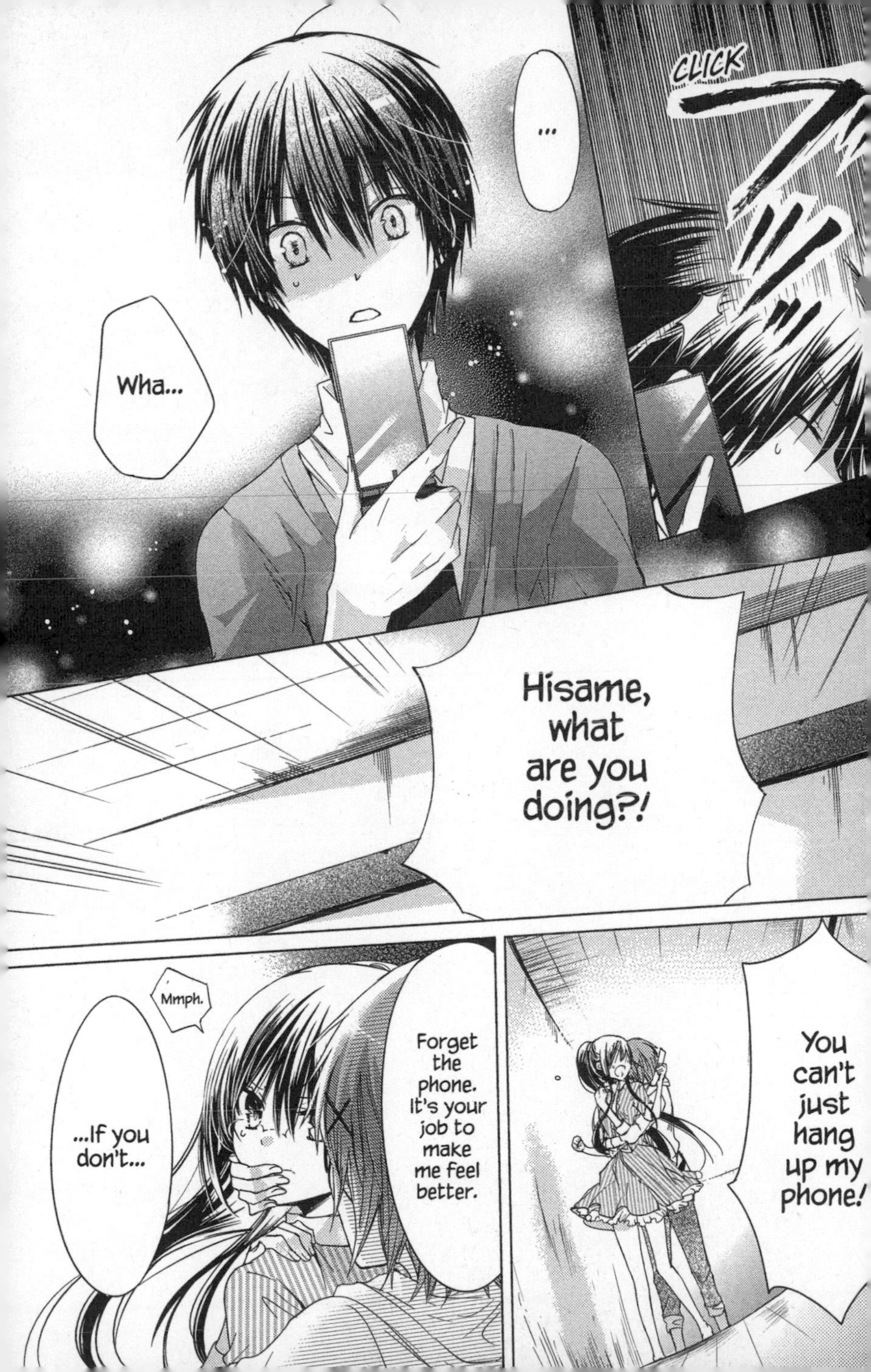
CLICK
...
Wha...
Hisame, what are you doing?!
You can't just hang up my phone!
Forget the phone. It's your job to make me feel better.
Mmph.
...If you don't...

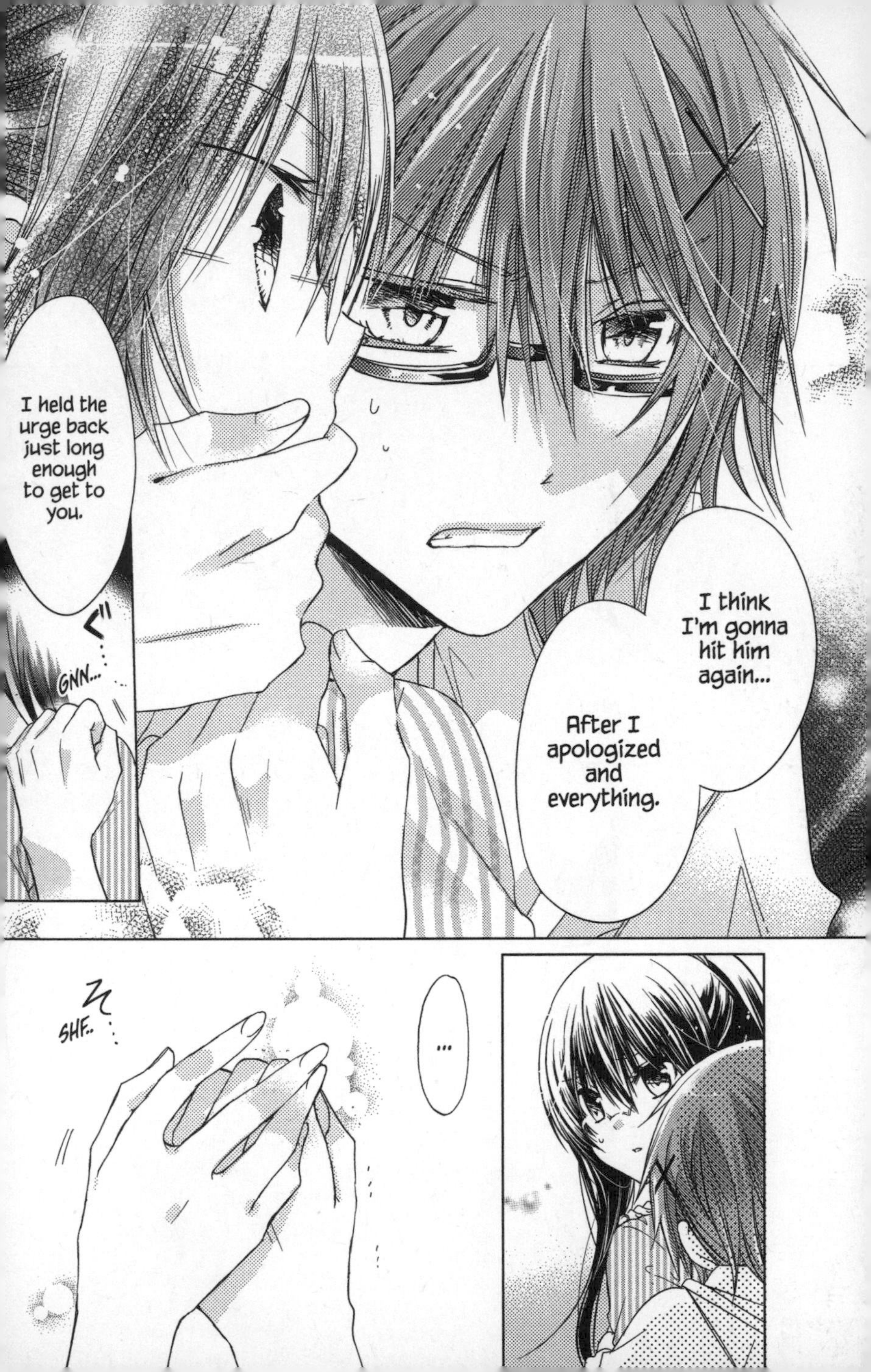
I think I'm gonna hit him again...
After I apologized and everything.
I held the urge back just long enough to get to you.
GNN...
...
SHF..

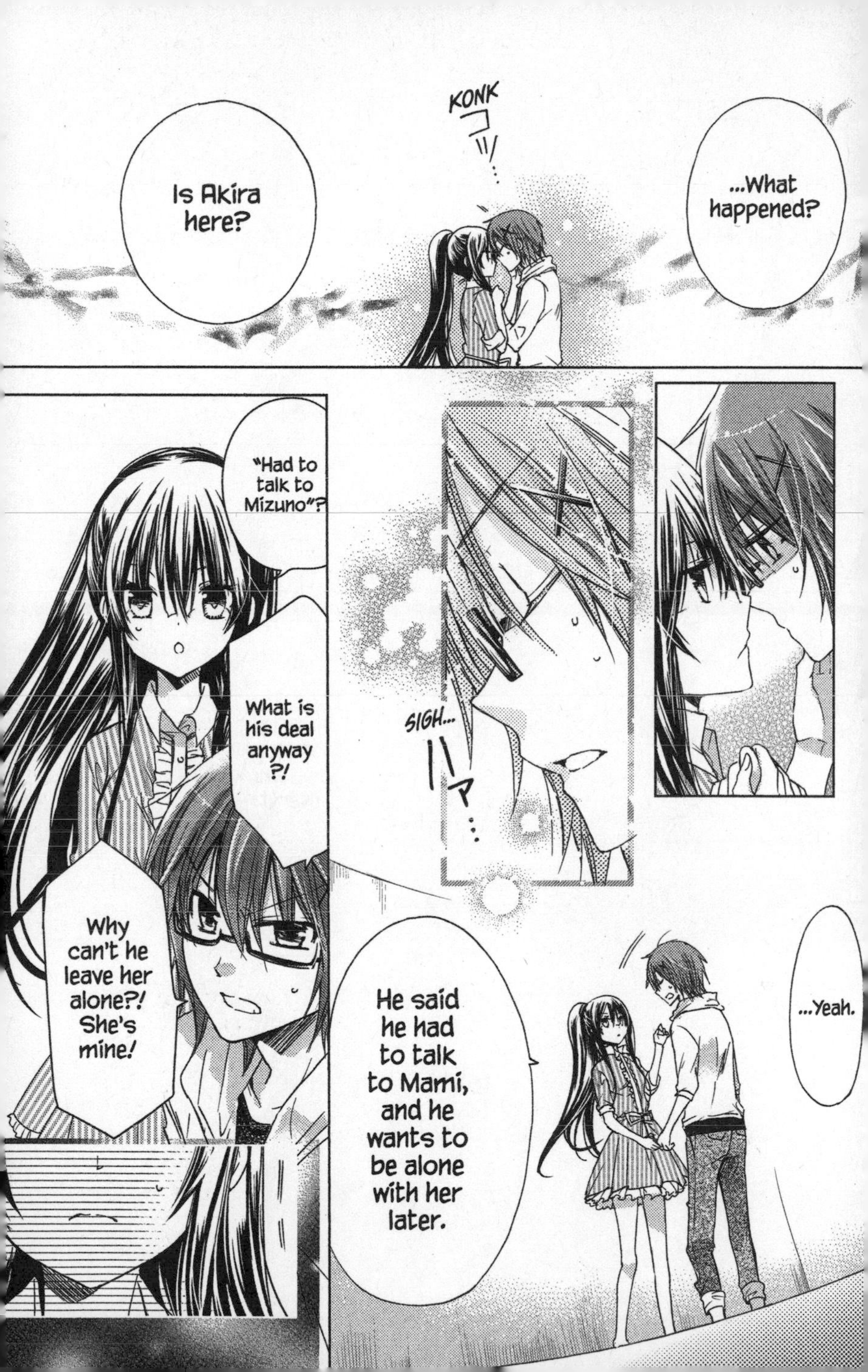
...What happened?
KONK
Is Akira here?
SIGH...
...Yeah.
He said he had to talk to Mami, and he wants to be alone with her later.
"Had to talk to Mizuno"?
What is his deal anyway?!
Why can't he leave her alone?! She's mine!

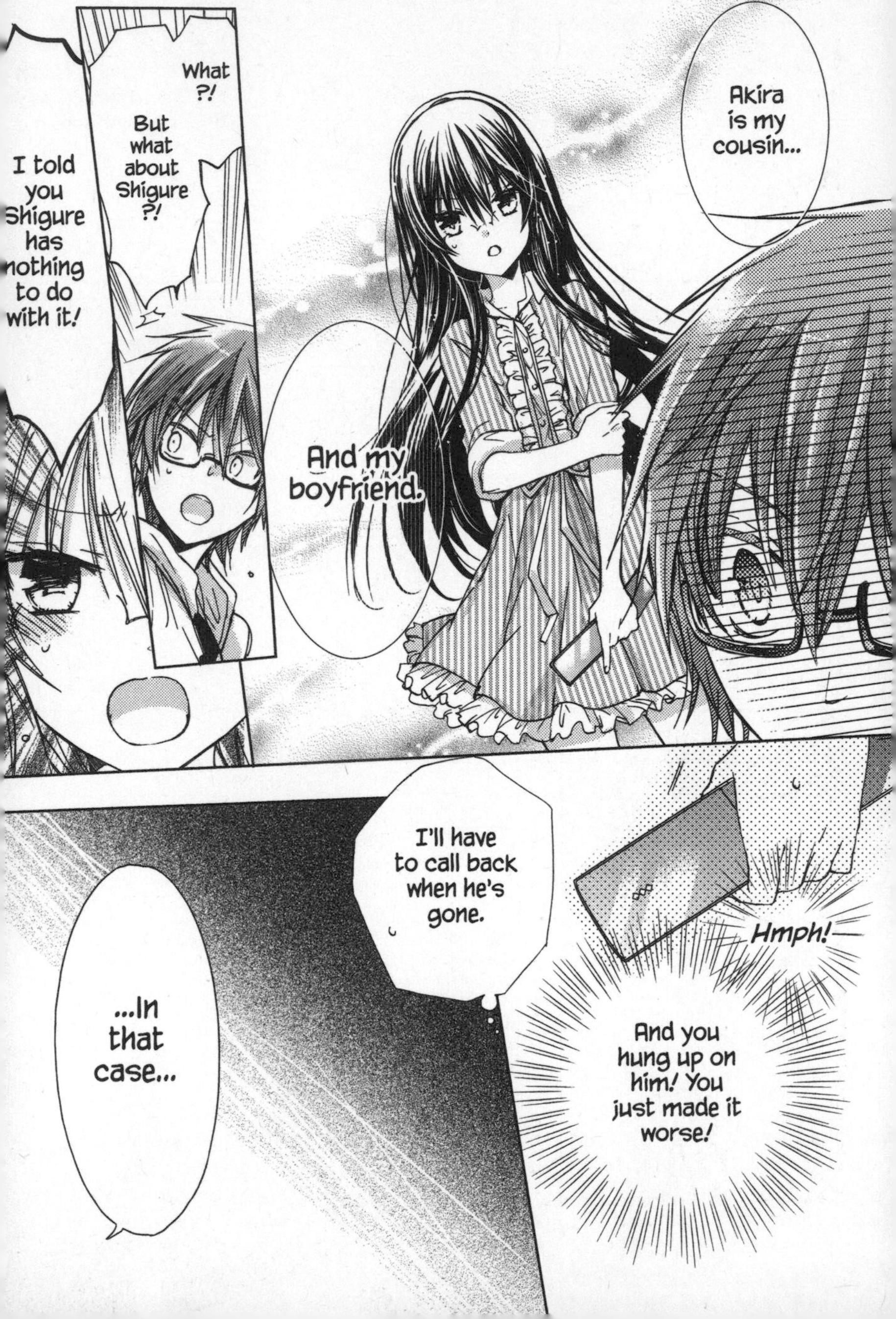
Akira is my cousin...
And my boyfriend.
What?!
But what about Shigure?!
I told you Shigure has nothing to do with it!
I'll have to call back when he's gone.
Hmph!
And you hung up on him! You just made it worse!
...In that case...

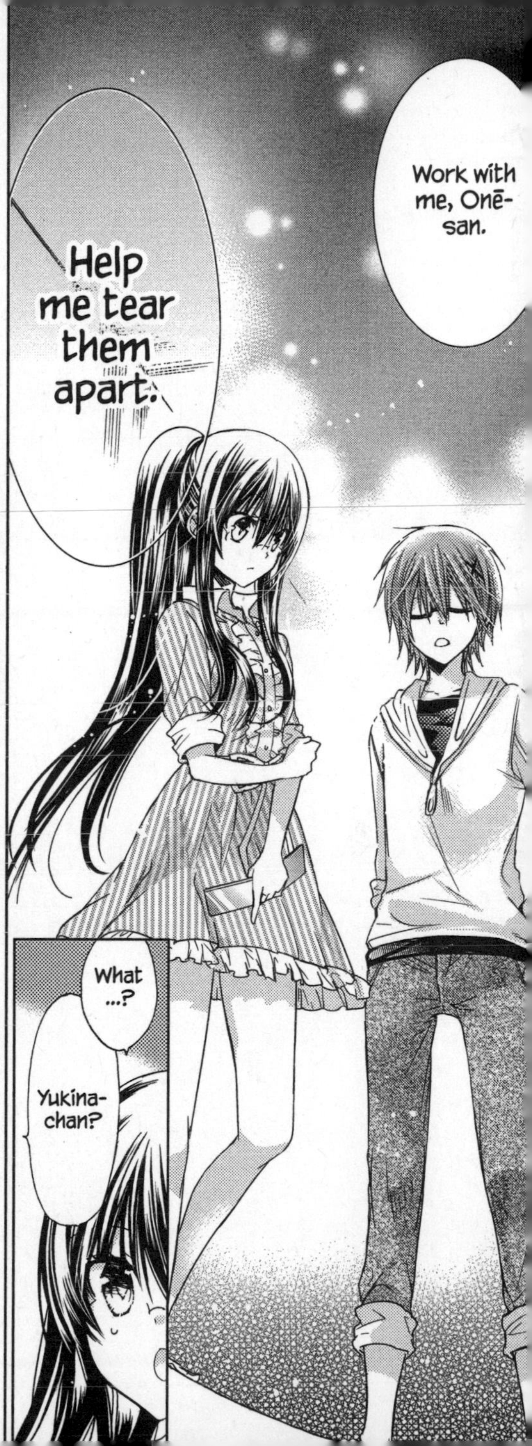
Work with me, Onē-san.
Help me tear them apart.
What ...?
Yukina-chan?

3

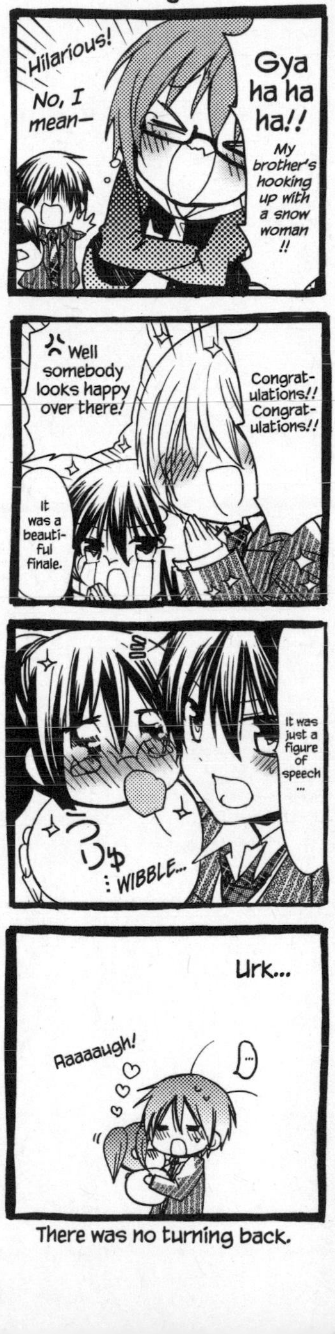
Gya ha ha ha!!
My brother's hooking up with a snow woman!!
Hilarious!
No, I mean—
Congratulations!! Congratulations!!
Well somebody looks happy over there!
It was a beautiful finale.
It was just a figure of speech ...
WIBBLE...
Urk...
...
Aaaaaugh!

There was no turning back.

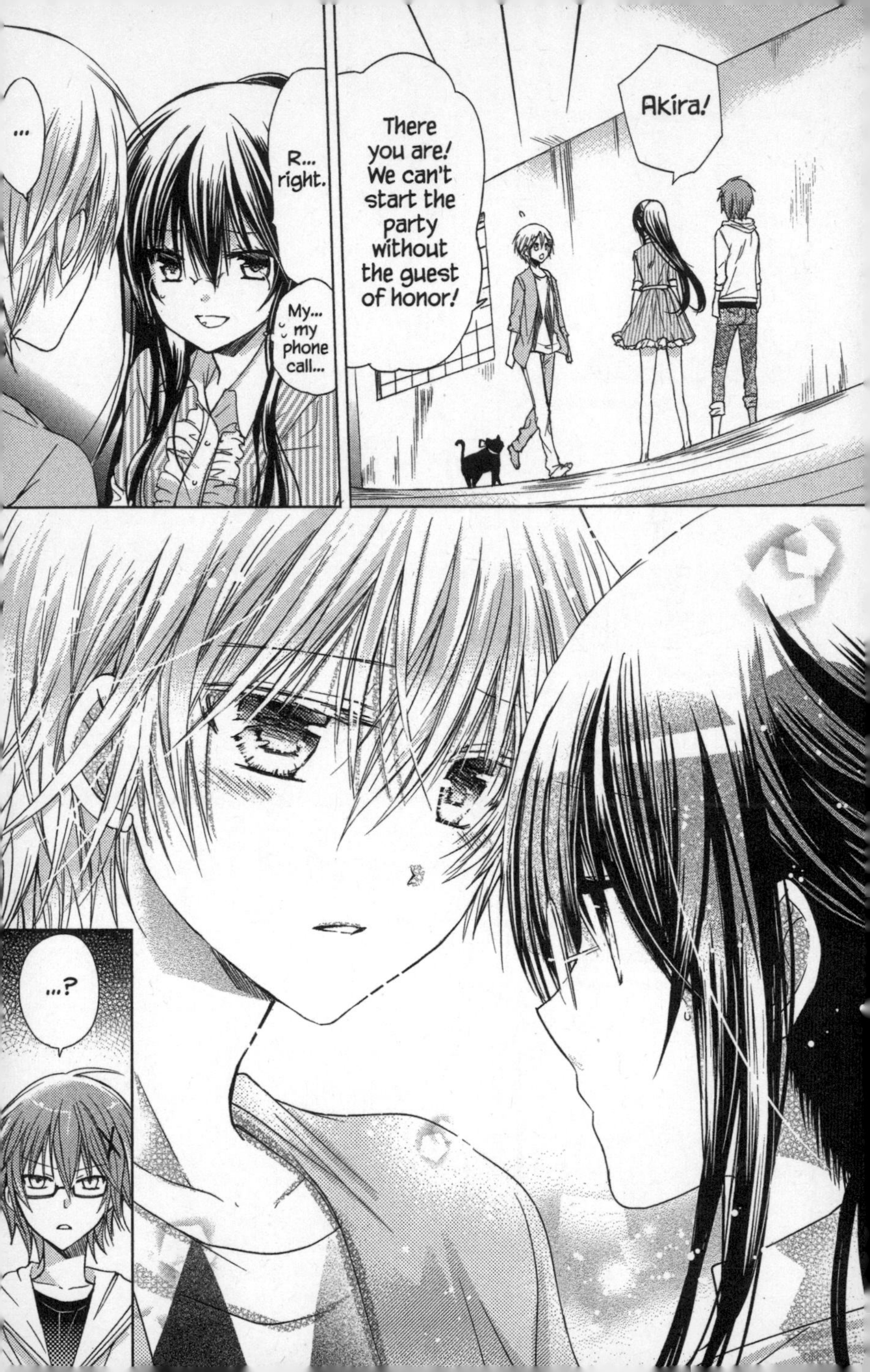
Akira!
There you are! We can't start the party without the guest of honor!
R... right.
My... my phone call...
...
...?

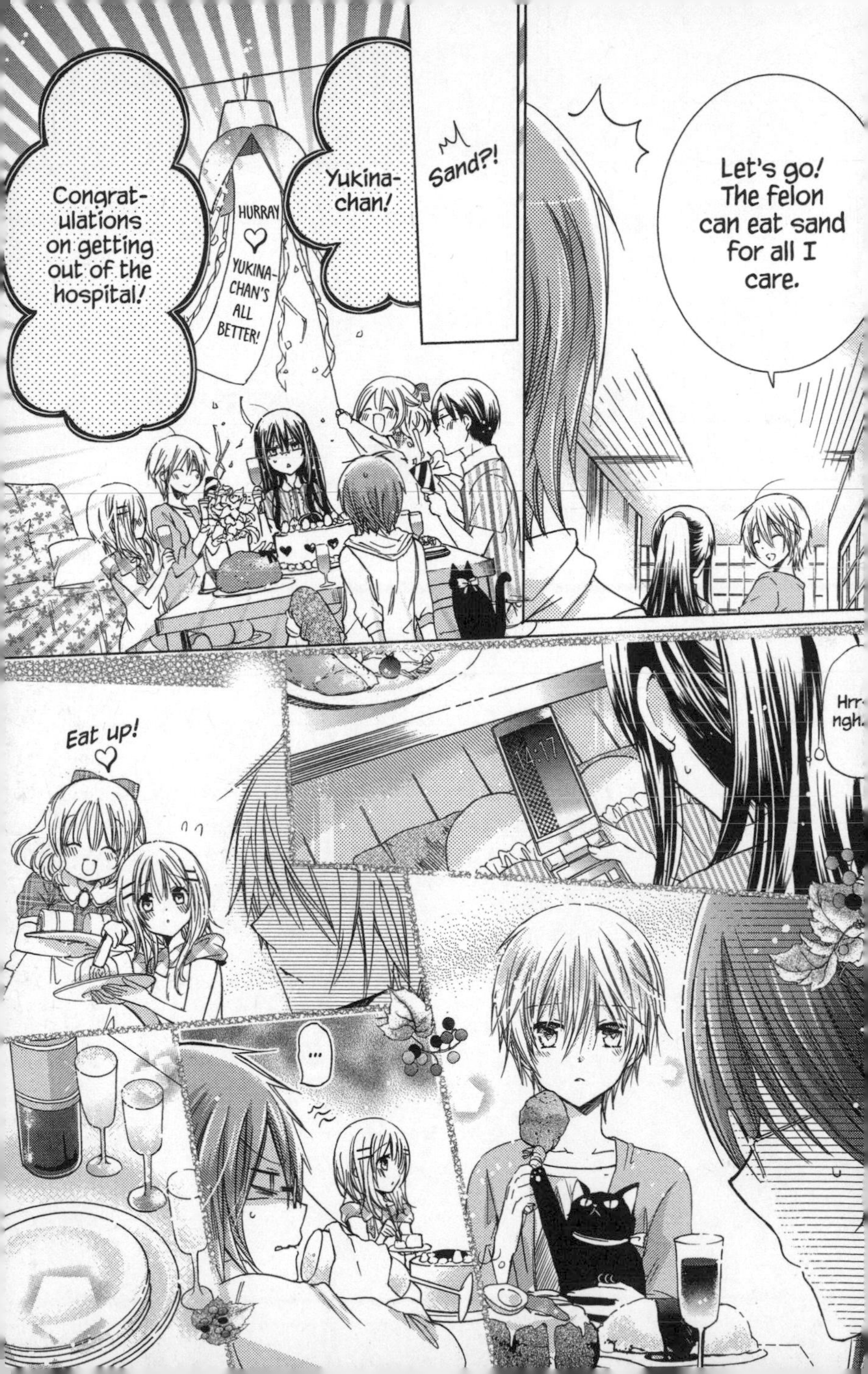

Let's go! The felon can eat sand for all I care.
Sand?!
Yukina-chan!
HURRAY ♥ YUKINA-CHAN'S ALL BETTER!
Congratulations on getting out of the hospital!
Hrr-ngh.
14:17
Eat up! ♥
...

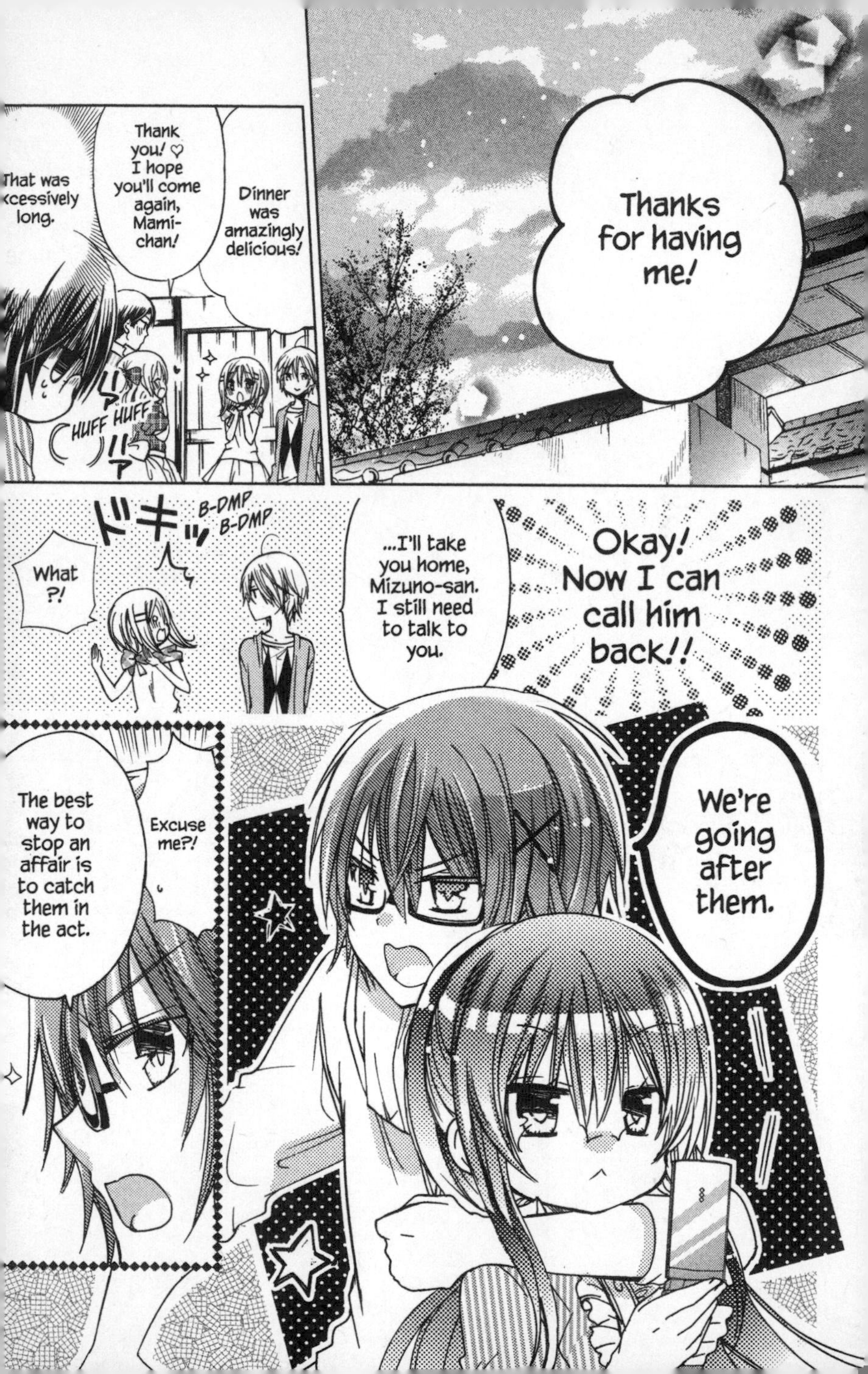
Thanks for having me!
Dinner was amazingly delicious!
Thank you! ♡ I hope you'll come again, Mami-chan!
That was xcessively long.
HUFF HUFF
Okay! Now I can call him back!!
...I'll take you home, Mizuno-san. I still need to talk to you.
B-DMP B-DMP
ドキッ
What?!
We're going after them.
Excuse me?!
The best way to stop an affair is to catch them in the act.

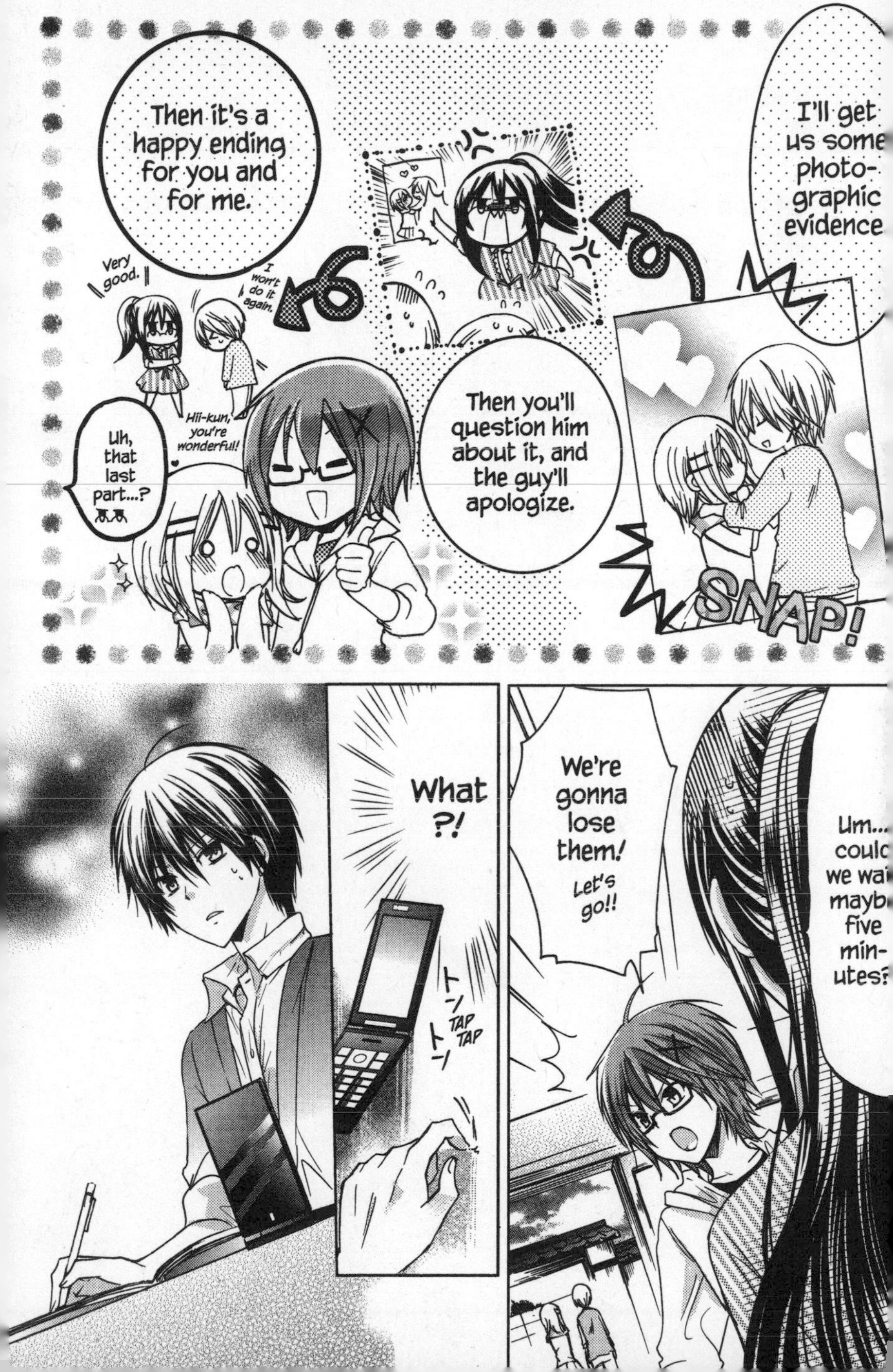
I'll get us some photo-graphic evidence
SNAP!
Then you'll question him about it, and the guy'll apologize.
Then it's a happy ending for you and for me.
I won't do it again.
Very good.
Hii-kun, you're wonderful!
Uh, that last part...?
Um... coul we wai mayb five min-utes?
We're gonna lose them!
Let's go!!
What?!
TAP TAP

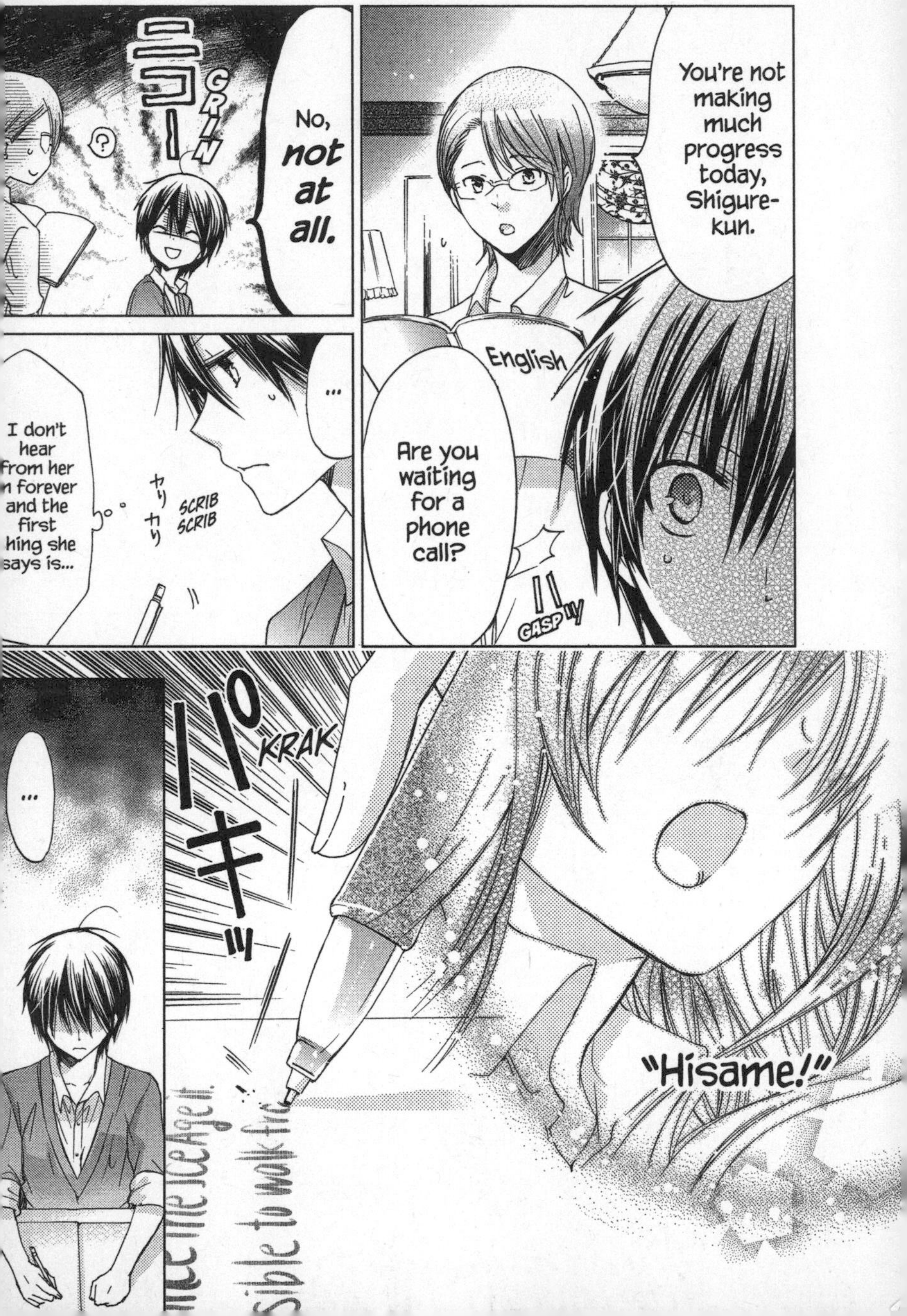
You're not making much progress today, Shigure-kun.
No, not at all.
GRIN
?
English
Are you waiting for a phone call?
GASP
...
I don't hear from her n forever and the first hing she says is...
SCRIB SCRIB
"Hisame!"
KRAK
...

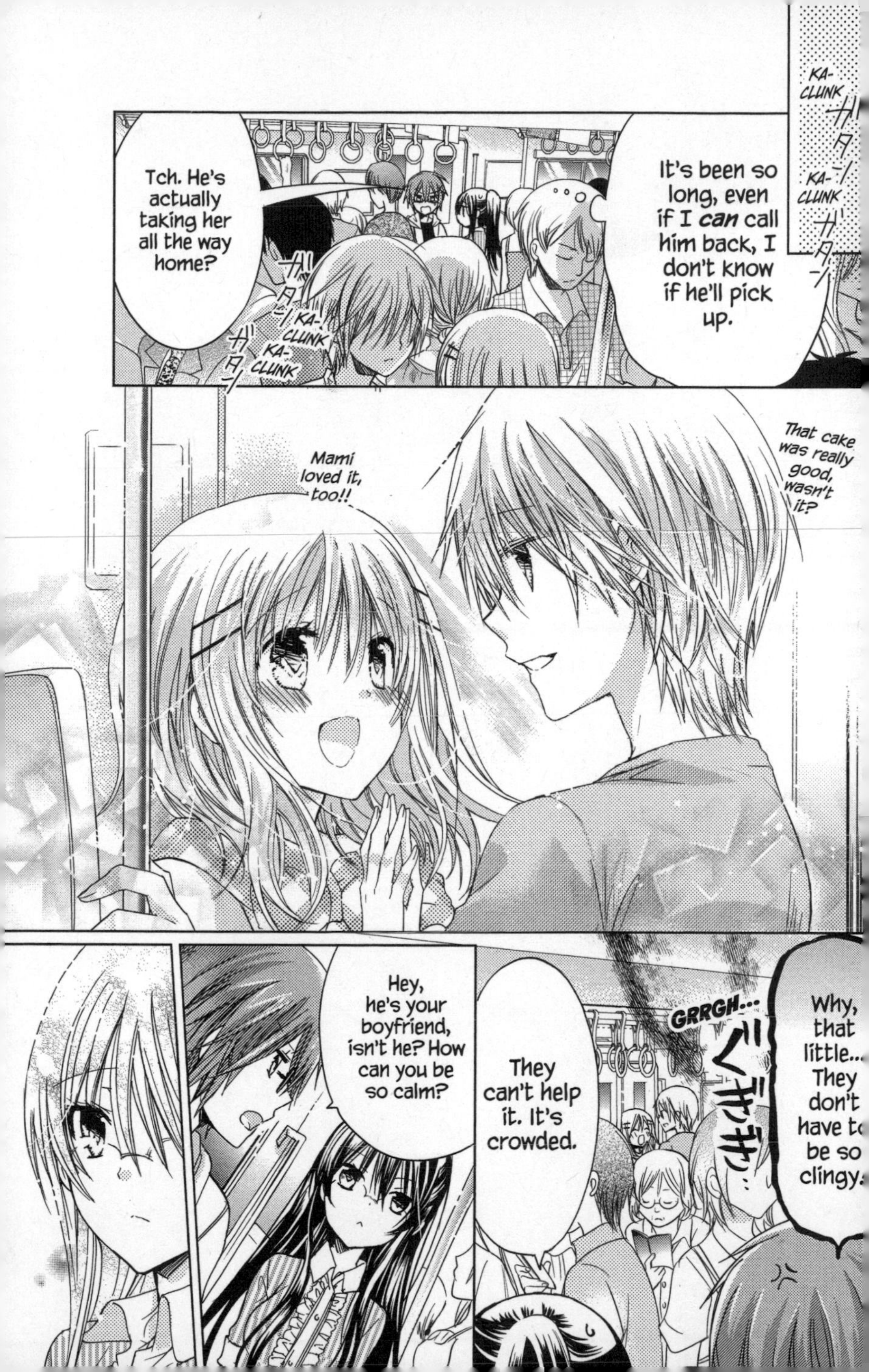
KA-CLUNK
KA-CLUNK
It's been so long, even if I *can* call him back, I don't know if he'll pick up.
Tch. He's actually taking her all the way home?
KA-CLUNK
KA-CLUNK
That cake was really good, wasn't it?
Mami loved it, too!!
Why, that little... They don't have to be so clingy.
GRRGH...
They can't help it. It's crowded.
Hey, he's your boyfriend, isn't he? How can you be so calm?

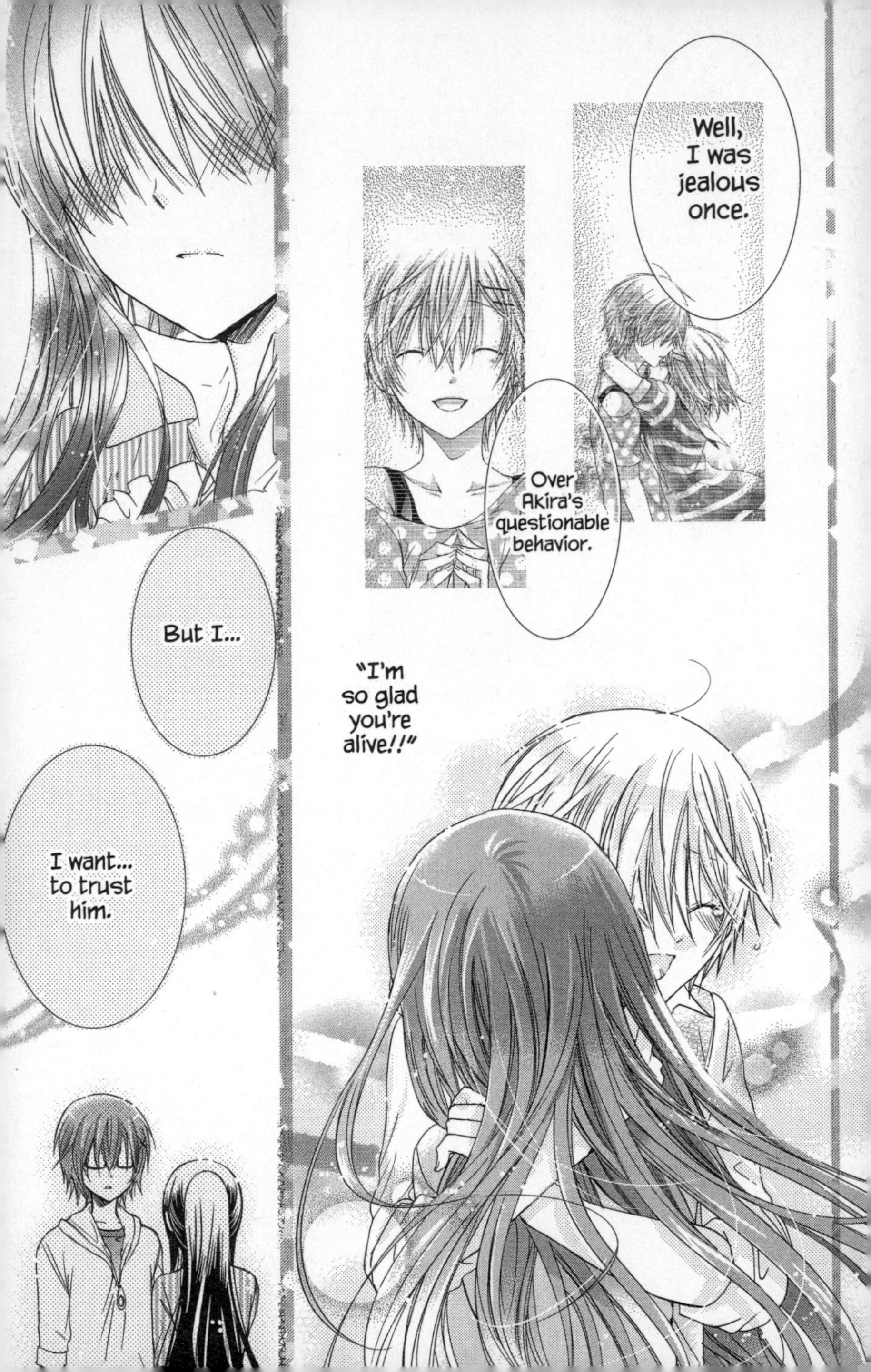
Well, I was jealous once.
Over Akira's questionable behavior.
"I'm so glad you're alive!!"
But I...
I want... to trust him.

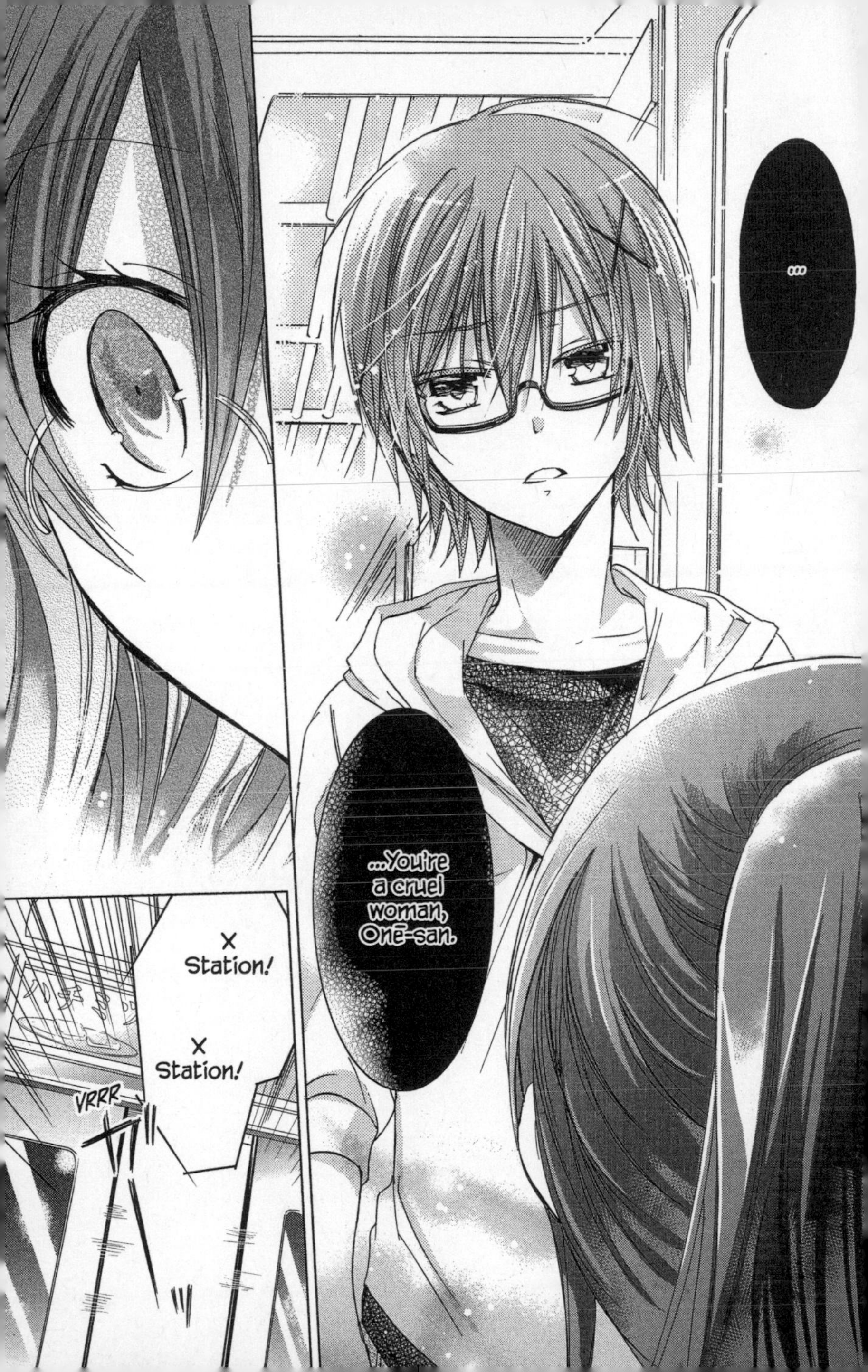
...
...You're a cruel woman, Onē-san.
X Station!
X Station!
VRRR

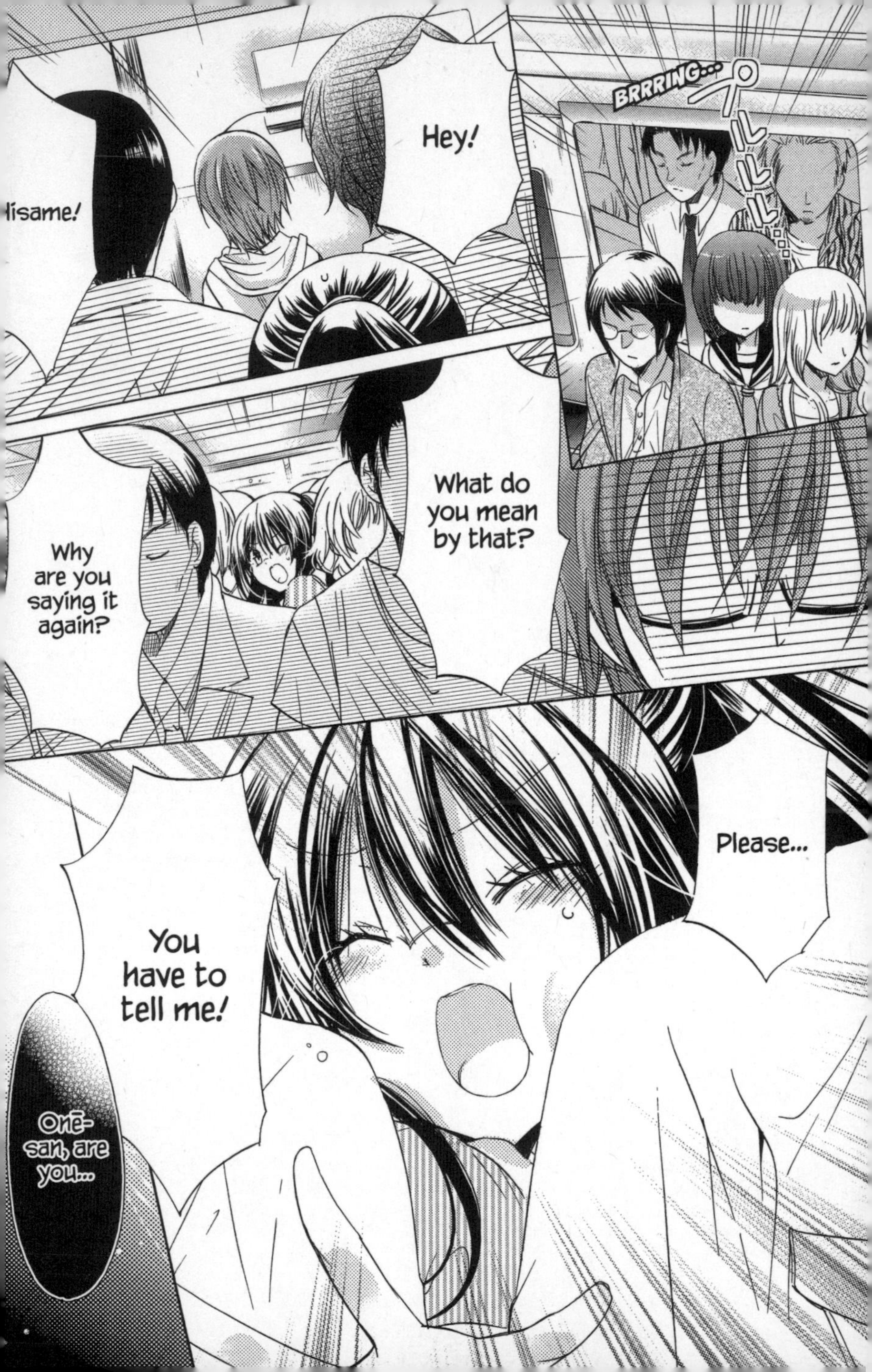

BRRRING...
Hey!
lisame!
What do you mean by that?
Why are you saying it again?
Please...
You have to tell me!
Onē-san, are you...

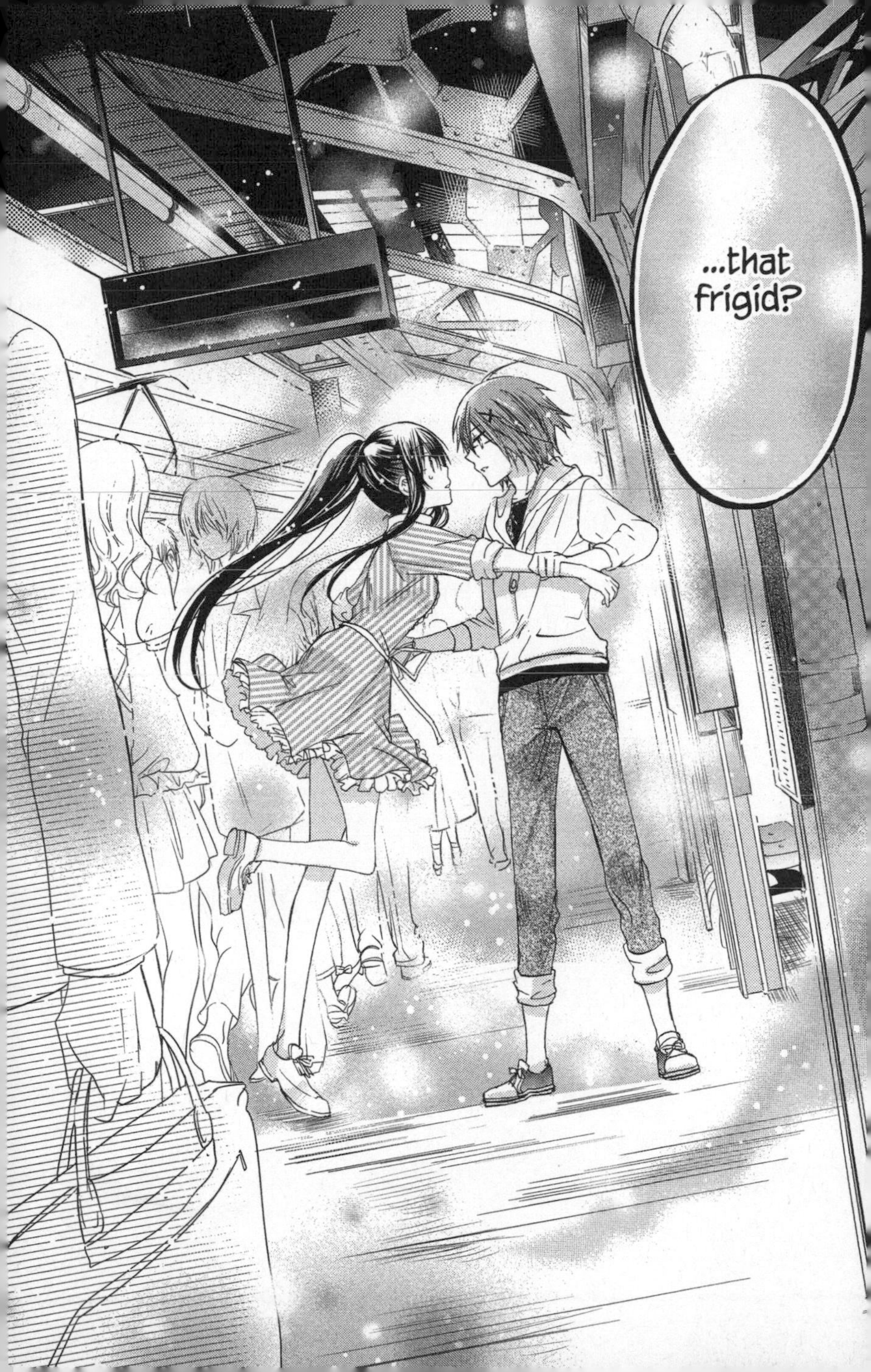
...that frigid?

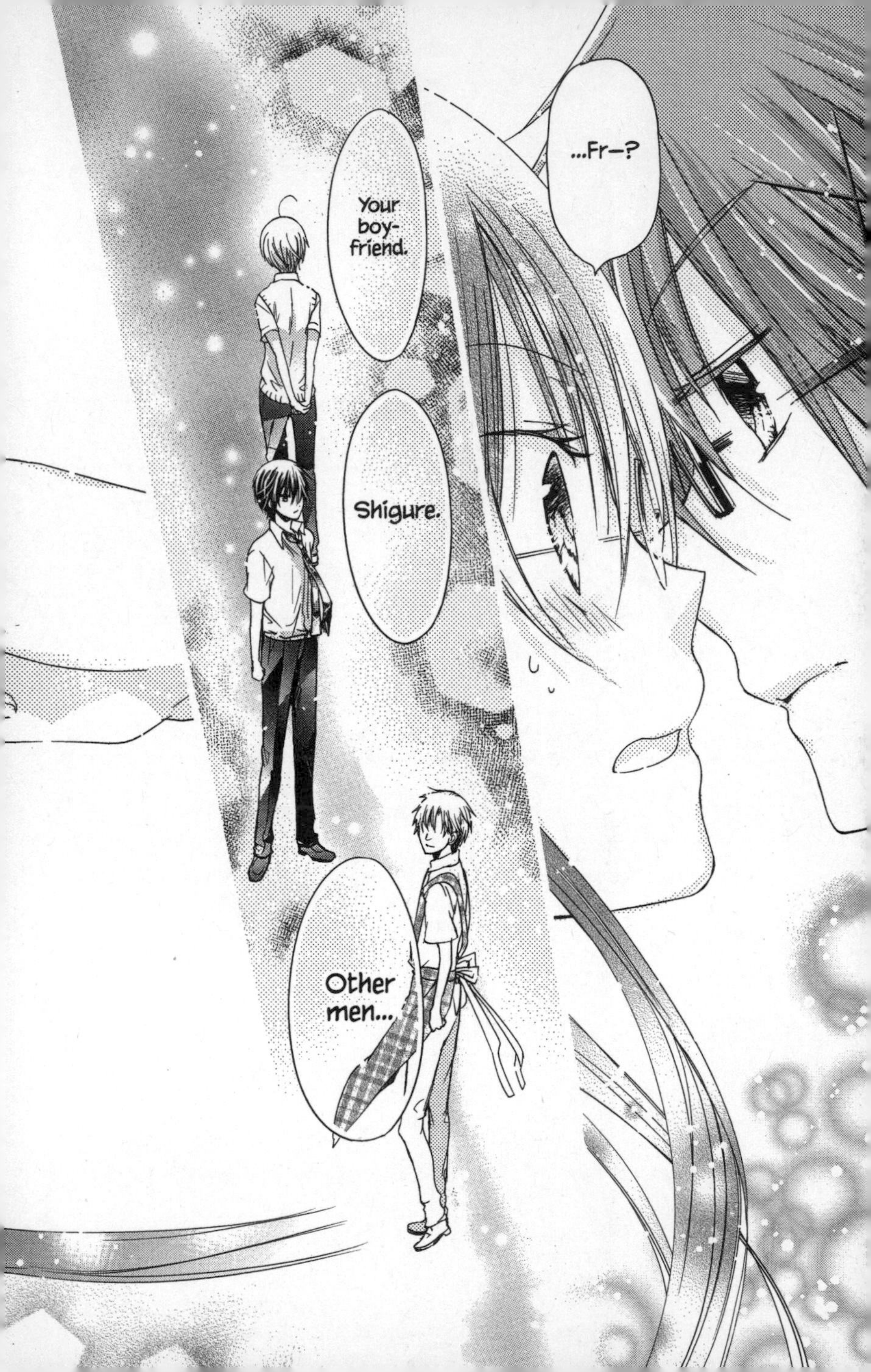
...Fr—?
Your boy-friend.
Shigure.
Other men...

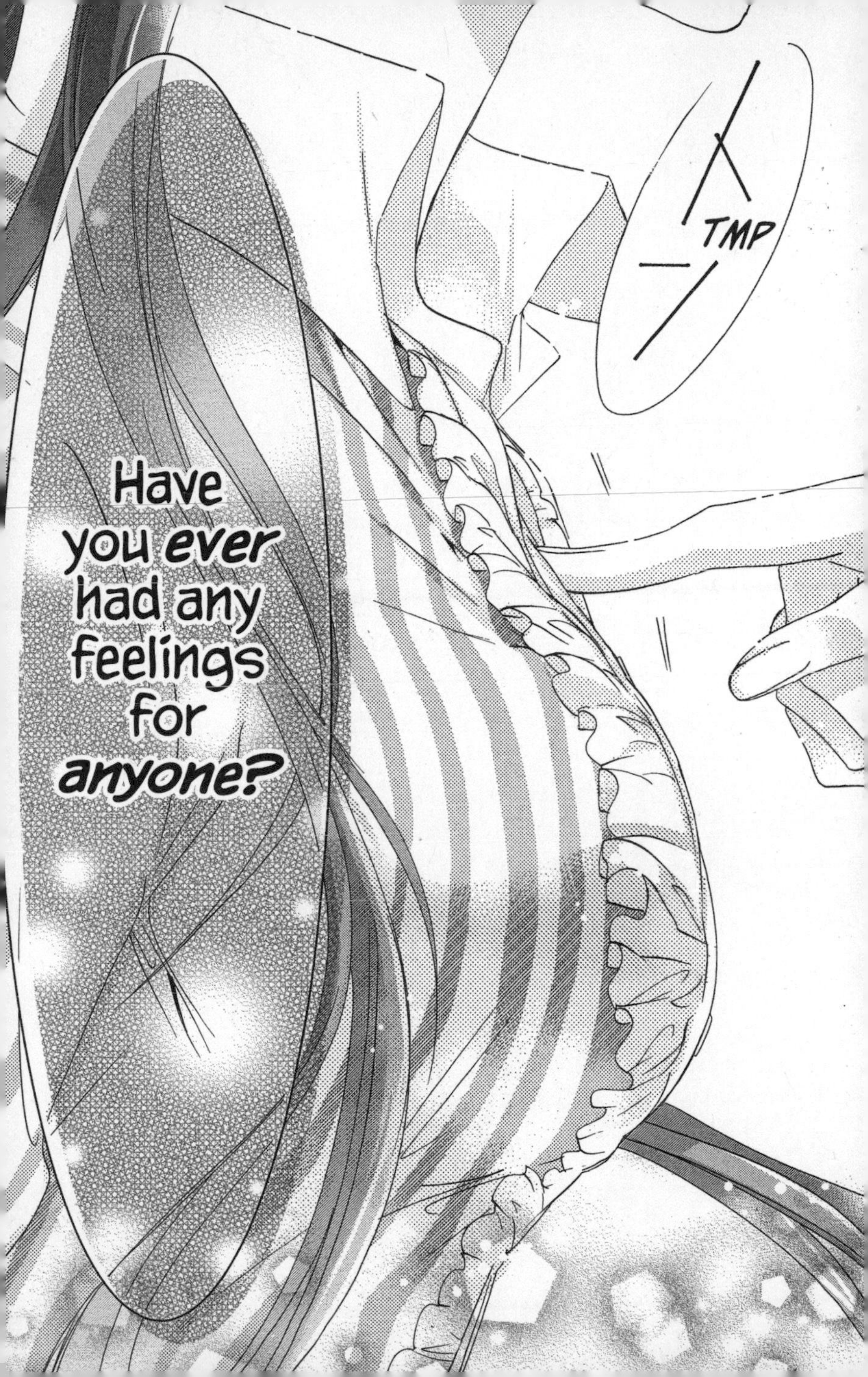
TMP
Have you ever had any feelings for anyone?

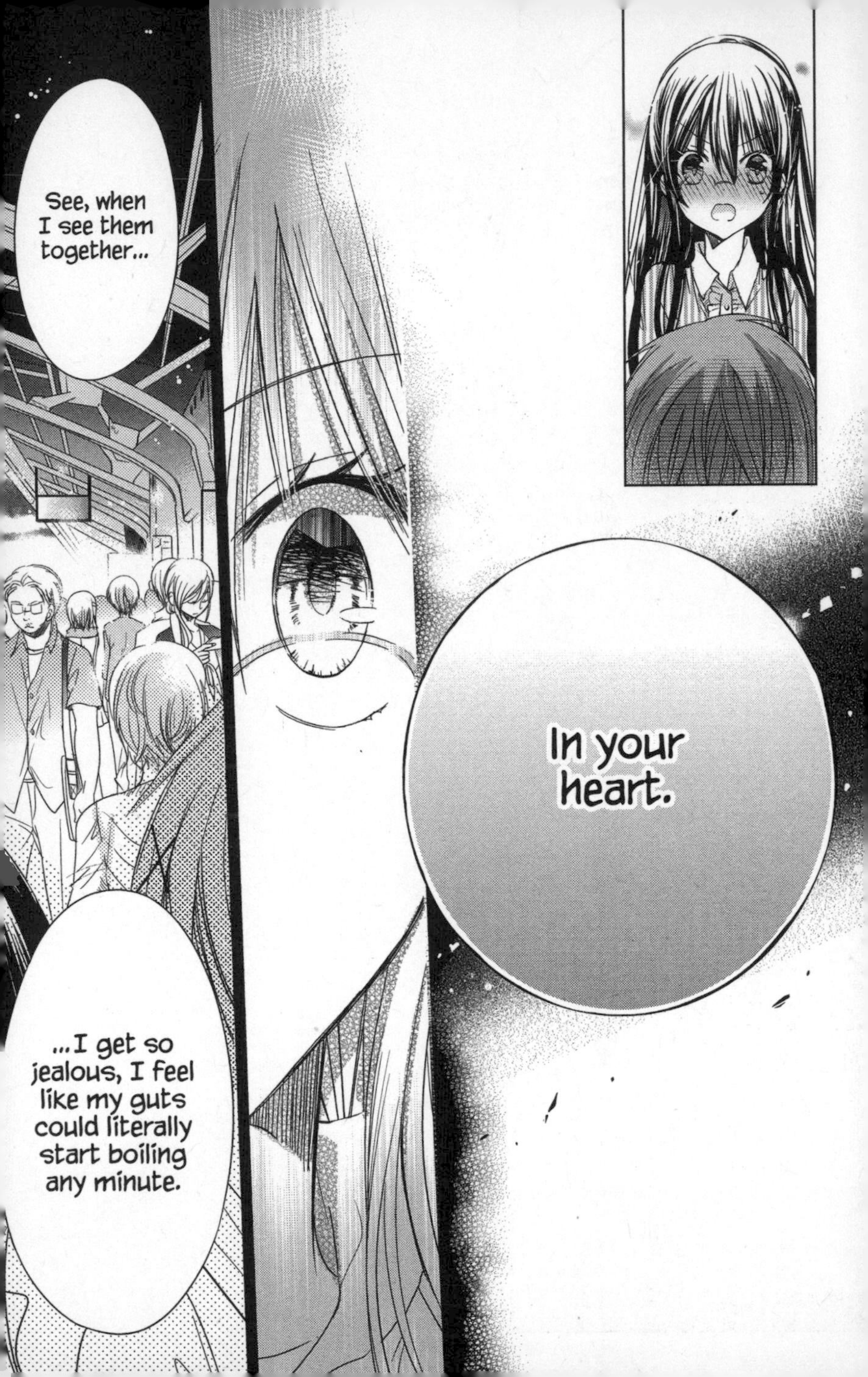
In your heart.
See, when I see them together...
...I get so jealous, I feel like my guts could literally start boiling any minute.

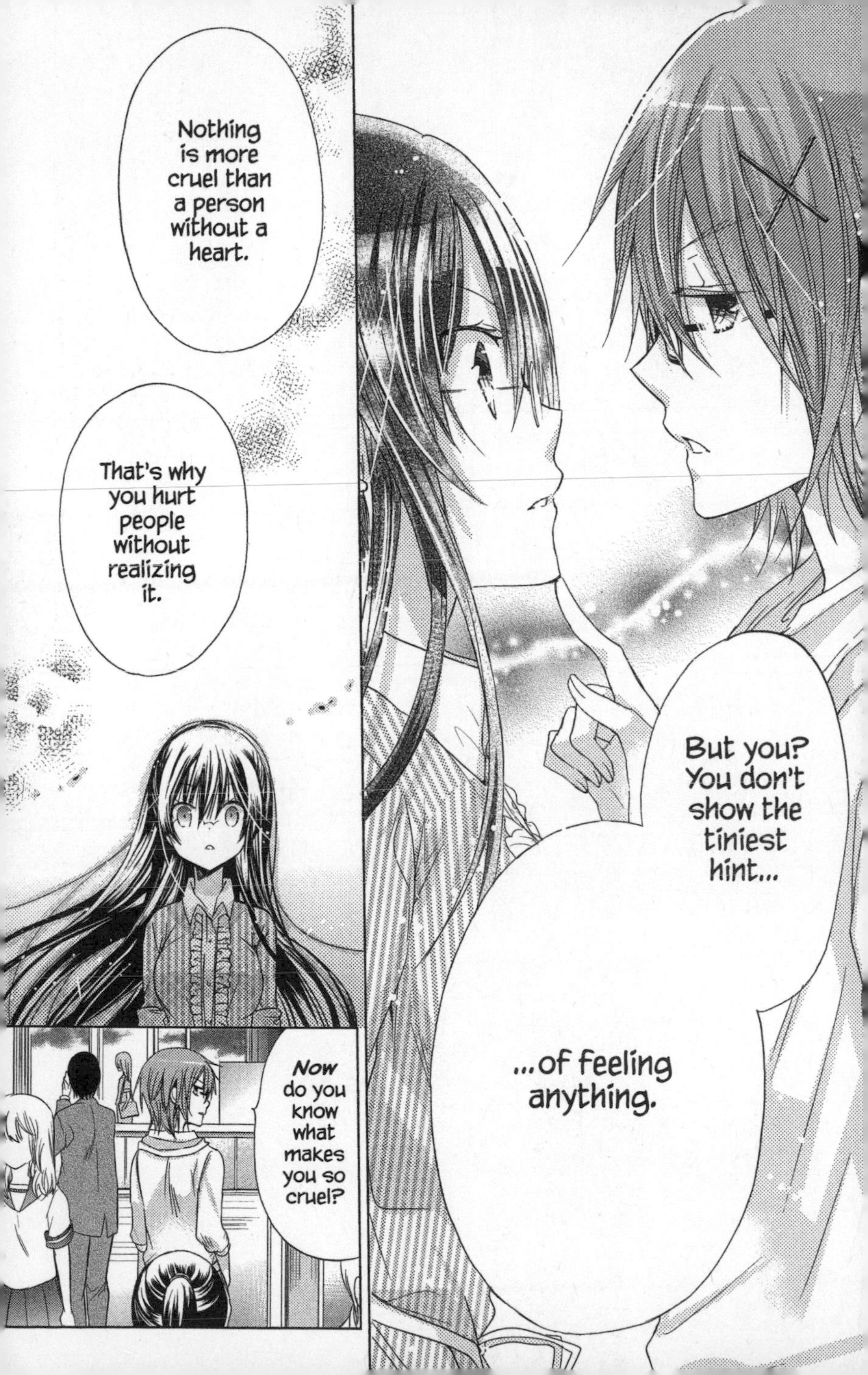
But you? You don't show the tiniest hint...
...of feeling anything.
Nothing is more cruel than a person without a heart.
That's why you hurt people without realizing it.
Now do you know what makes you so cruel?

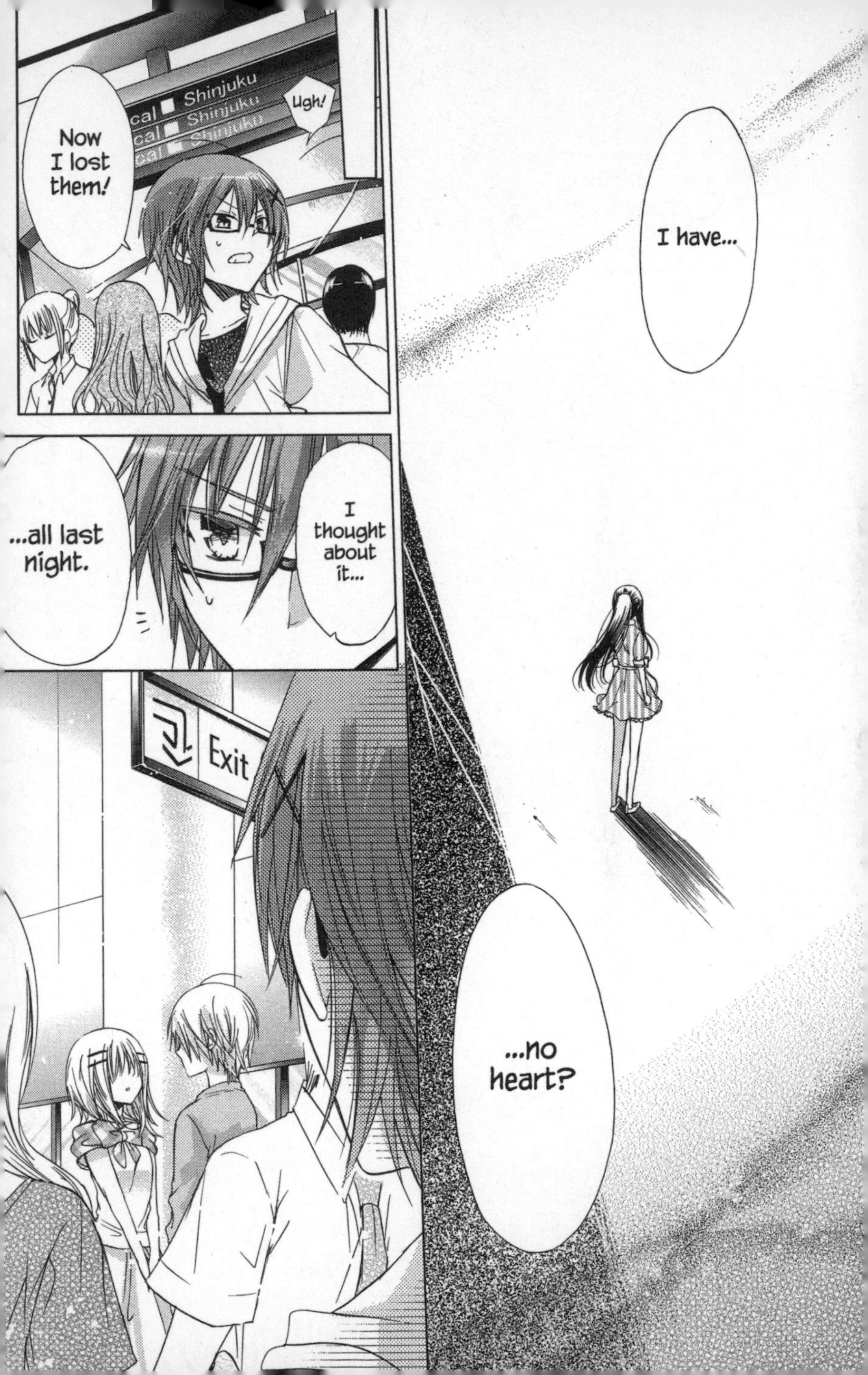
I have...
...no heart?
Ugh!
Now I lost them!
Shinjuku
Shinjuku
Shinjuku
I thought about it...
...all last night.
Exit

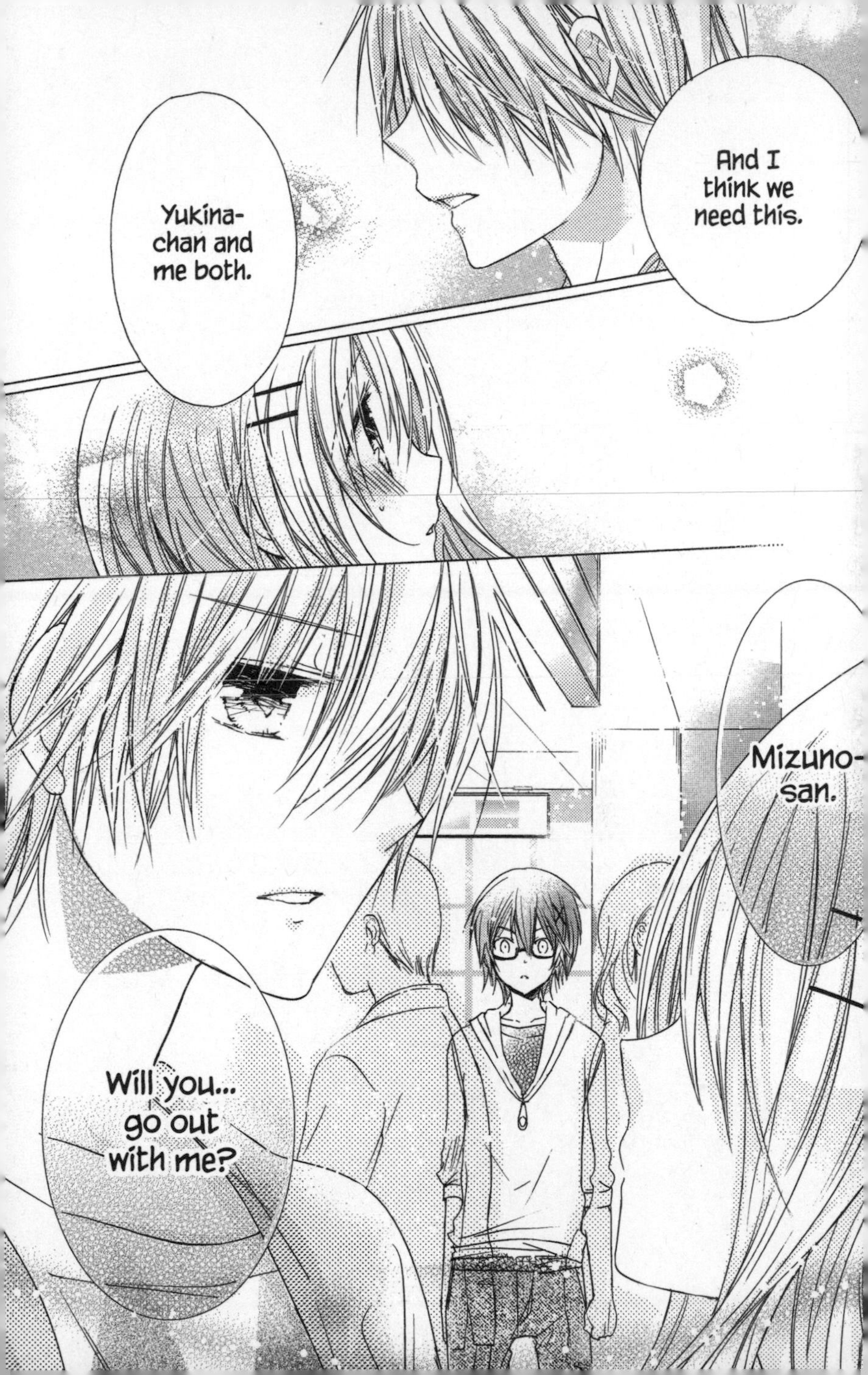
And I think we need this.
Yukina-chan and me both.
Mizuno-san.
Will you... go out with me?

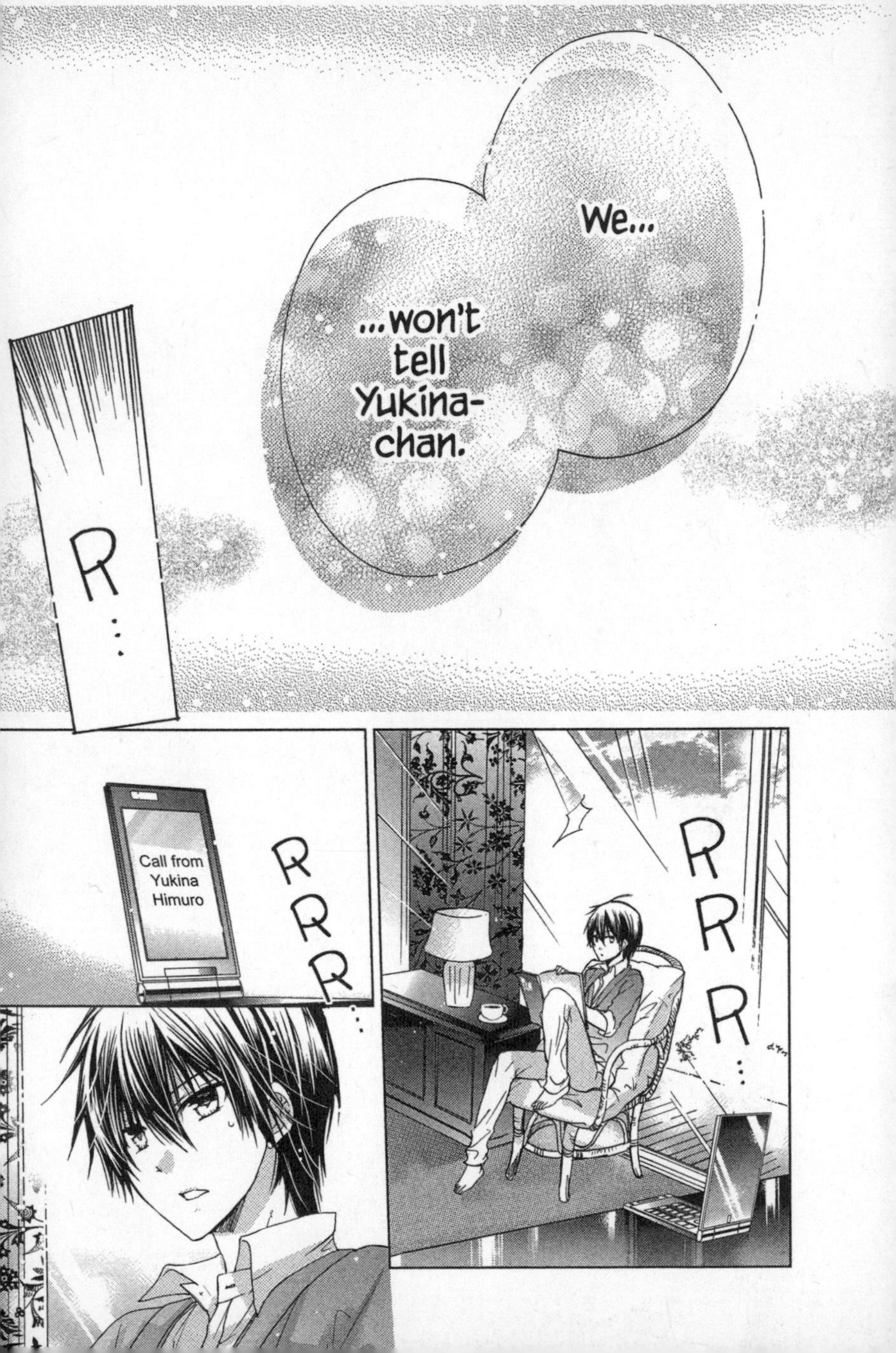
We...
...won't tell Yukina-chan.
R...
RRR...
Call from Yukina Himuro
RRR...

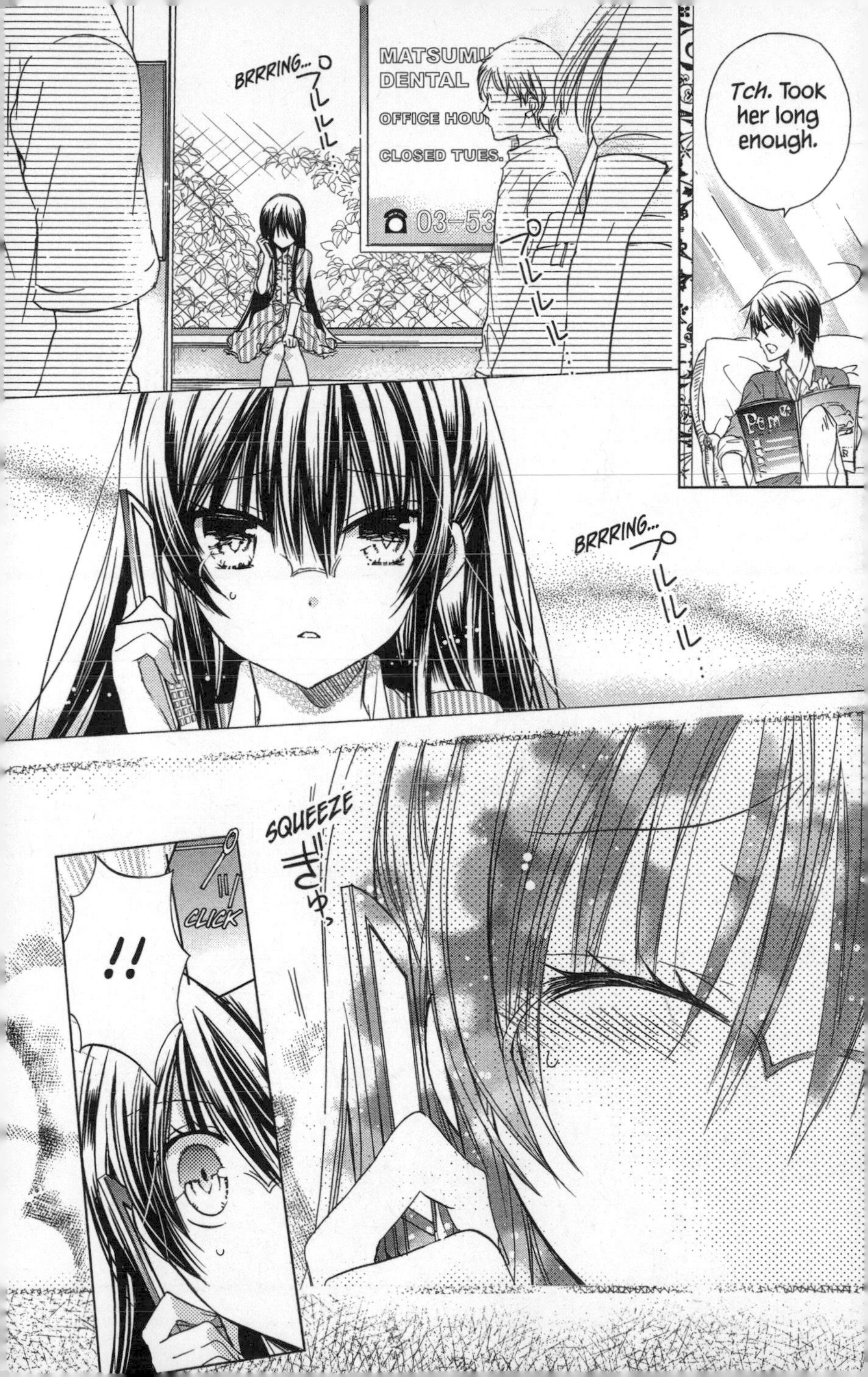
Tch. Took her long enough.
MATSUMU
DENTAL
OFFICE HOU
CLOSED TUES.
03-53
BRRRING...
プルルル
BRRRING...
プルルル…
SQUEEZE
ぎゅっ
CLICK
!!

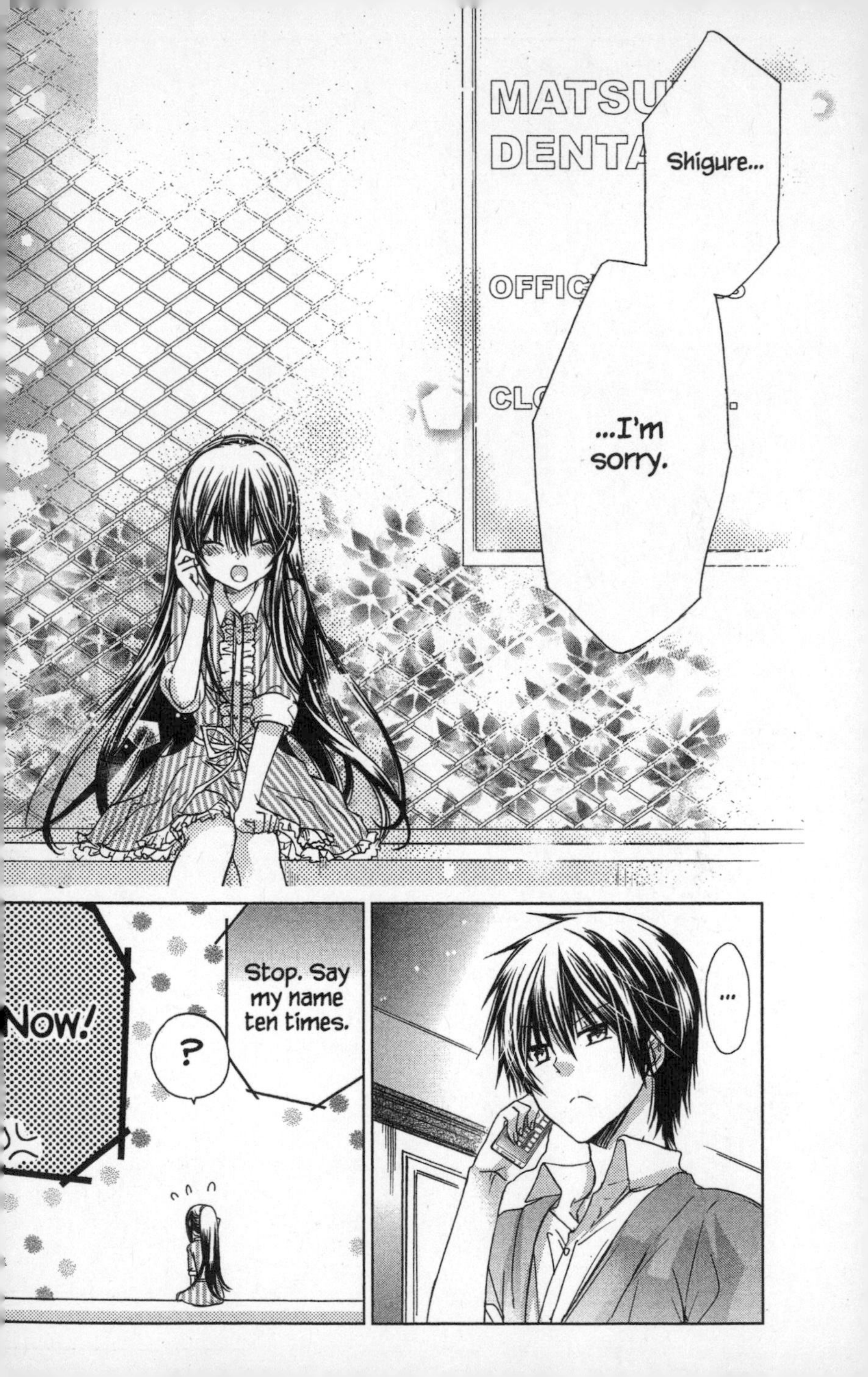
Shigure...
...I'm sorry.
...
Stop. Say my name ten times.
?
Now!

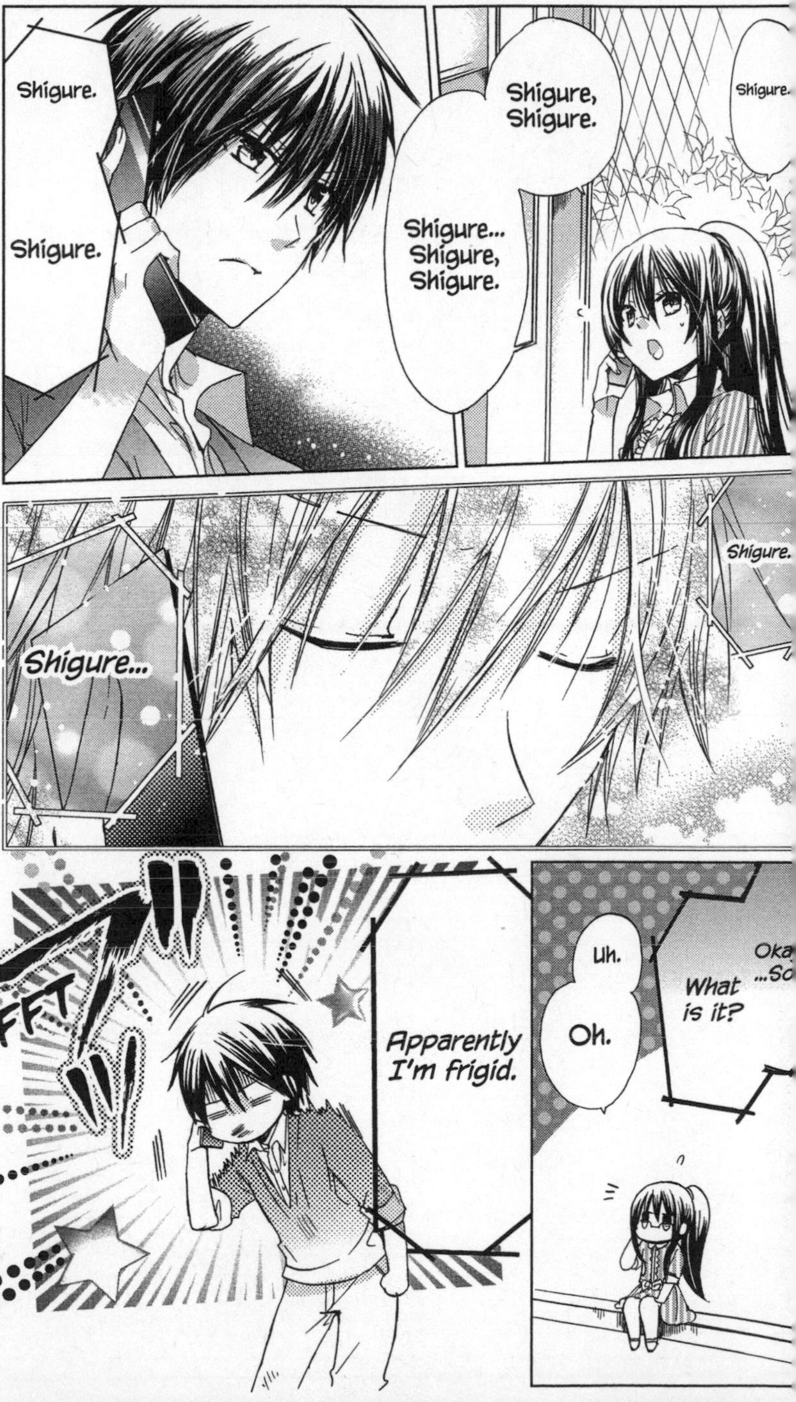
Shigure.
Shigure, Shigure.
Shigure... Shigure, Shigure.
Shigure.
Shigure.
Shigure.
Shigure...
What is it?
Uh.
Oh.
Apparently I'm frigid.
PFFT

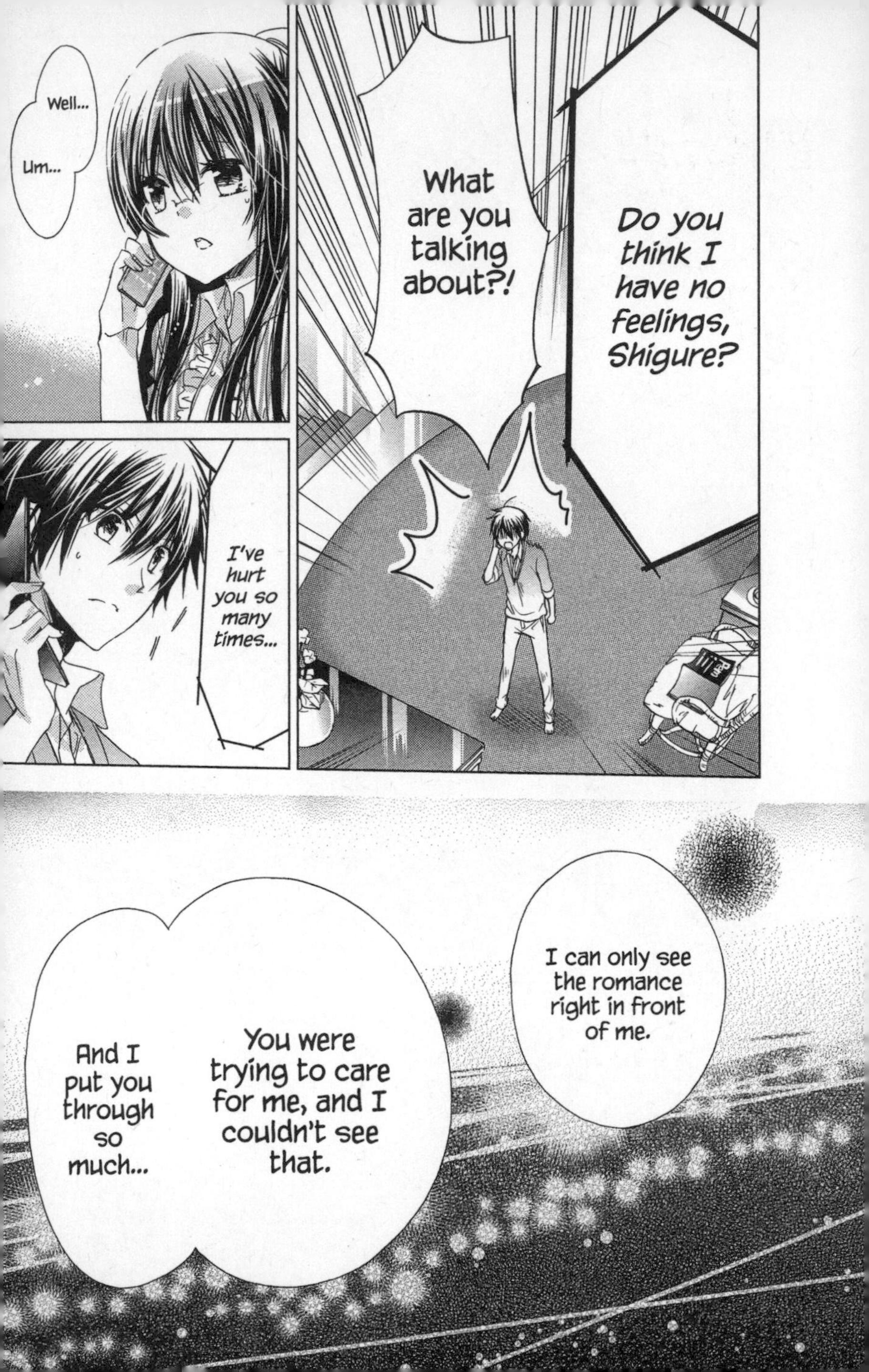
Do you think I have no feelings, Shigure?
What are you talking about?!
Well...
Um...
I've hurt you so many times...
I can only see the romance right in front of me.
You were trying to care for me, and I couldn't see that.
And I put you through so much...

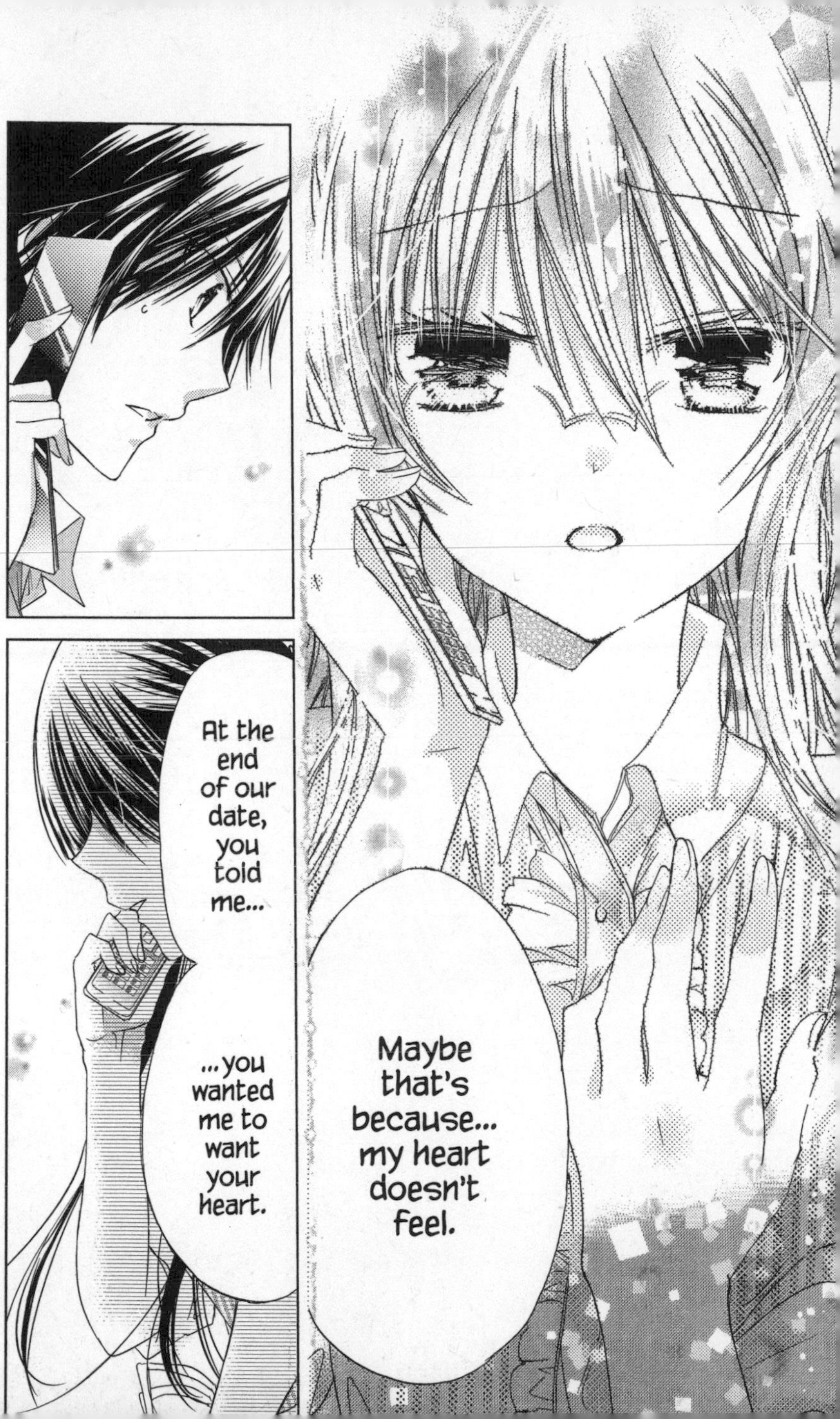
Maybe that's because... my heart doesn't feel.
At the end of our date, you told me...
...you wanted me to want your heart.

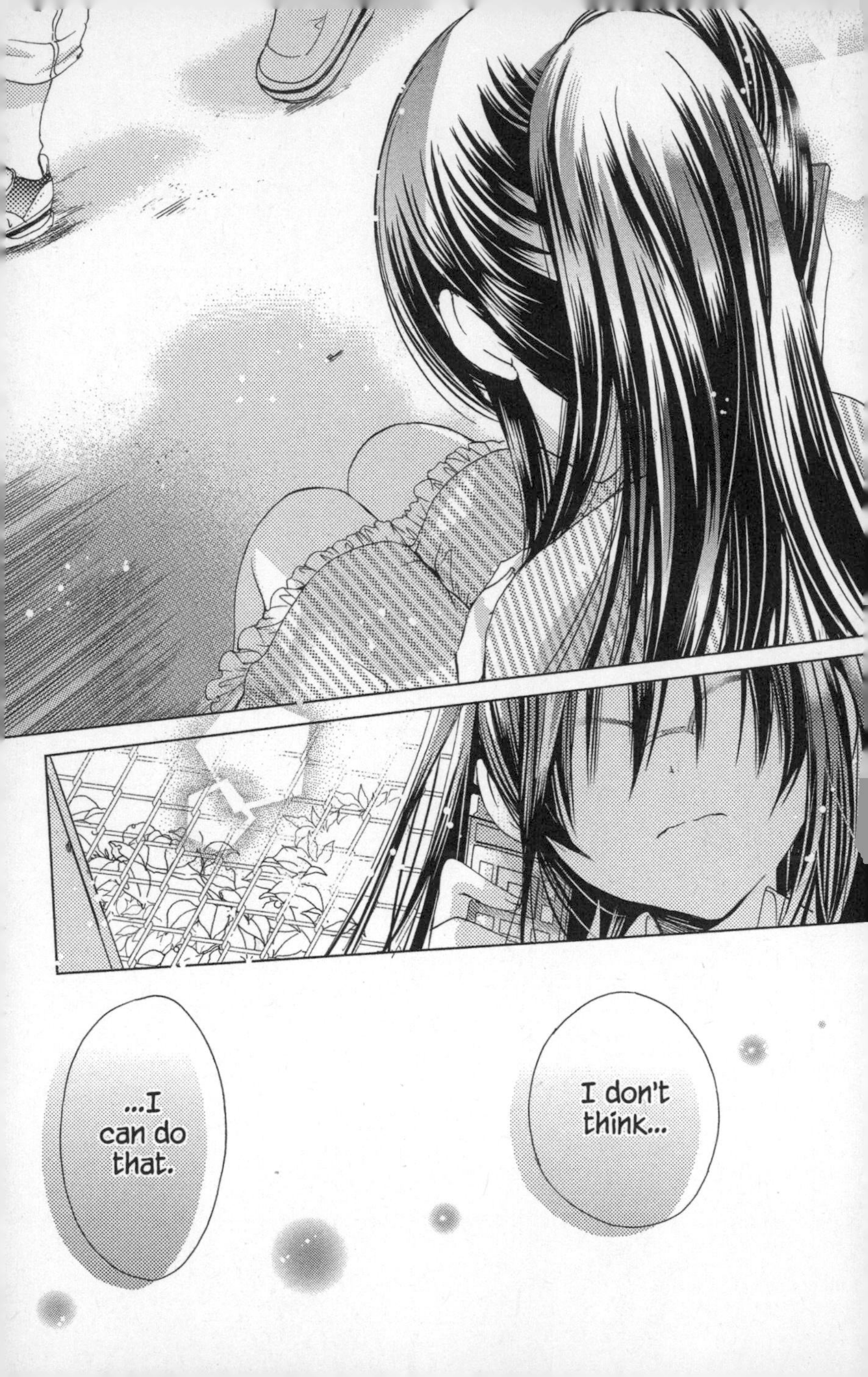
I don't think...
...I can do that.

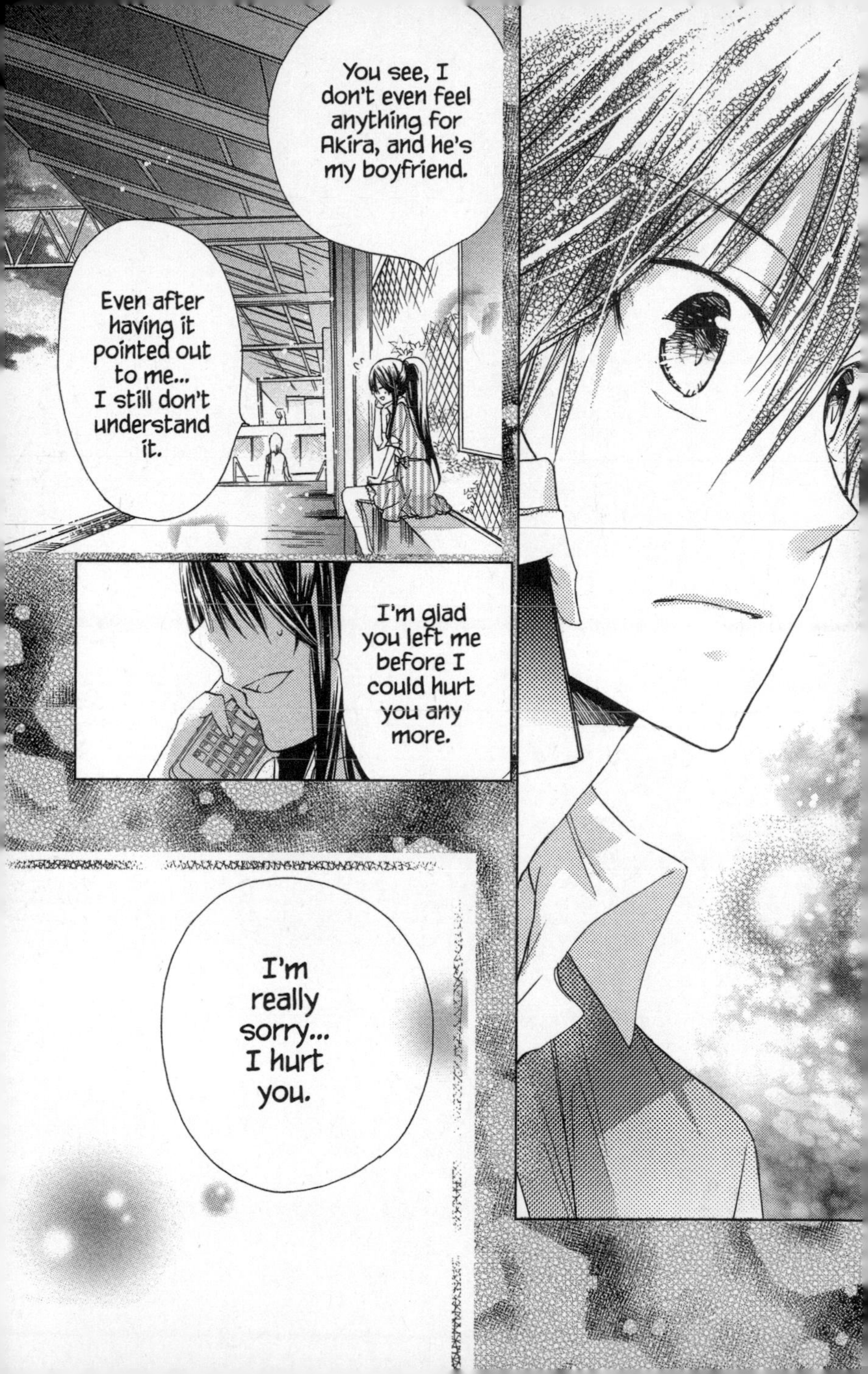
You see, I don't even feel anything for Akira, and he's my boyfriend.
Even after having it pointed out to me... I still don't understand it.
I'm glad you left me before I could hurt you any more.
I'm really sorry... I hurt you.

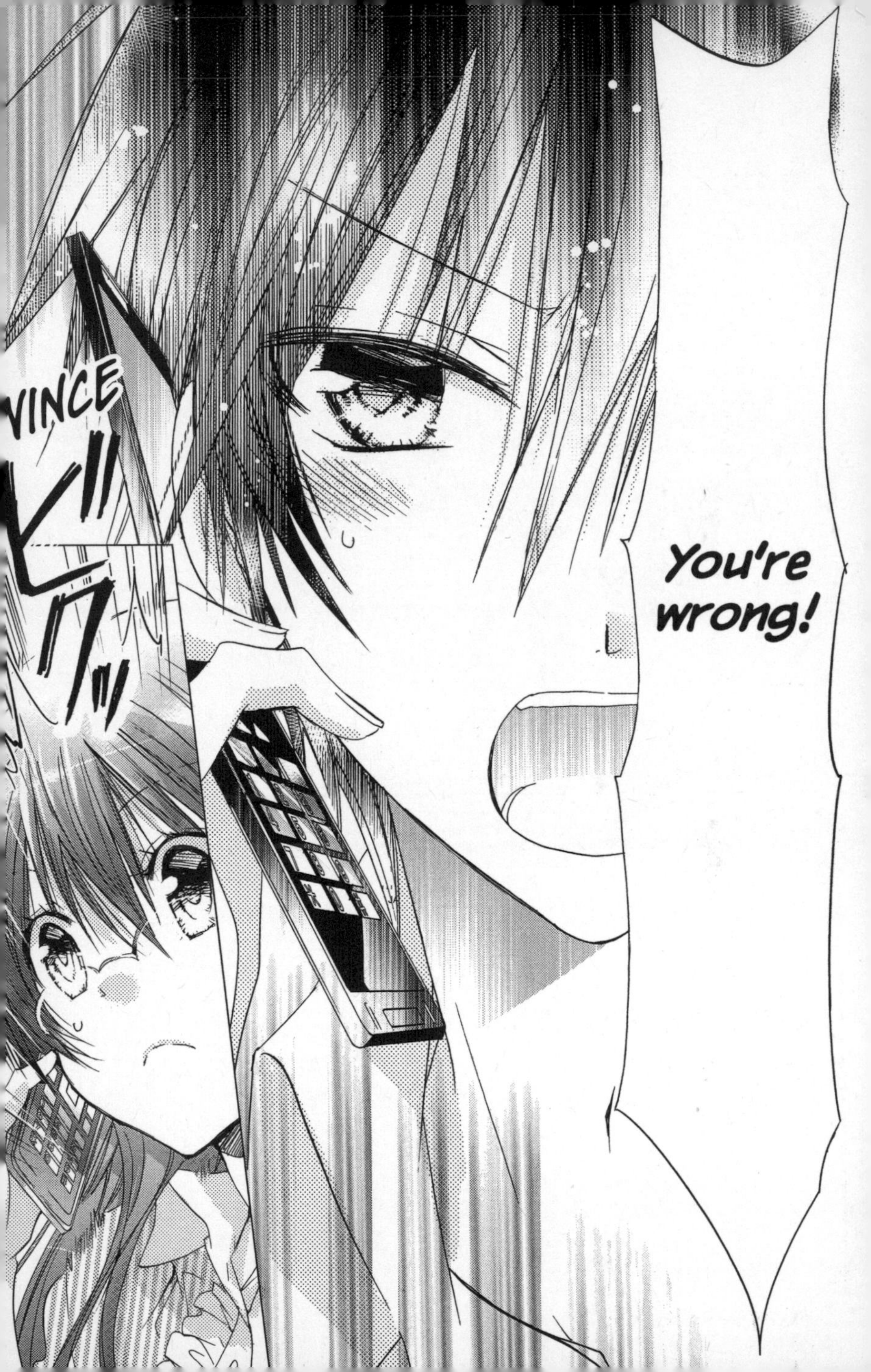
You're wrong!
VINCE

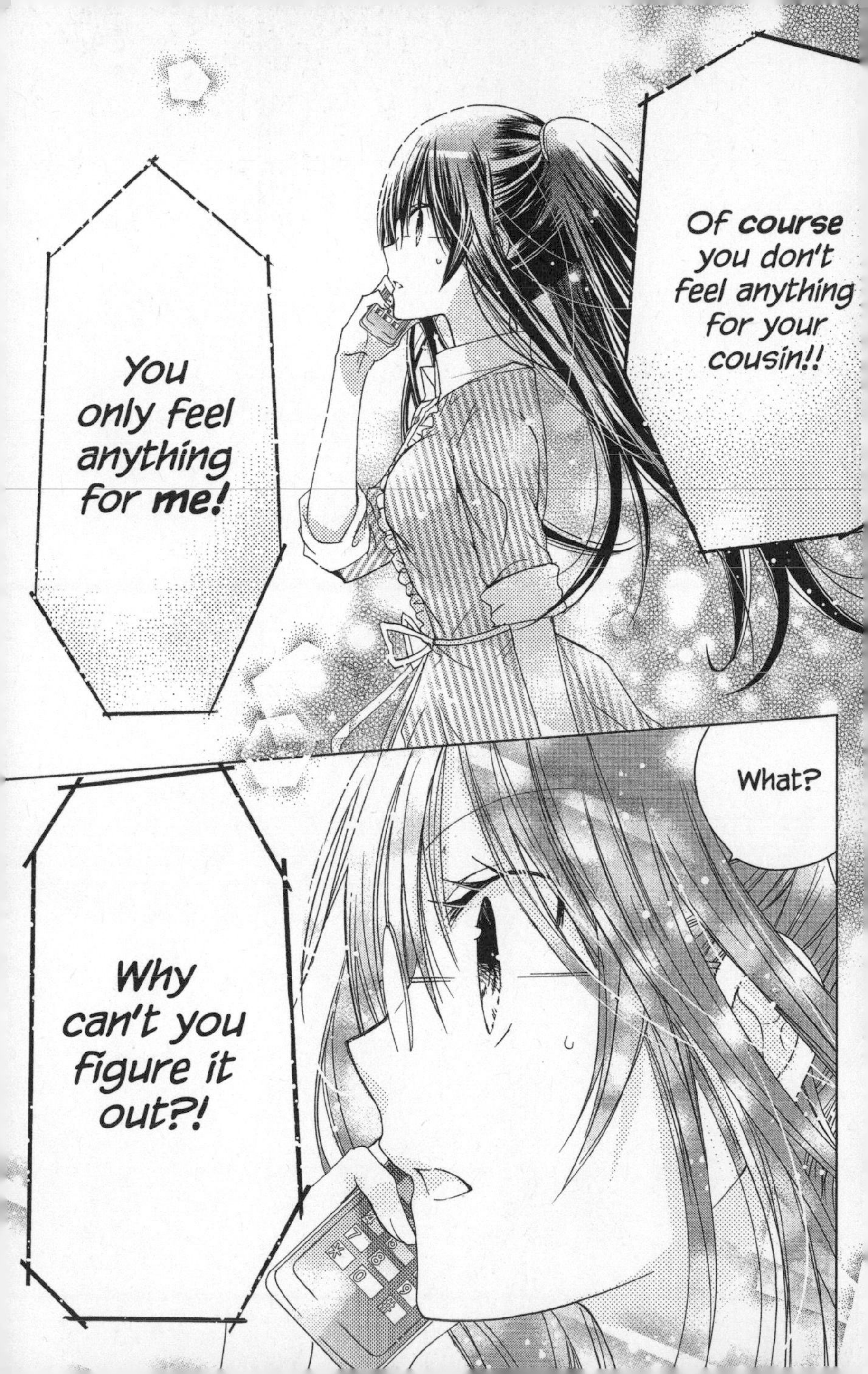
Of course you don't feel anything for your cousin!!
You only feel anything for me!
What?
Why can't you figure it out?!

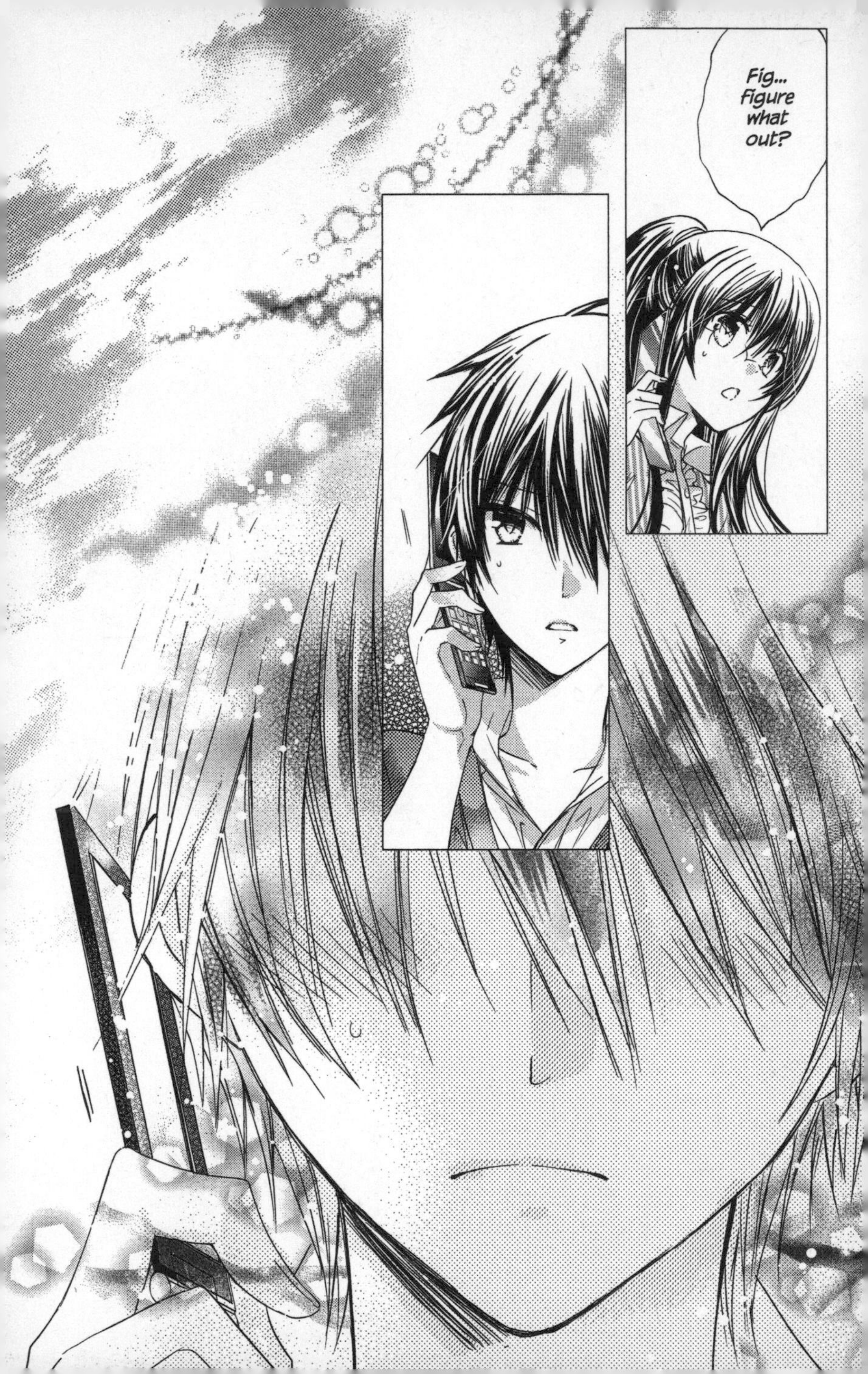
Fig... figure what out?

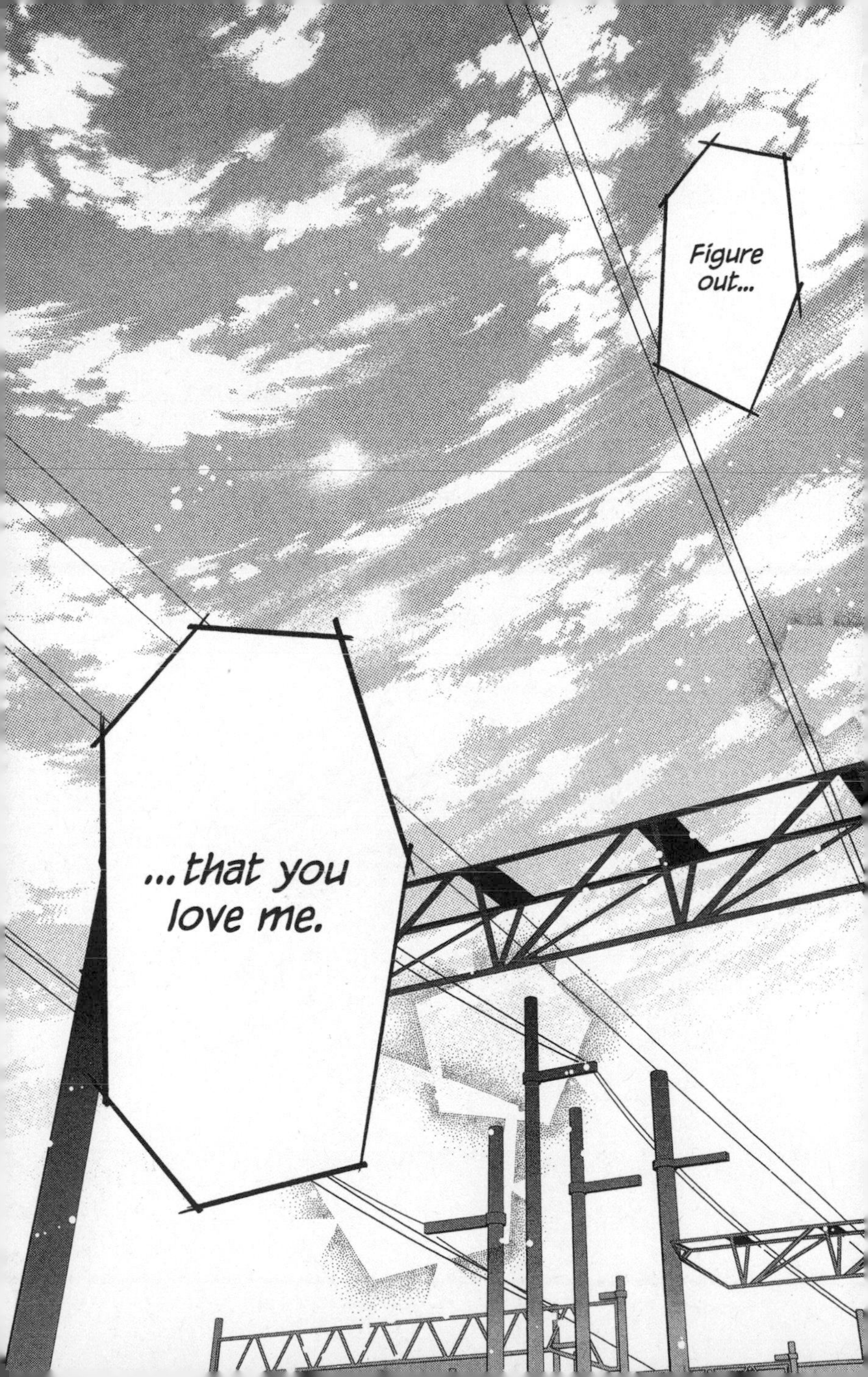
Figure out...
...that you love me.

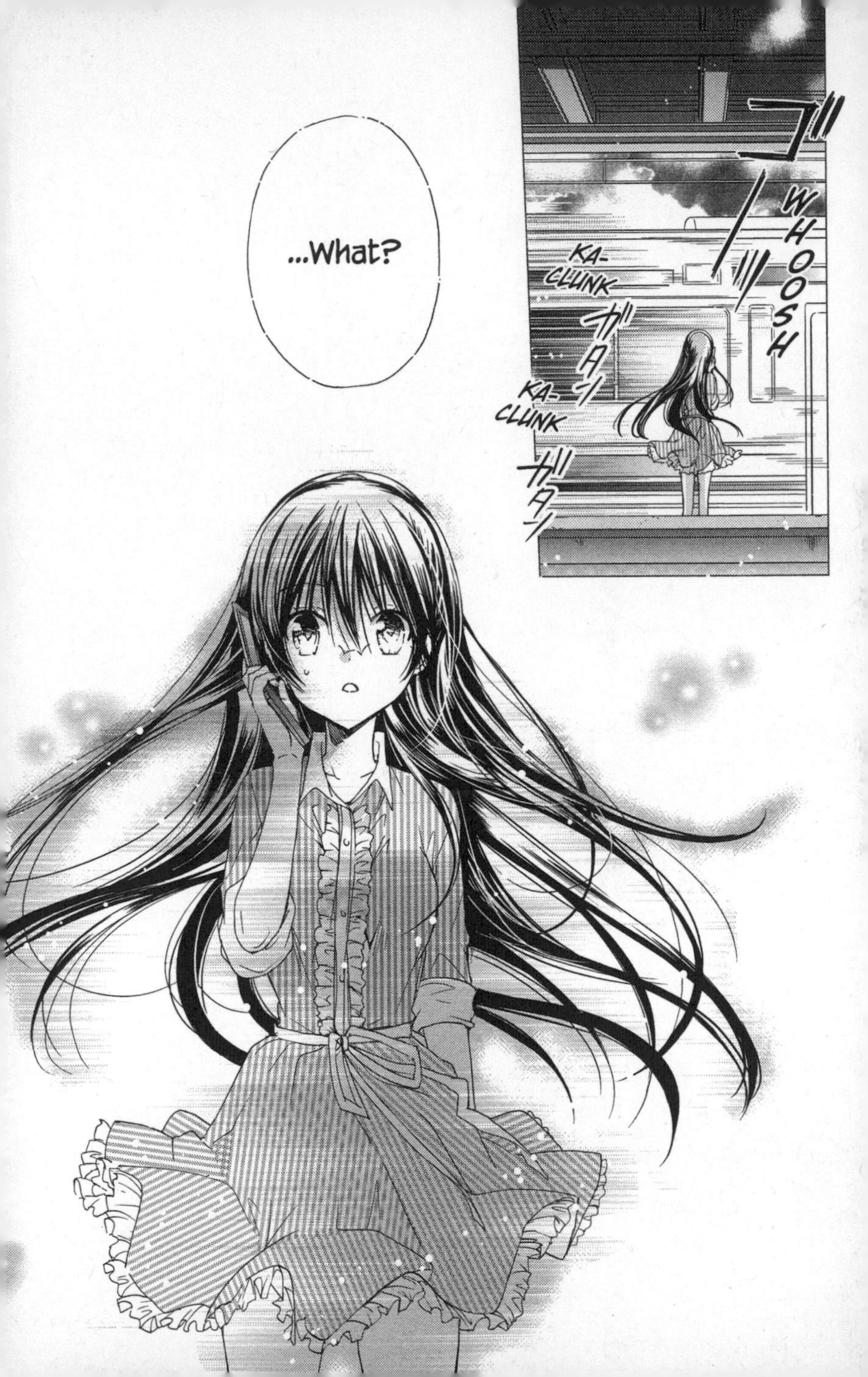
WHOOSH
KA-CLUNK
KA-CLUNK
...What?

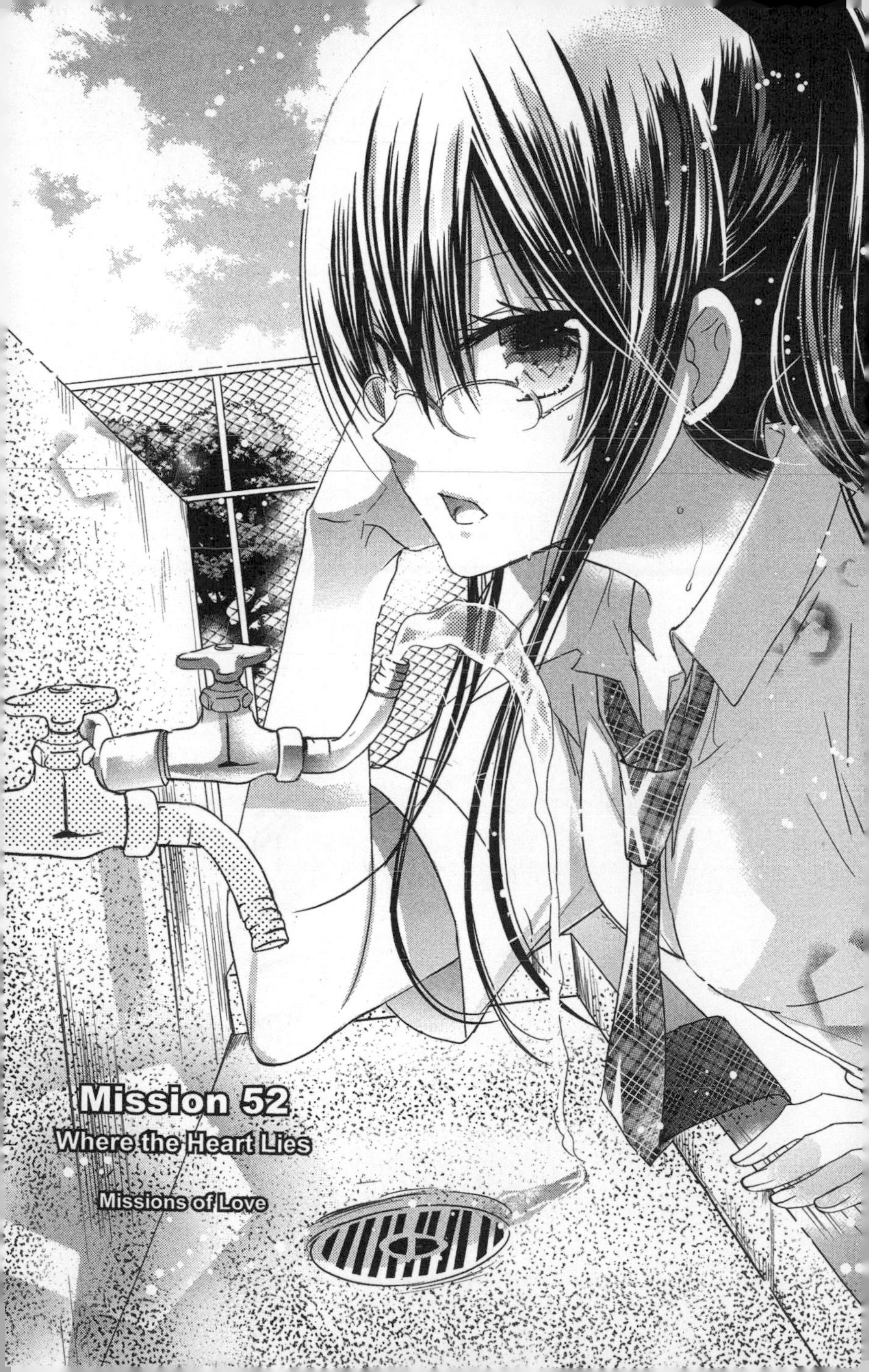
Mission 52
Where the Heart Lies
Missions of Love

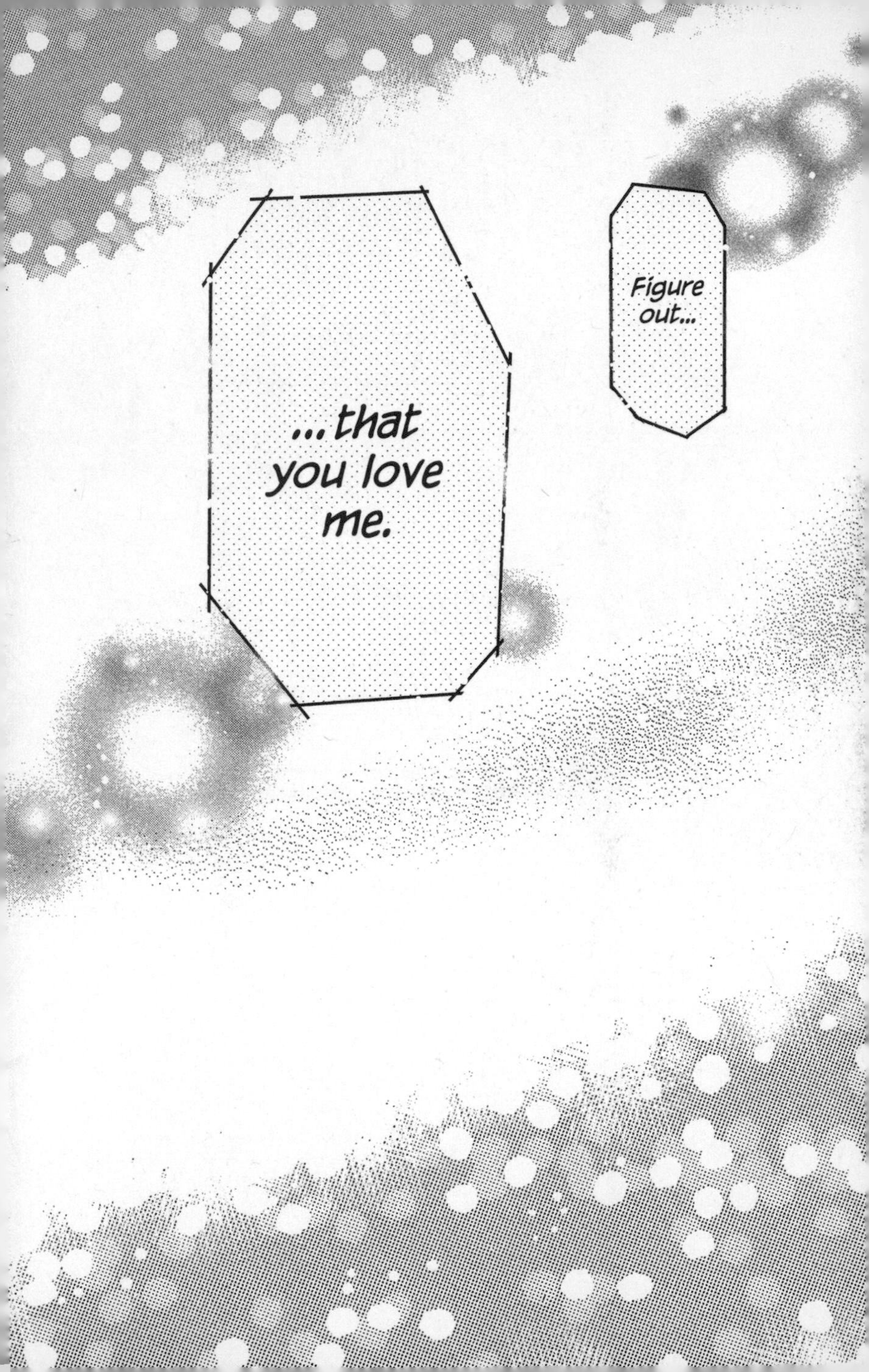
Figure out...
...that you love me.

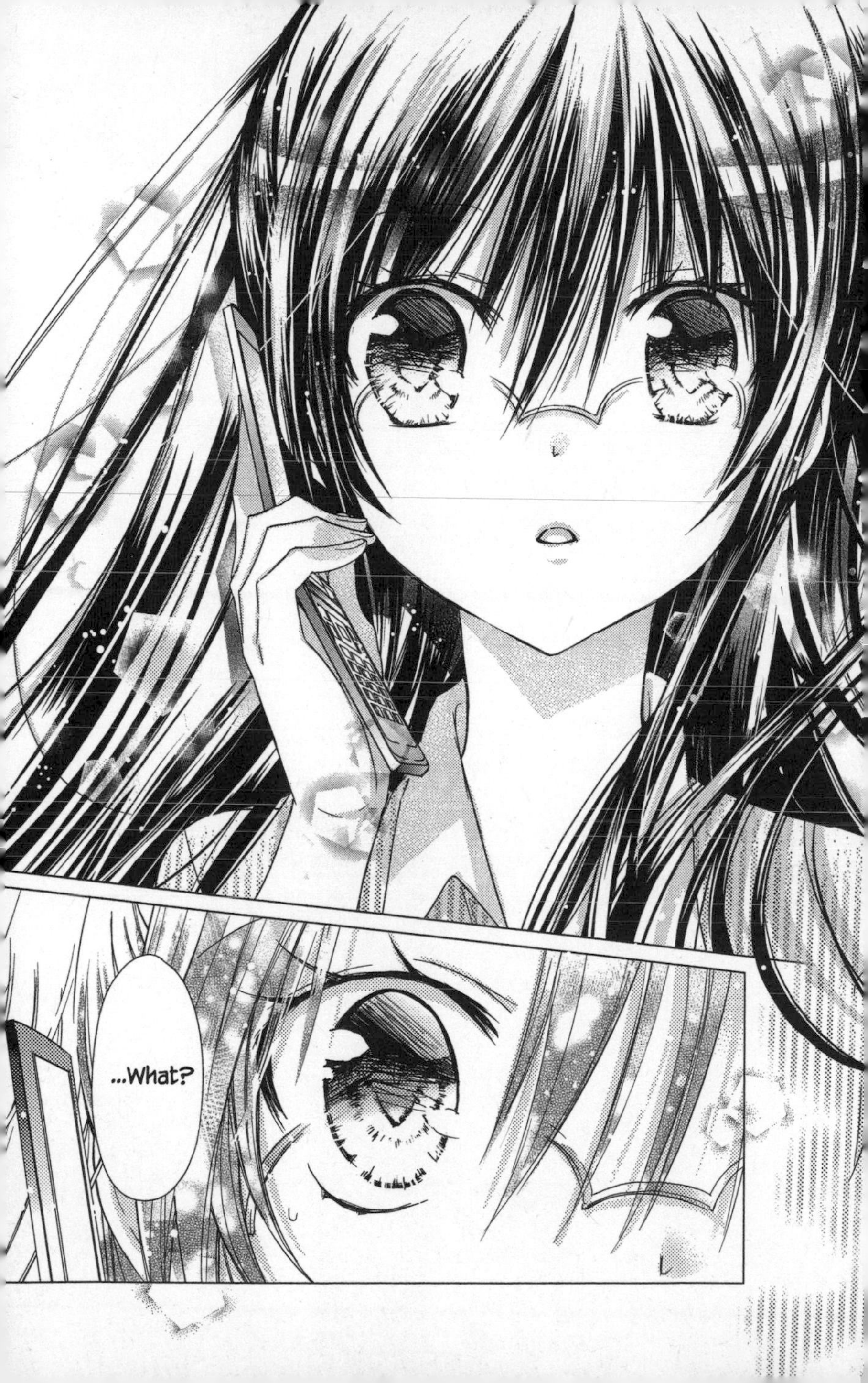
...What?

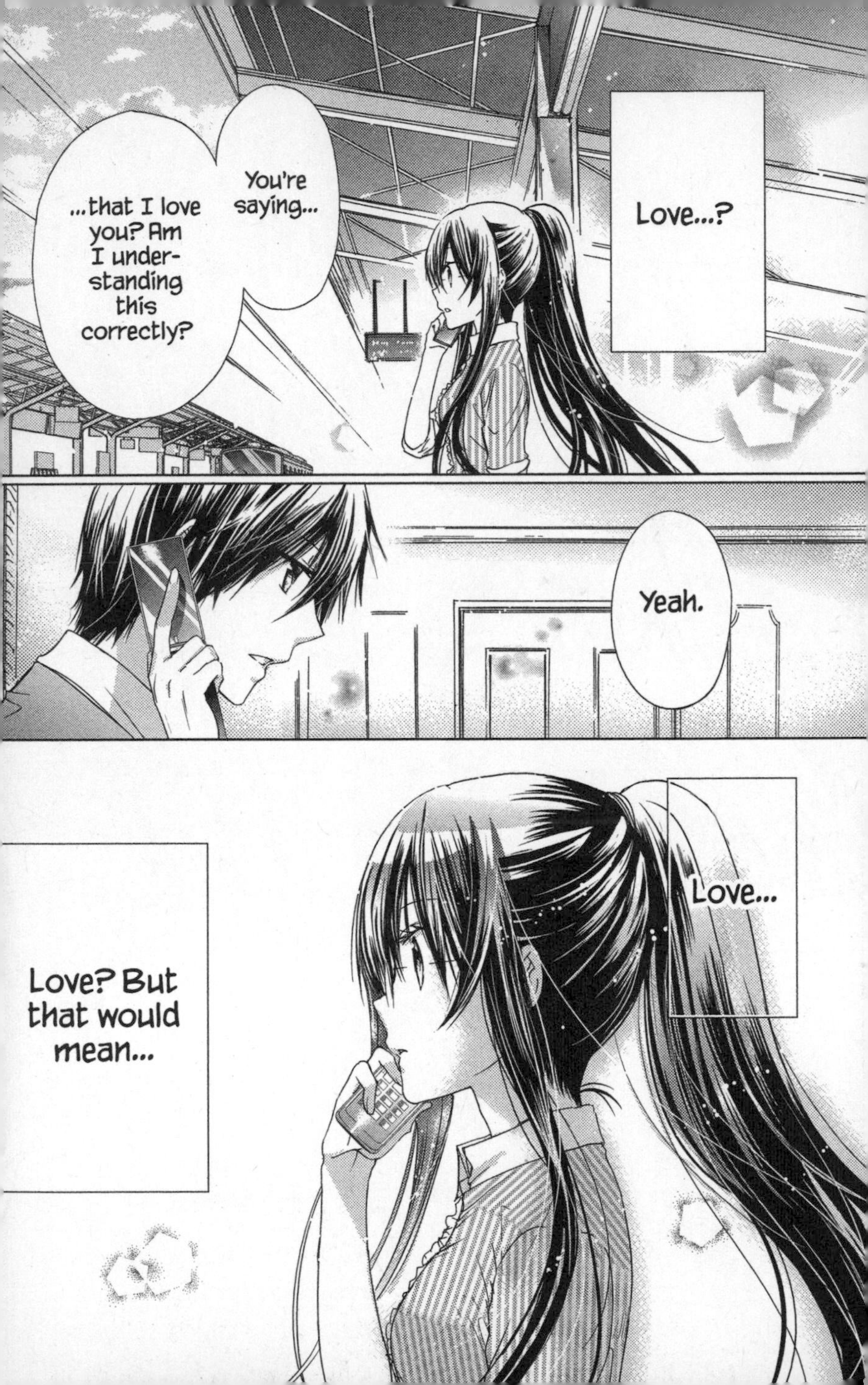
Love...?
You're saying...
...that I love you? Am I under-standing this correctly?
Yeah.
Love...
Love? But that would mean...

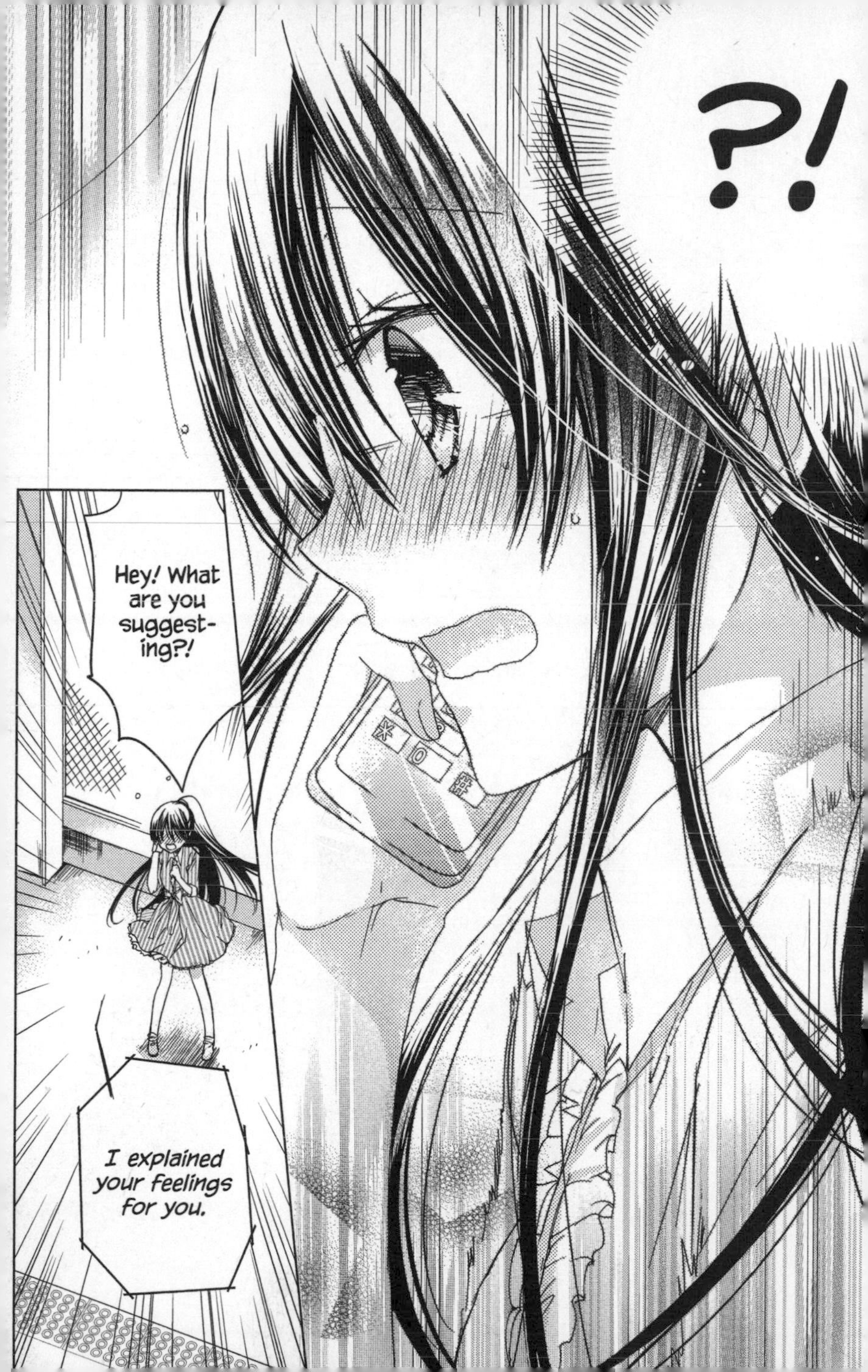
?!
Hey! What are you suggest-ing?!
I explained your feelings for you.

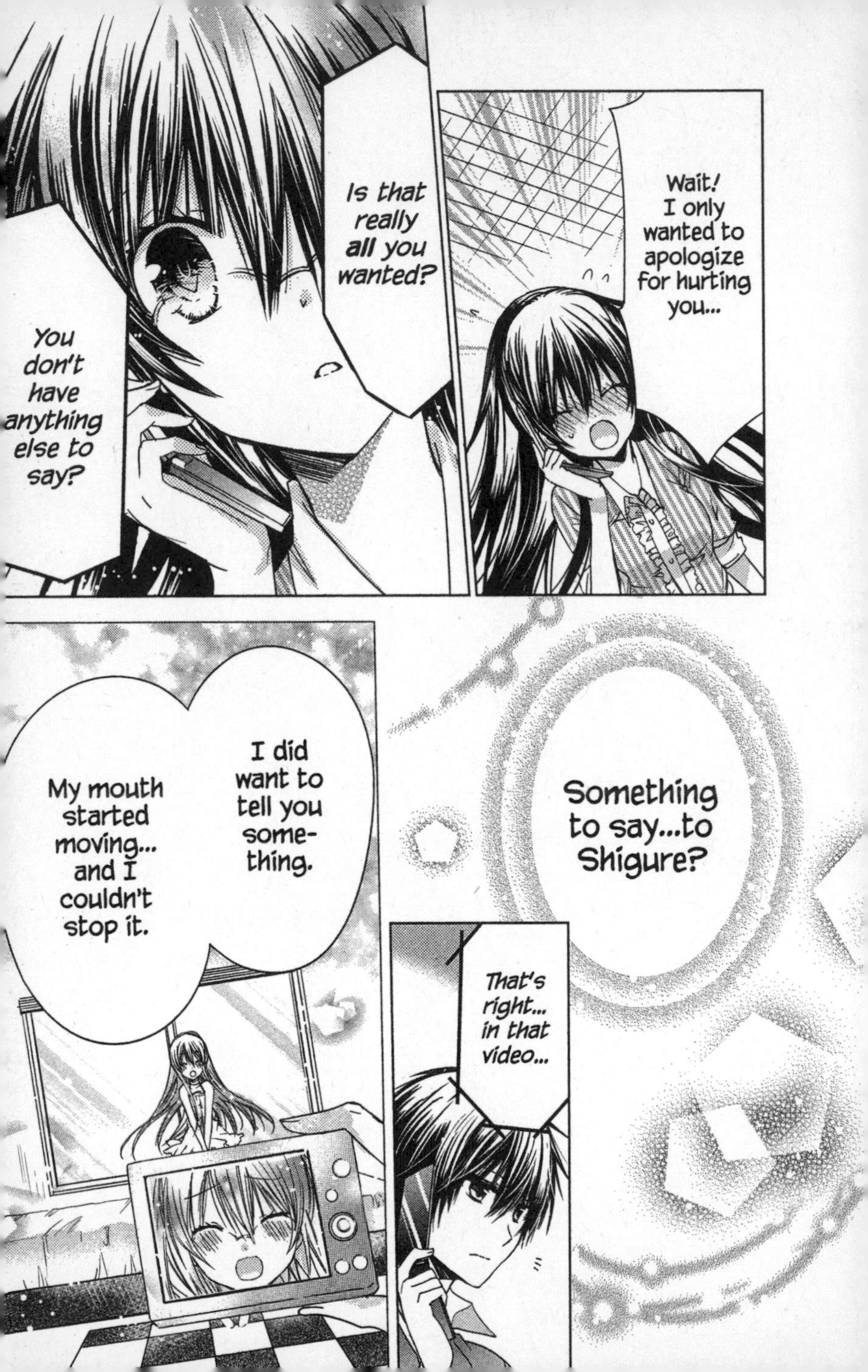
Wait! I only wanted to apologize for hurting you...
Is that really all you wanted?
You don't have anything else to say?
Something to say...to Shigure?
That's right... in that video...
I did want to tell you some-thing.
My mouth started moving... and I couldn't stop it.

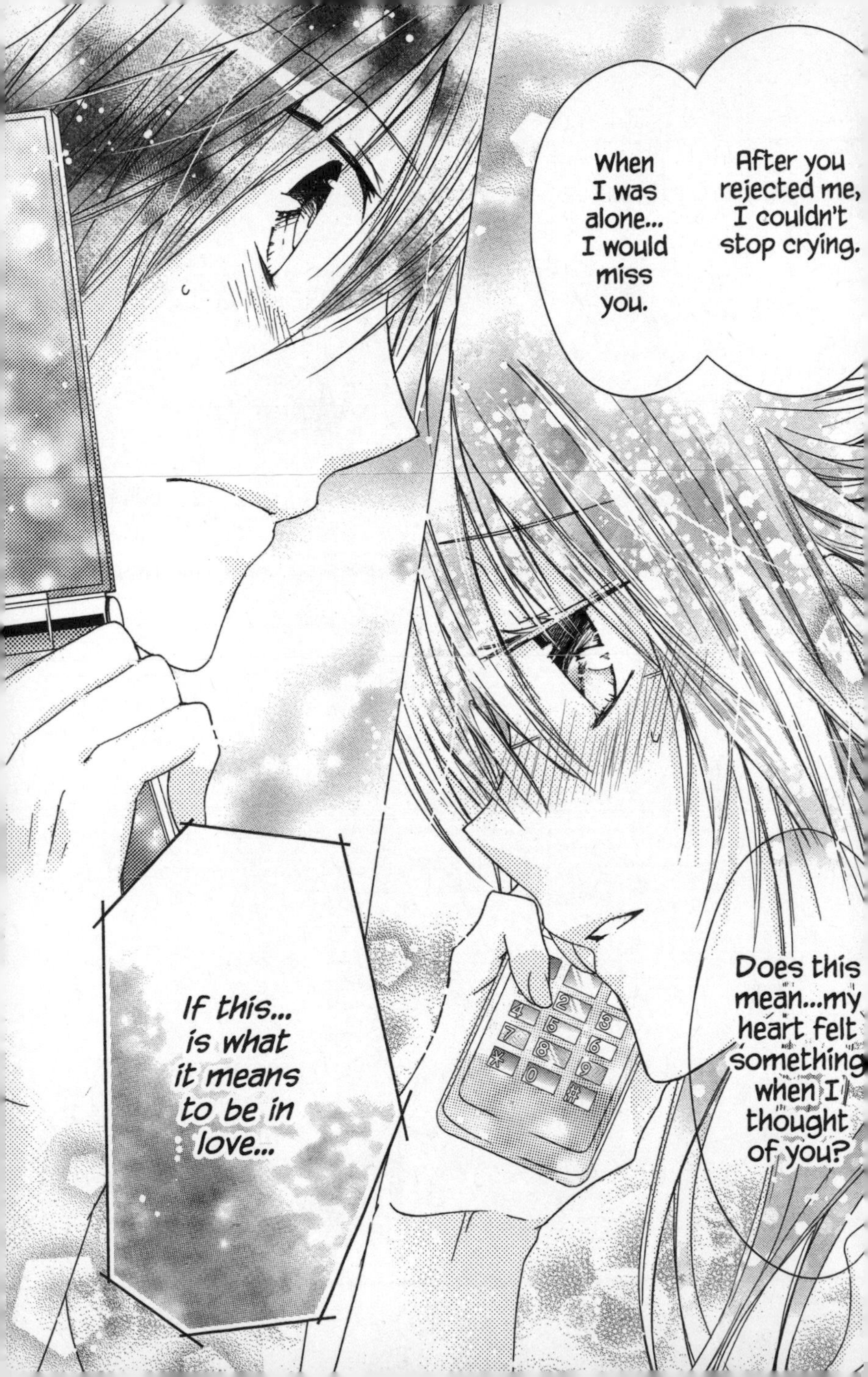
After you rejected me, I couldn't stop crying.
When I was alone... I would miss you.
Does this mean...my heart felt something when I thought of you?
If this... is what it means to be in love...

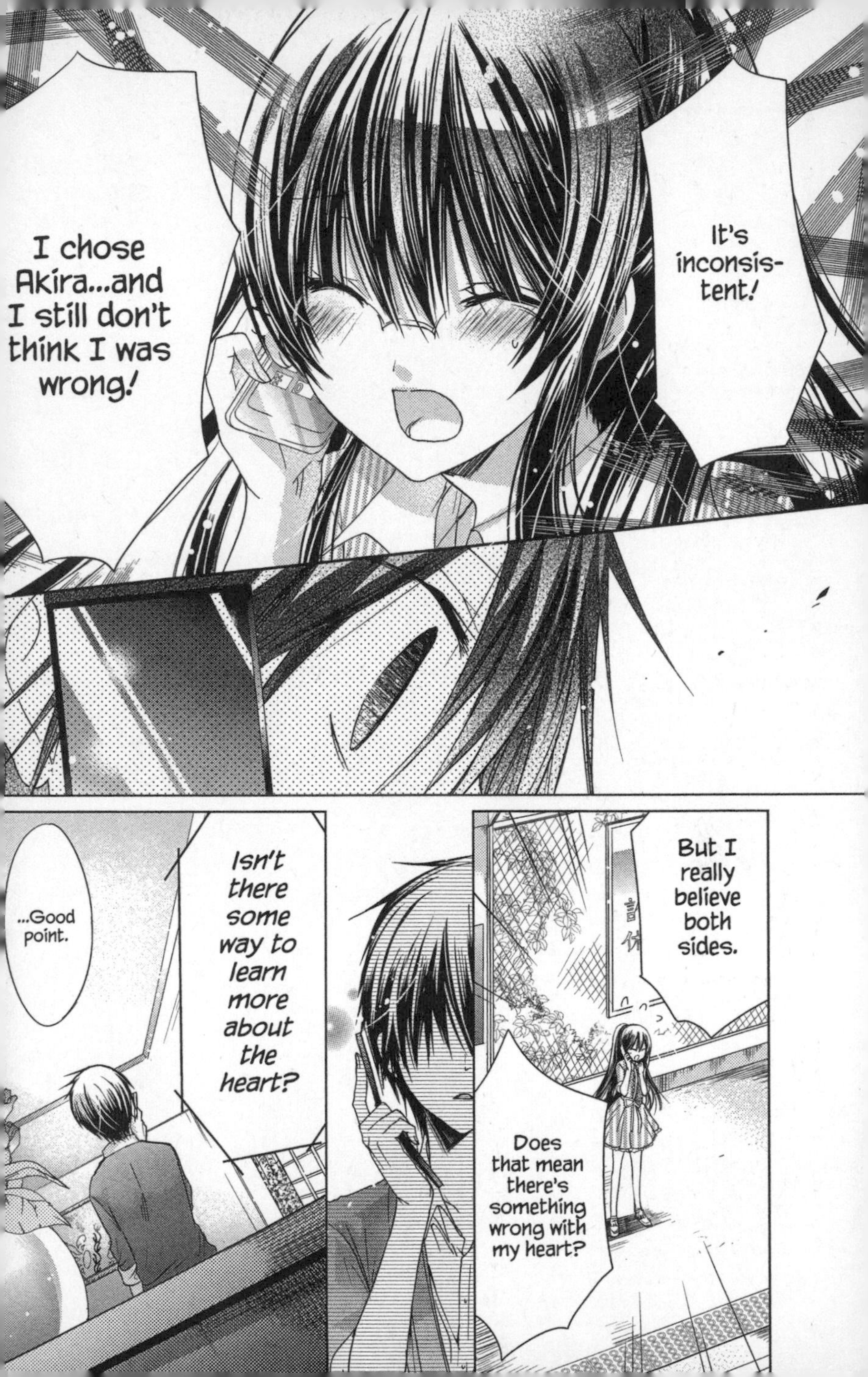

It's inconsistent!
I chose Akira...and I still don't think I was wrong!
But I really believe both sides.
Does that mean there's something wrong with my heart?
Isn't there some way to learn more about the heart?
...Good point.

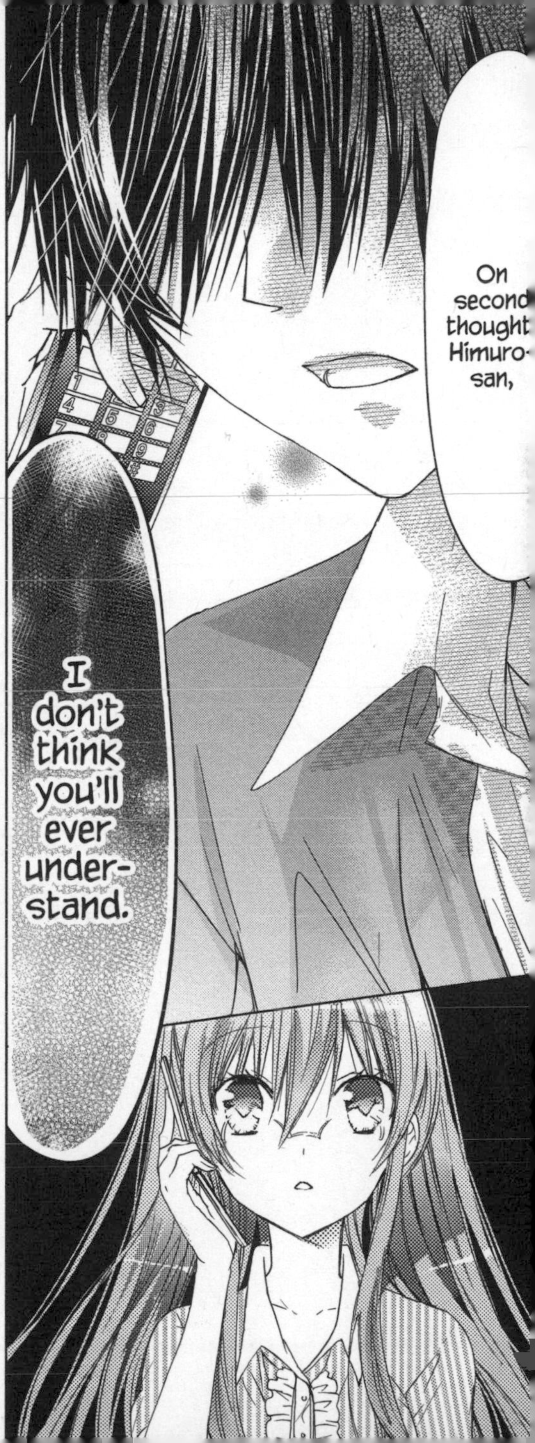
On second thought Himuro-san,
I don't think you'll ever under-stand.

4

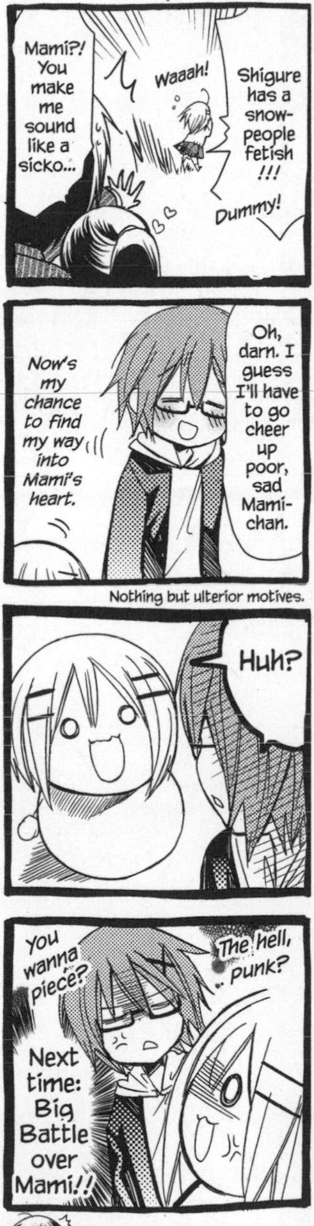
Shigure has a snow-people fetish!!!
Waaah!
Mami?! You make me sound like a sicko...
Dummy!
Oh, darn. I guess I'll have to go cheer up poor, sad Mami-chan.
Now's my chance to find my way into Mami's heart.
Huh?
The hell, punk?
You wanna piece?
Next time: Big Battle over Mami!!

Nothing but ulterior motives.

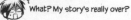

What? My story's really over?

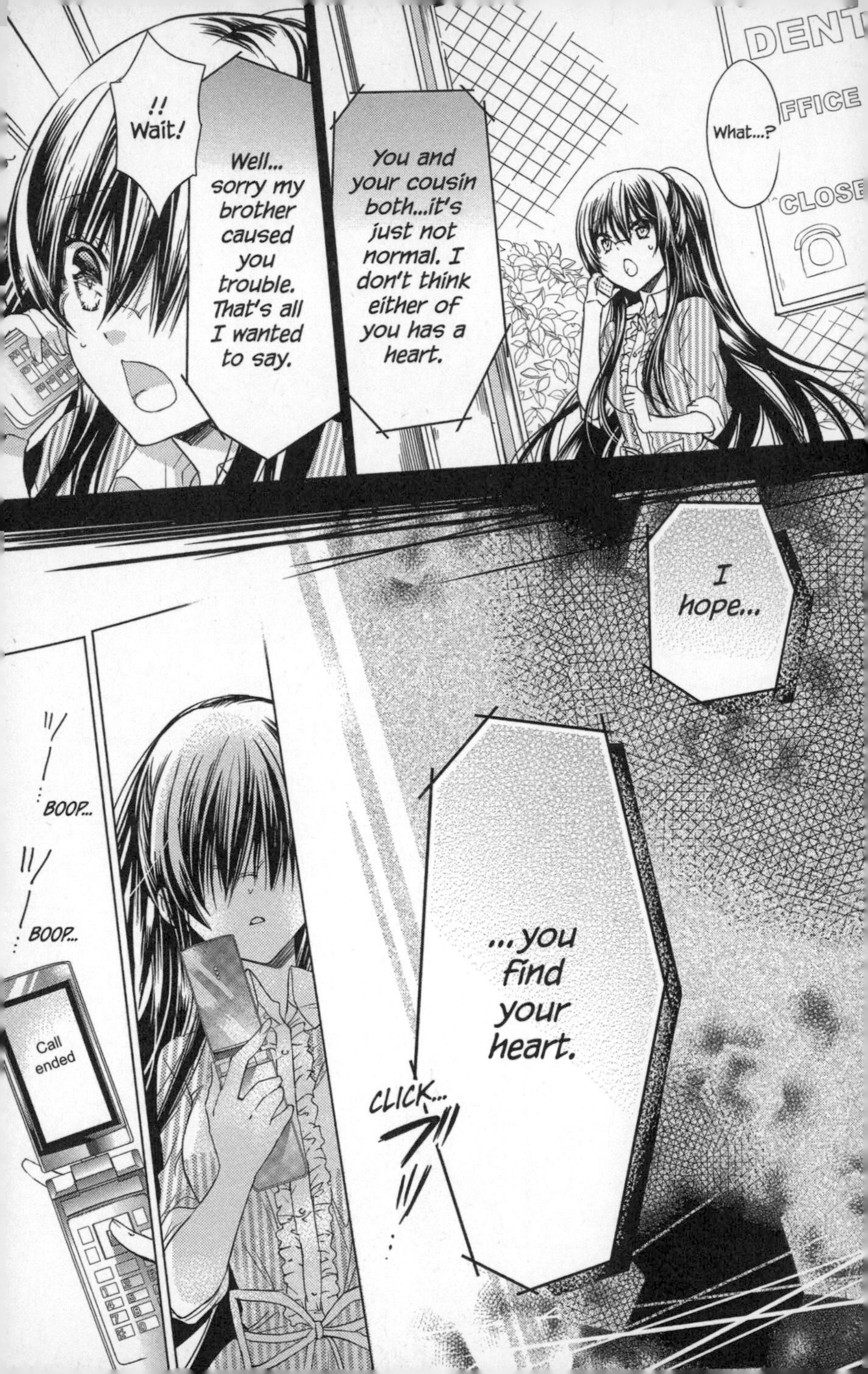
DENT
FFICE
CLOSE
What...?
You and your cousin both...it's just not normal. I don't think either of you has a heart.
Well... sorry my brother caused you trouble. That's all I wanted to say.
!! Wait!
I hope...
...you find your heart.
CLICK...
BOOP...
BOOP...
Call ended

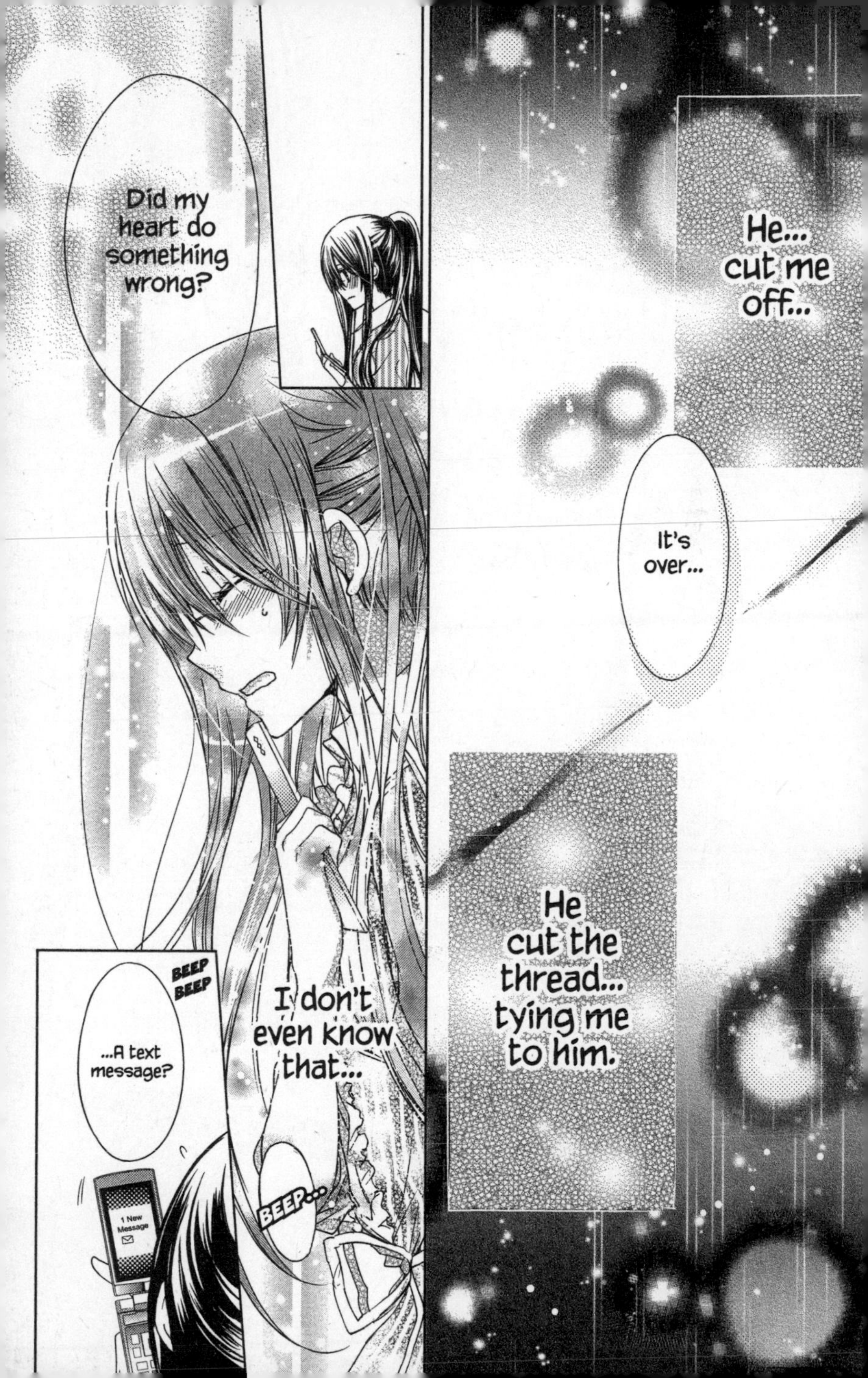
He... cut me off...
It's over...
He cut the thread... tying me to him.
Did my heart do something wrong?
I don't even know that...
BEEP...
BEEP BEEP
...A text message?
1 New Message

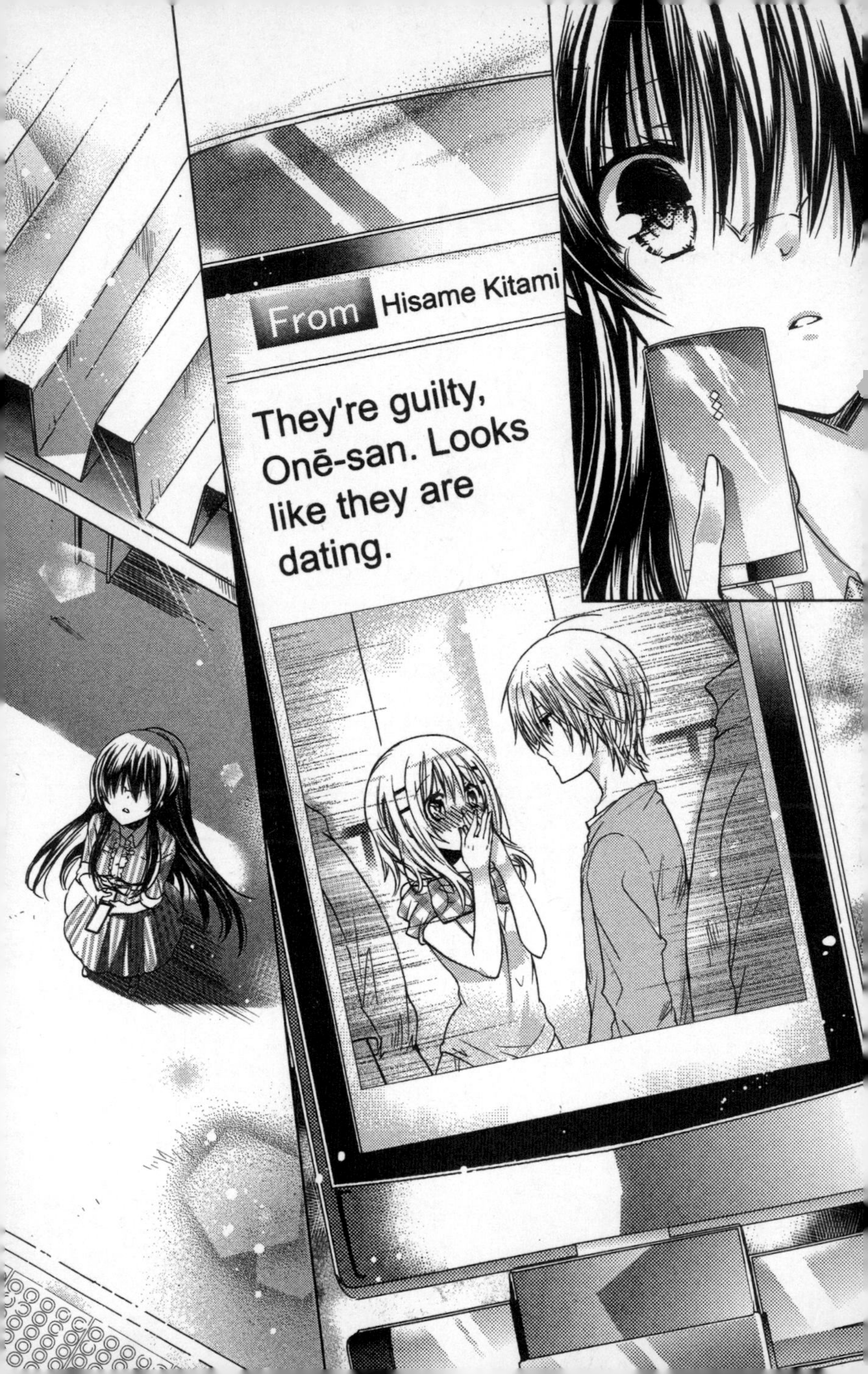
From Hisame Kitami
They're guilty, Onē-san. Looks like they are dating.

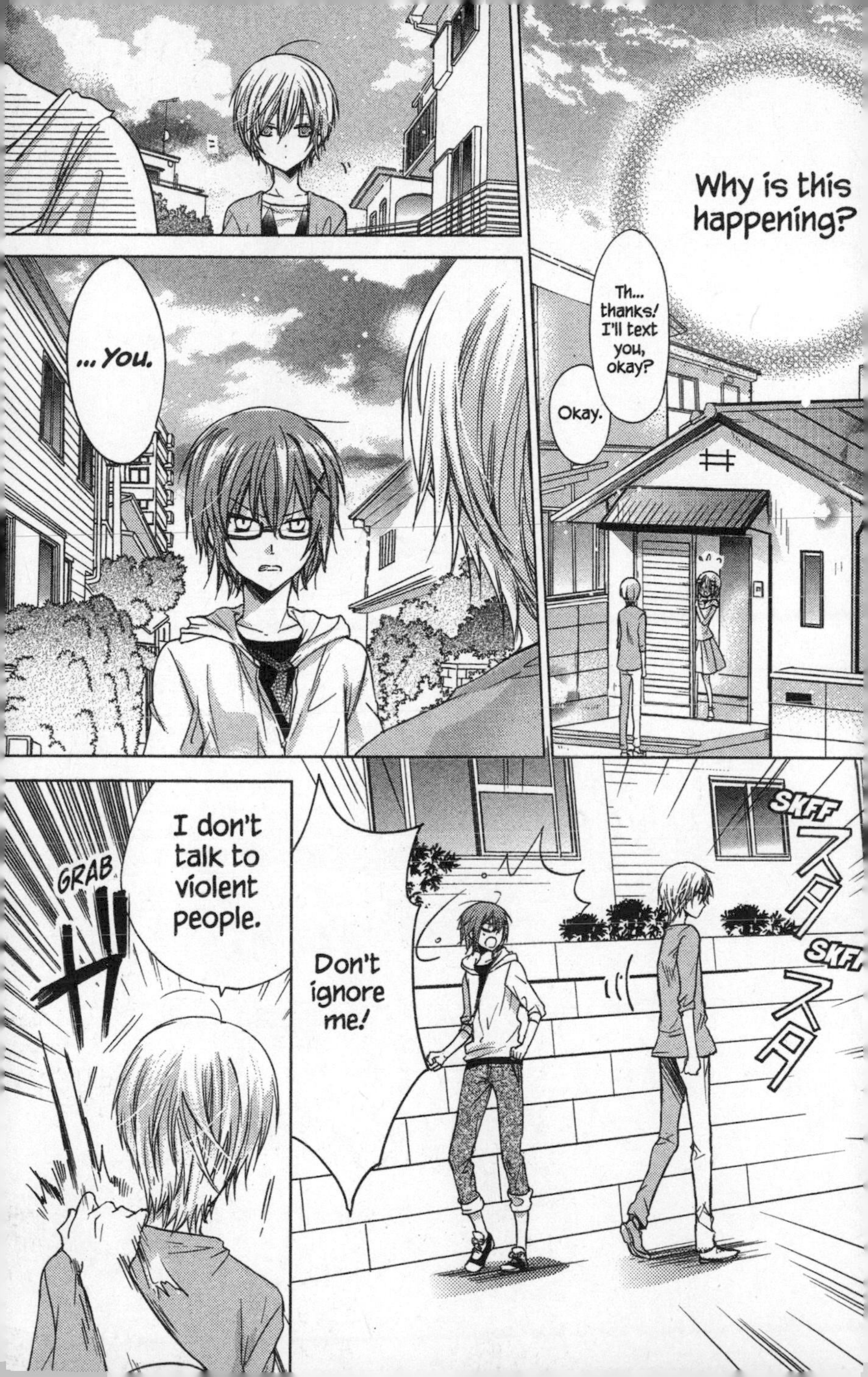
Why is this happening?
Th... thanks! I'll text you, okay?
Okay.
...You.
SKFF
SKFF
Don't ignore me!
I don't talk to violent people.
GRAB

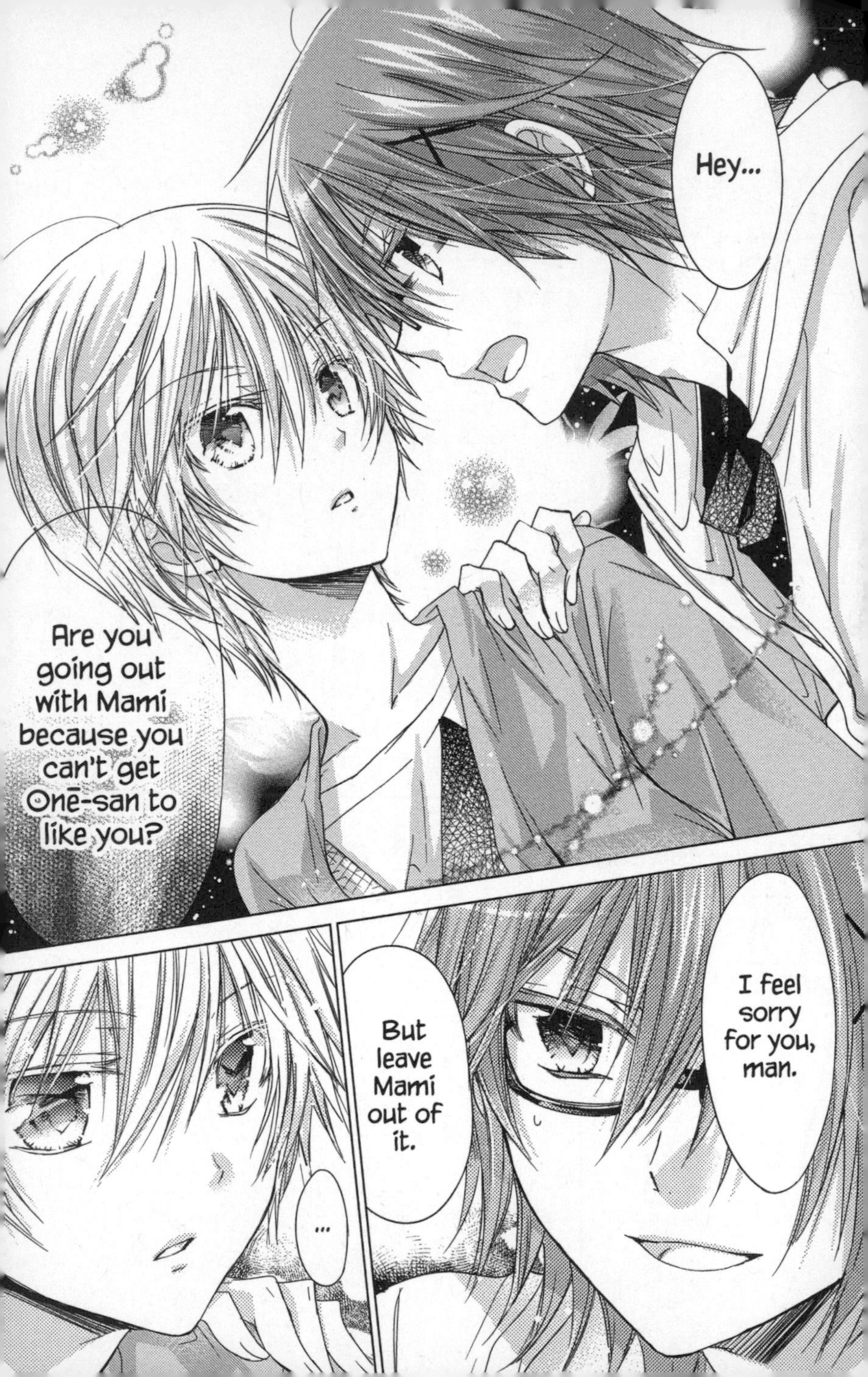
Hey...
Are you going out with Mami because you can't get Onē-san to like you?
I feel sorry for you, man.
But leave Mami out of it.
...

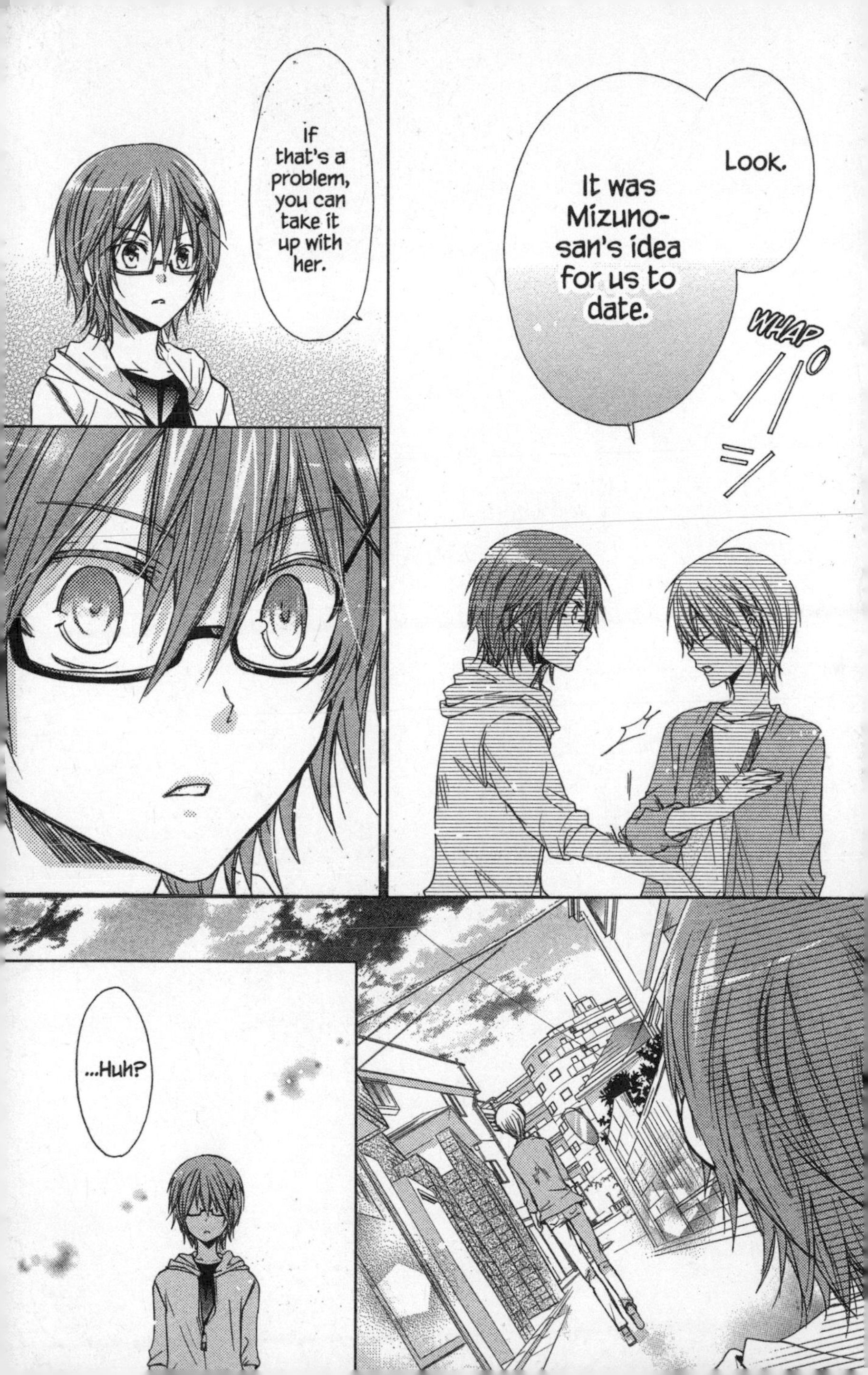
Look.
It was Mizuno-san's idea for us to date.
WHAP
If that's a problem, you can take it up with her.
...Huh?

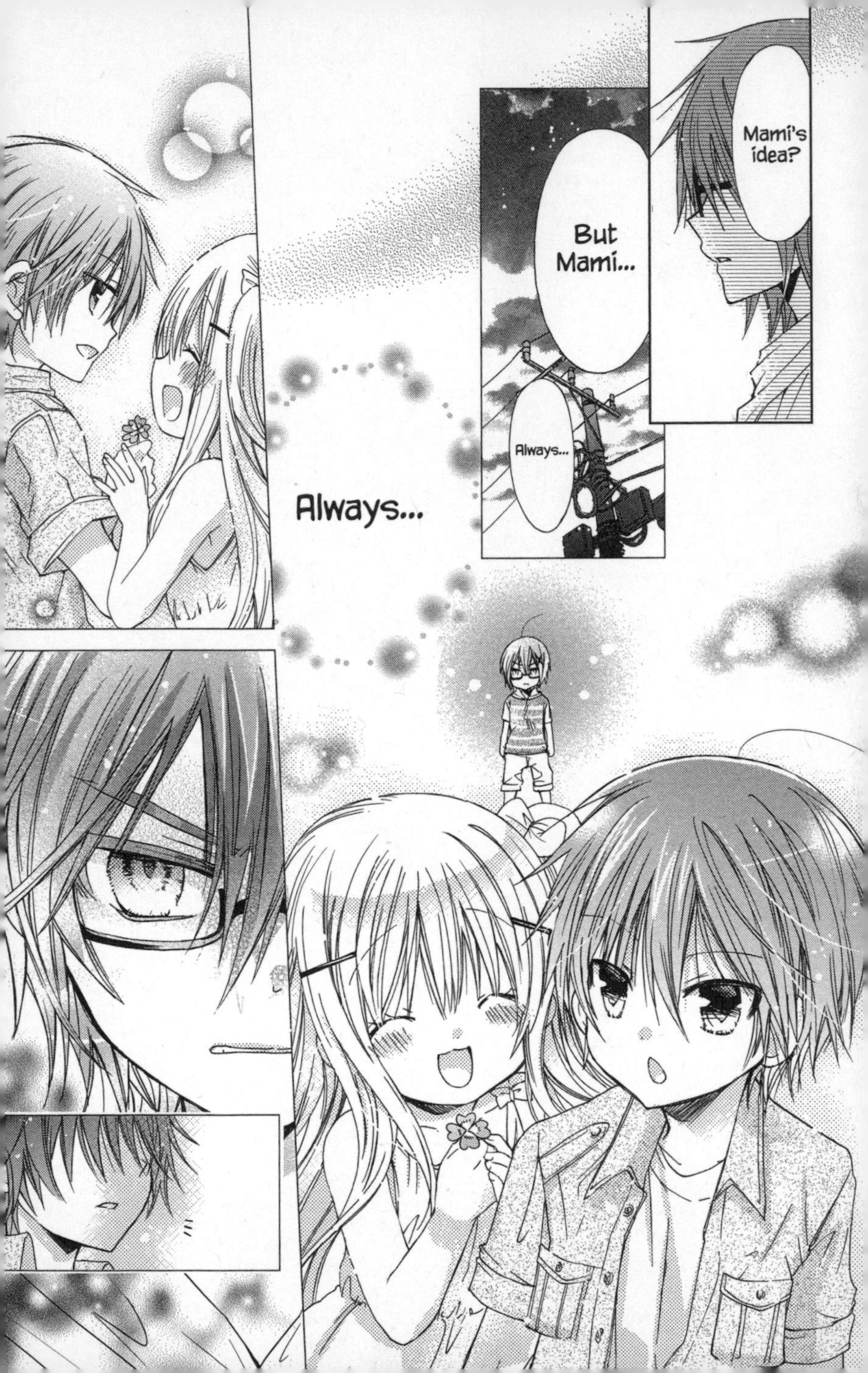
Mami's idea?
But Mami...
Always...
Always...

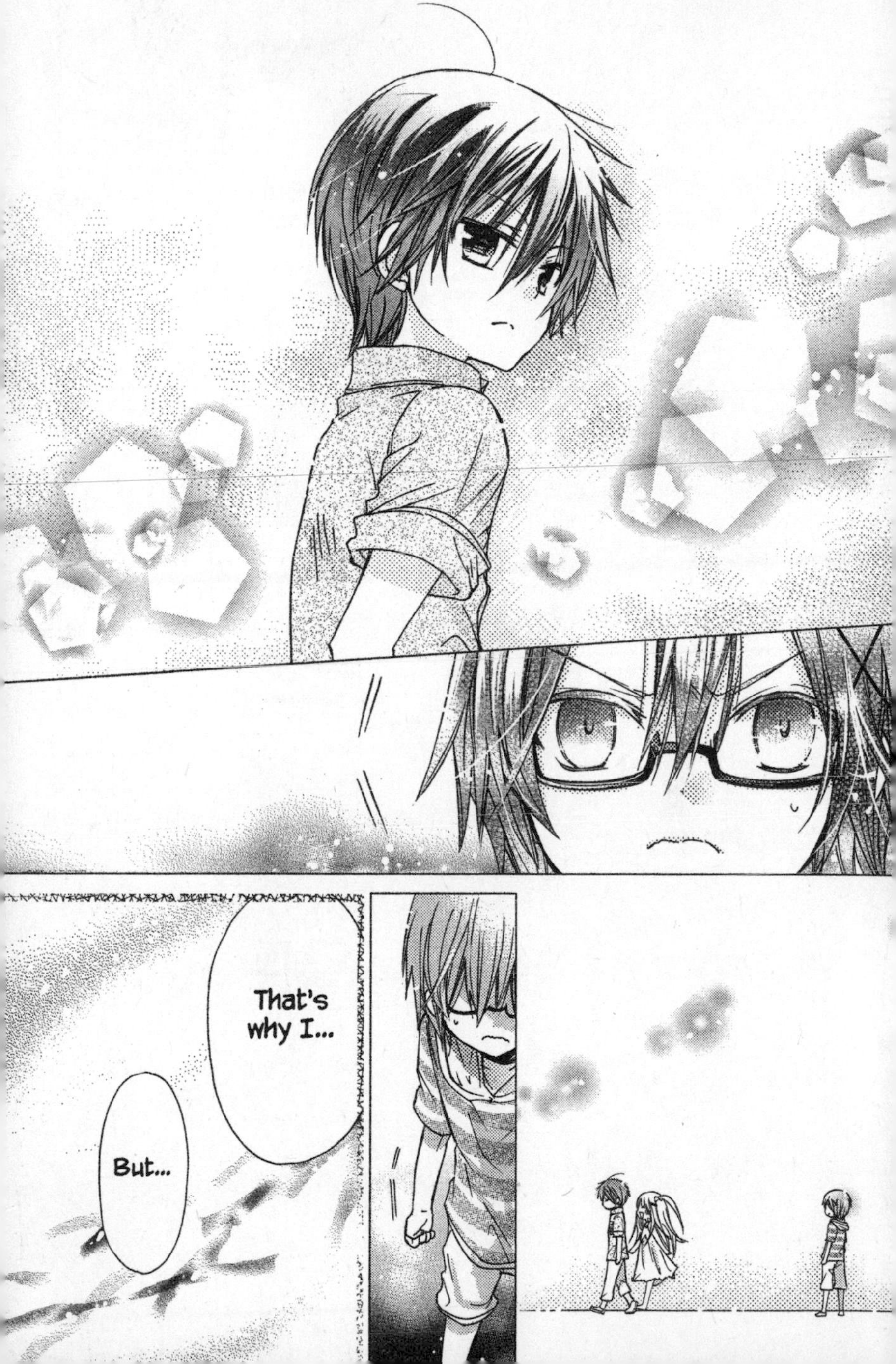
That's why I...
But...

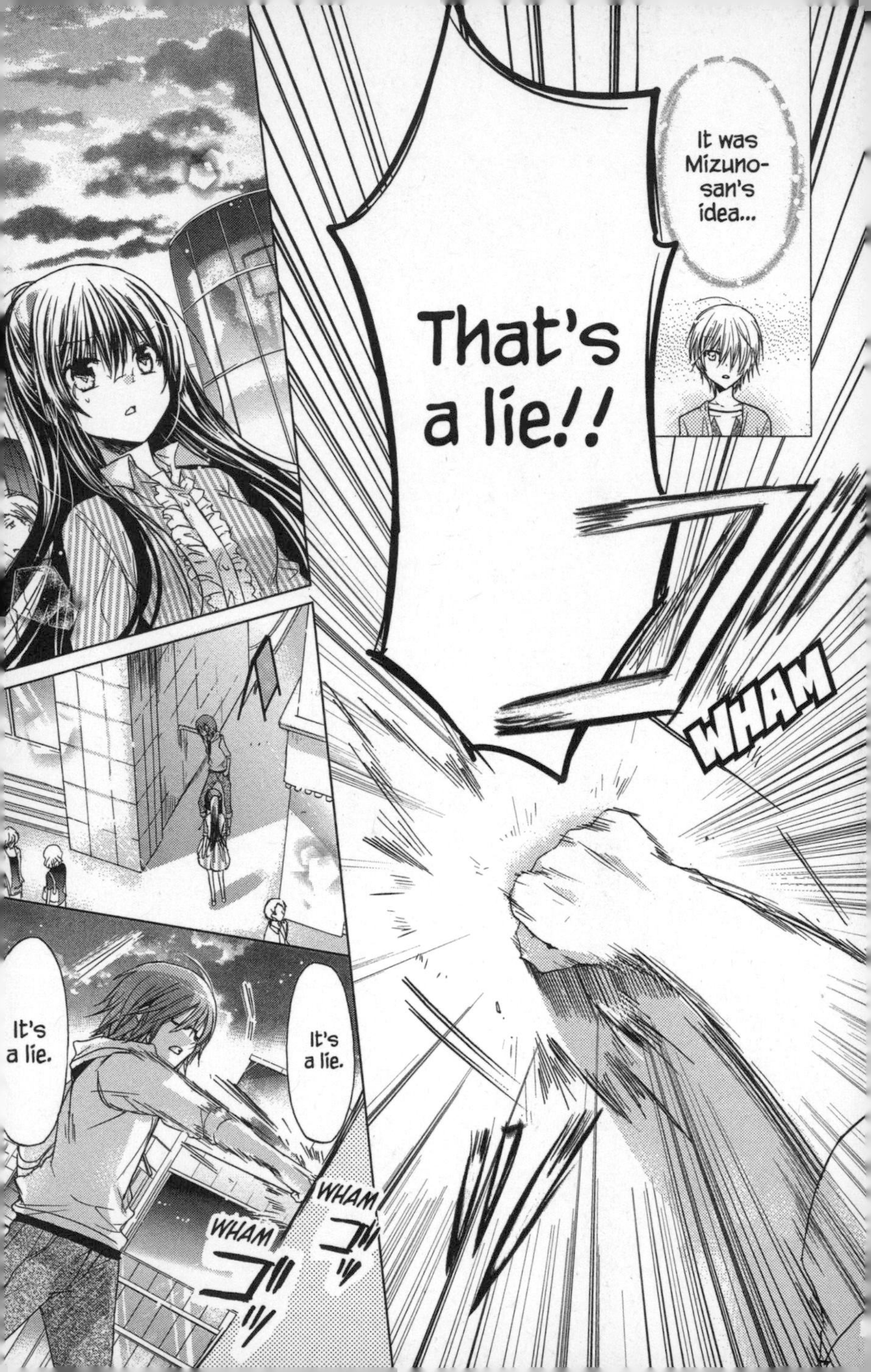
It was Mizuno-san's idea...
That's a lie!!
WHAM
It's a lie.
It's a lie.
WHAM
WHAM

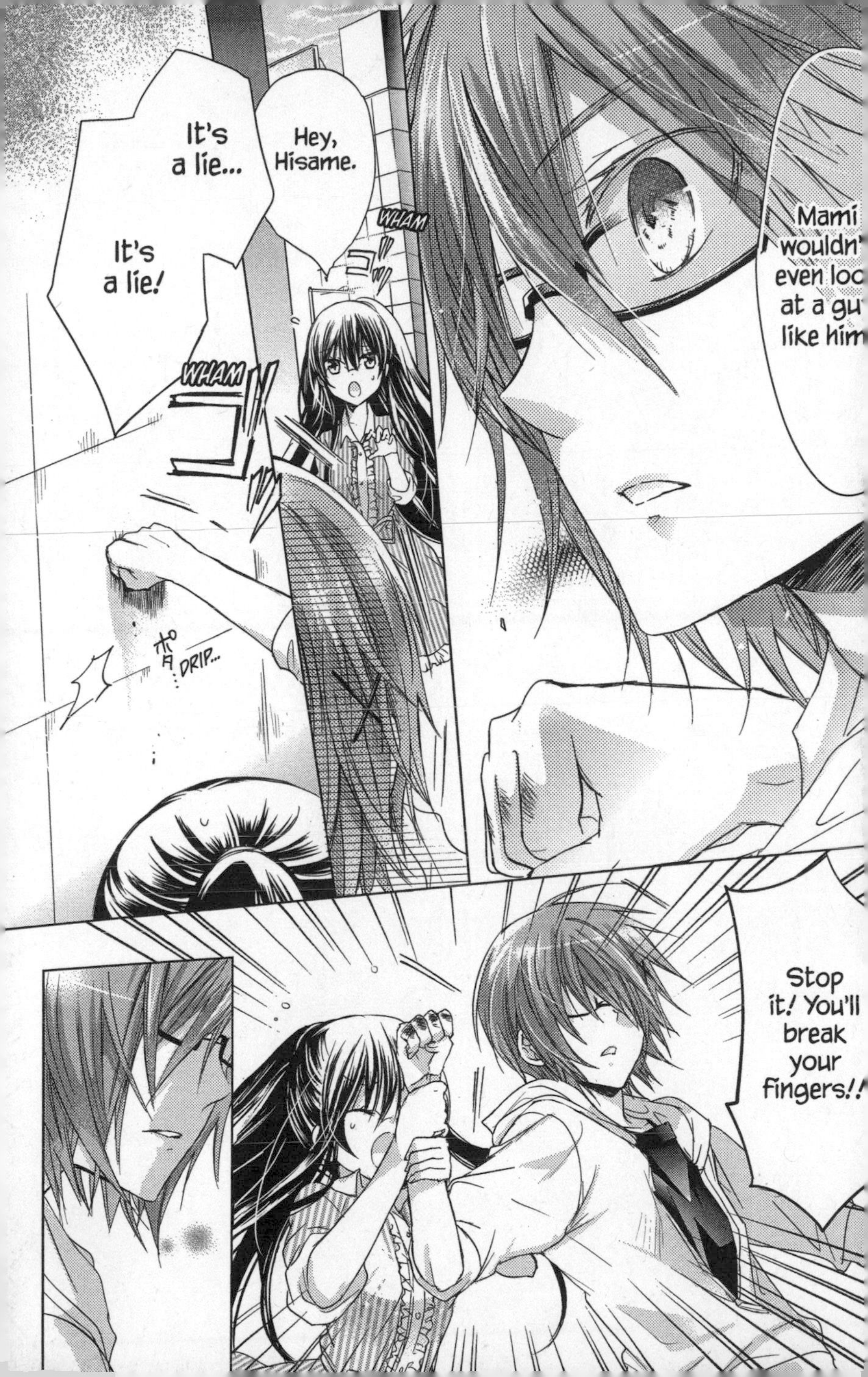
Mami wouldn' even loo at a gu like him
Hey, Hisame.
WHAM
It's a lie...
It's a lie!
WHAM
DRIP...
Stop it! You'll break your fingers!!

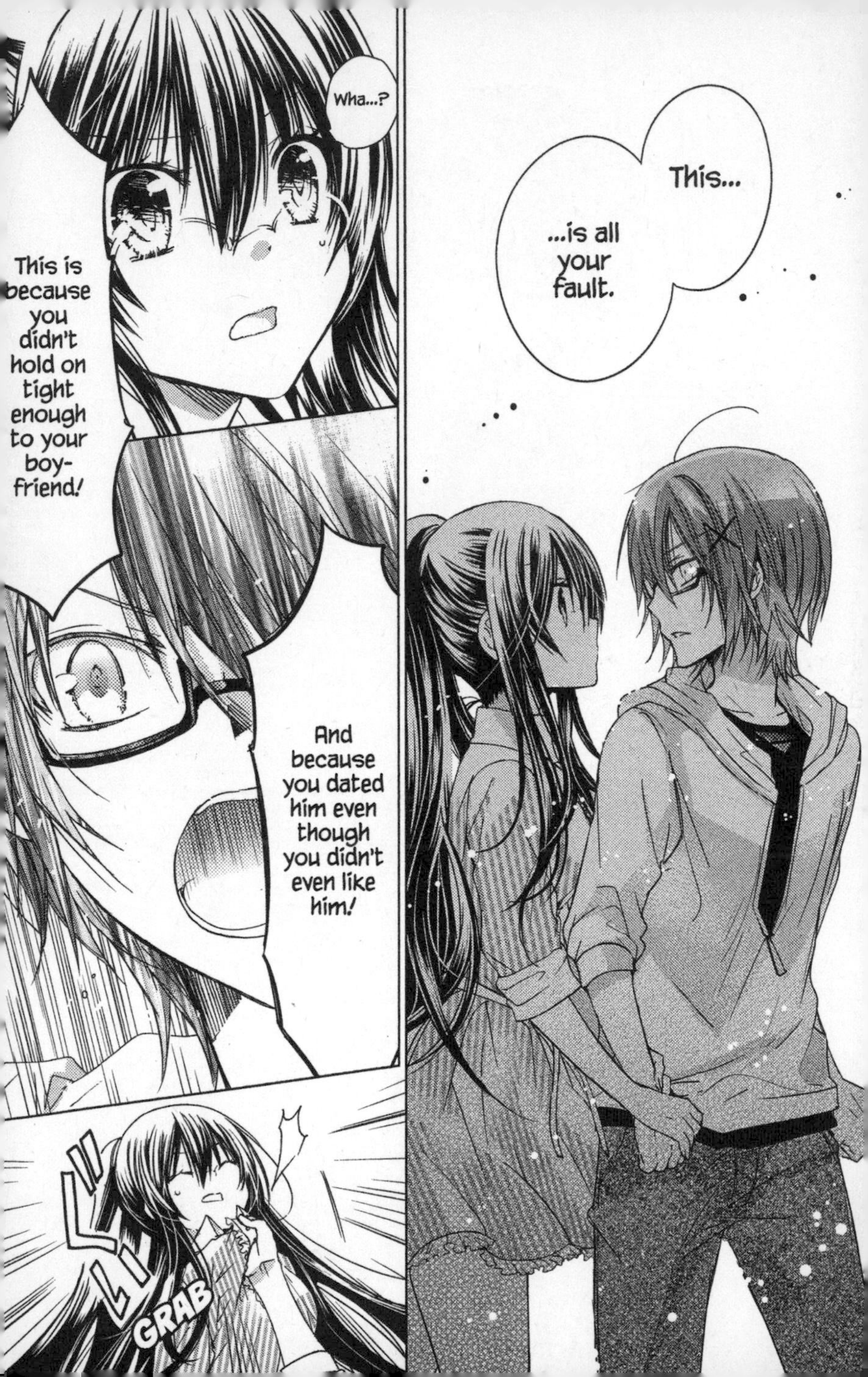
This...
...is all your fault.
Wha...?
This is because you didn't hold on tight enough to your boy-friend!
And because you dated him even though you didn't even like him!
GRAB

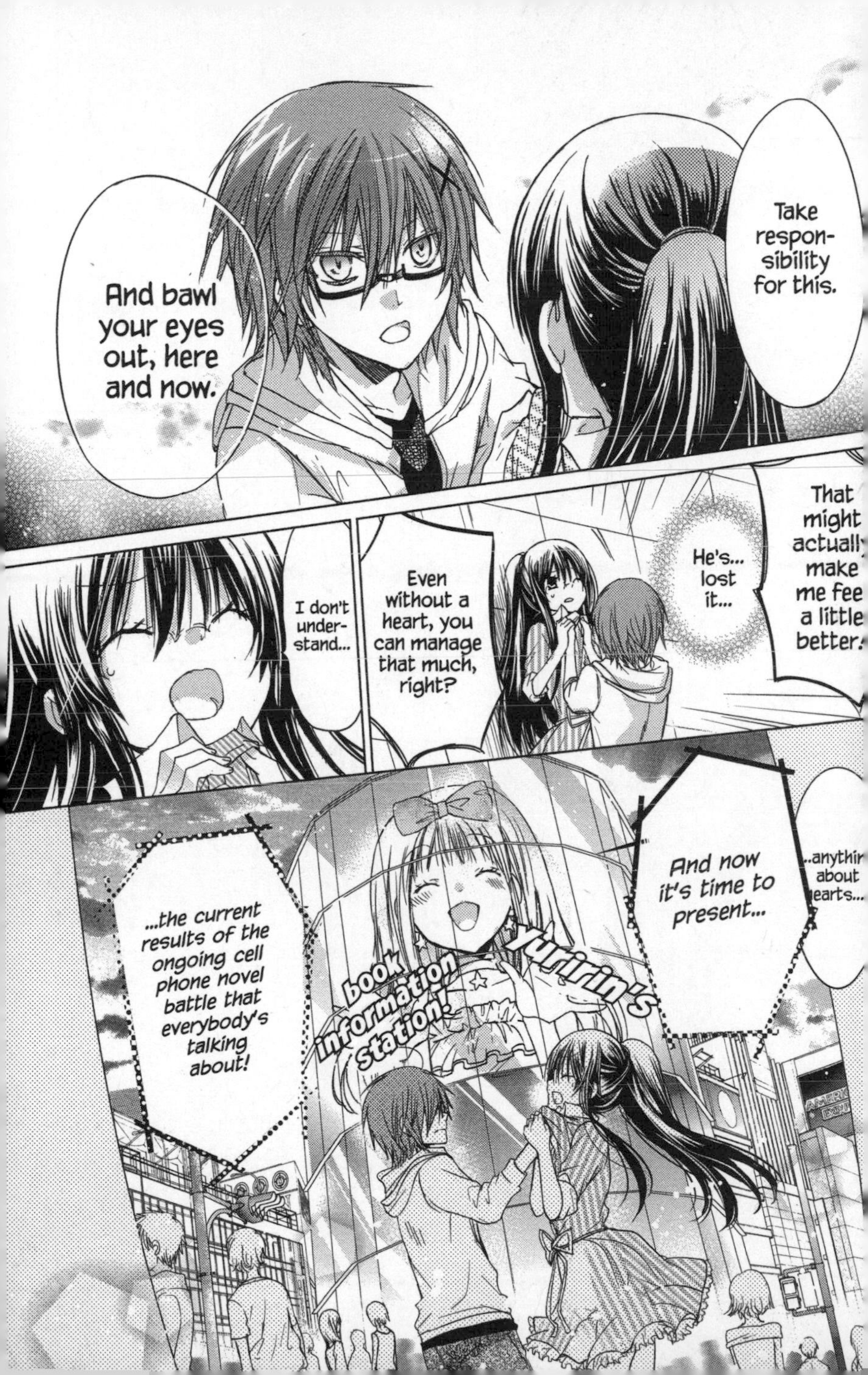
Take responsibility for this.
And bawl your eyes out, here and now.
That might actuall make me fee a little better.
He's... lost it...
Even without a heart, you can manage that much, right?
I don't under-stand...
...anythir about earts...
And now it's time to present...
Yuririn's book information Station!
...the current results of the ongoing cell phone novel battle that everybody's talking about!

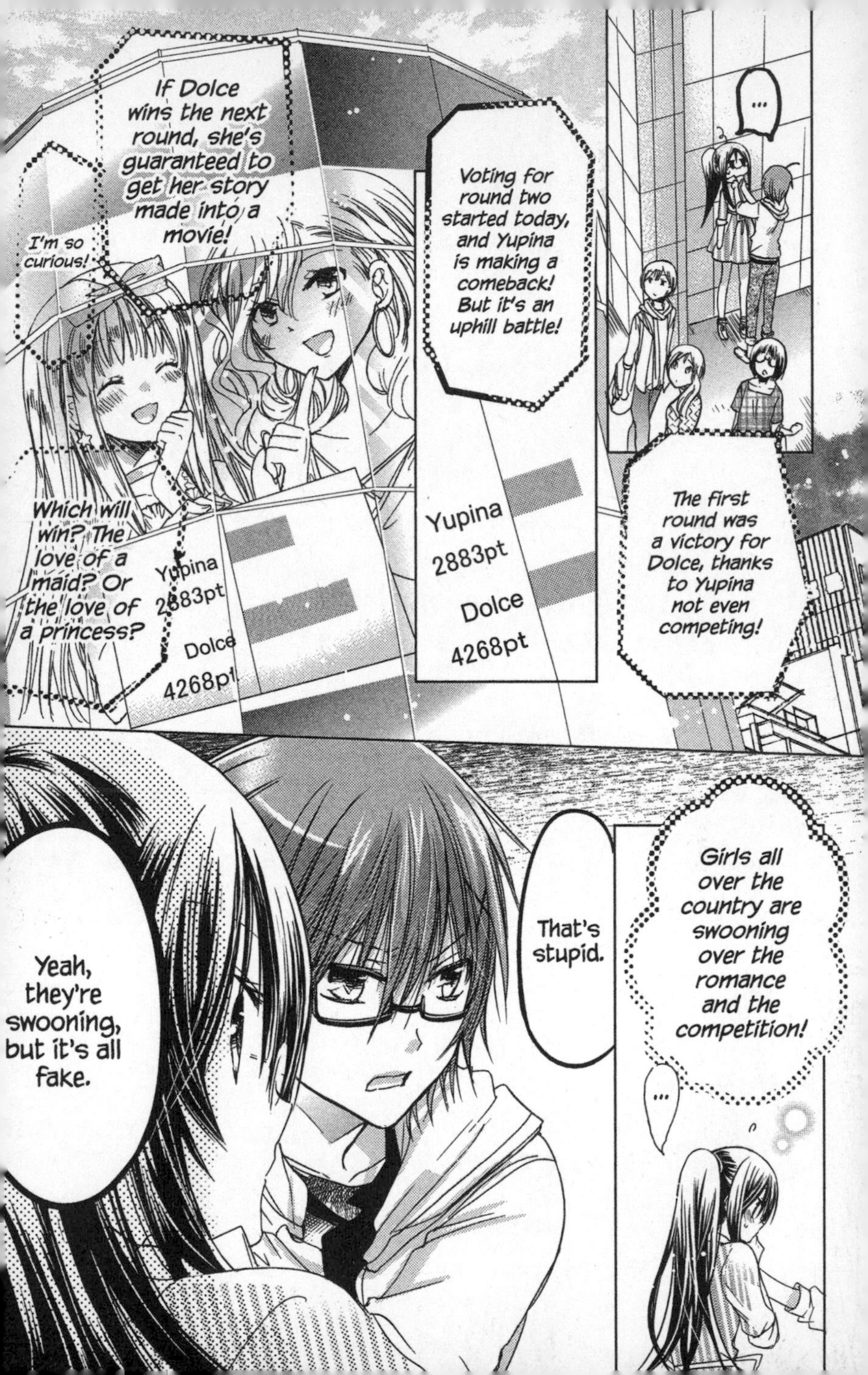
...
Voting for round two started today, and Yupina is making a comeback! But it's an uphill battle!
Yupina
2883pt
Dolce
4268pt
If Dolce wins the next round, she's guaranteed to get her story made into a movie!
I'm so curious!
The first round was a victory for Dolce, thanks to Yupina not even competing!
Which will win? The love of a maid? Or the love of a princess?
Yupina
2883pt
Dolce
4268pt
Girls all over the country are swooning over the romance and the competition!
...
That's stupid.
Yeah, they're swooning, but it's all fake.

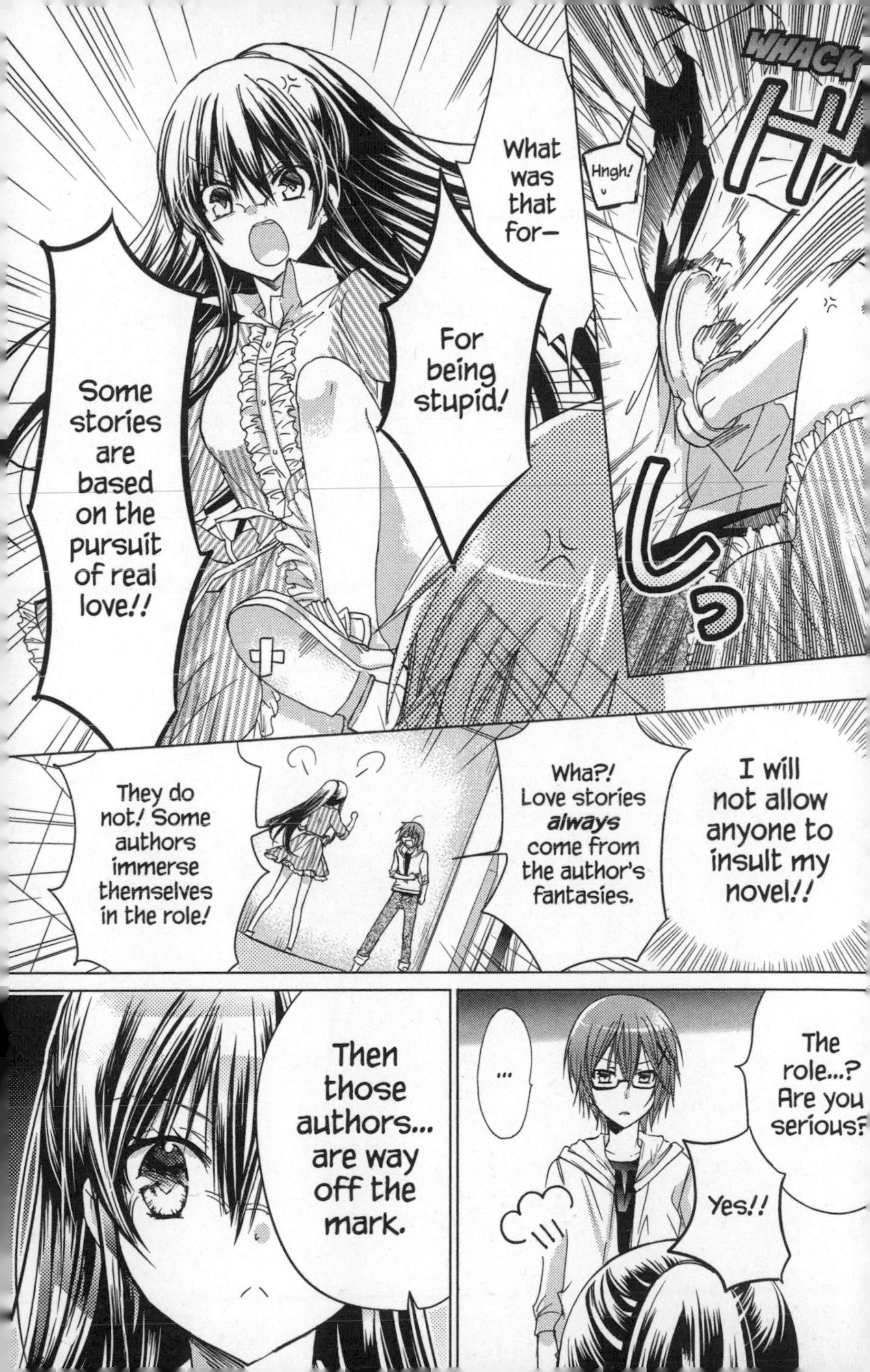
WHACK
Hngh!
What was that for—
For being stupid!
Some stories are based on the pursuit of real love!!
I will not allow anyone to insult my novel!!
Wha?! Love stories *always* come from the author's fantasies.
They do not! Some authors immerse themselves in the role!
The role...? Are you serious?
...
Yes!!
Then those authors... are way off the mark.

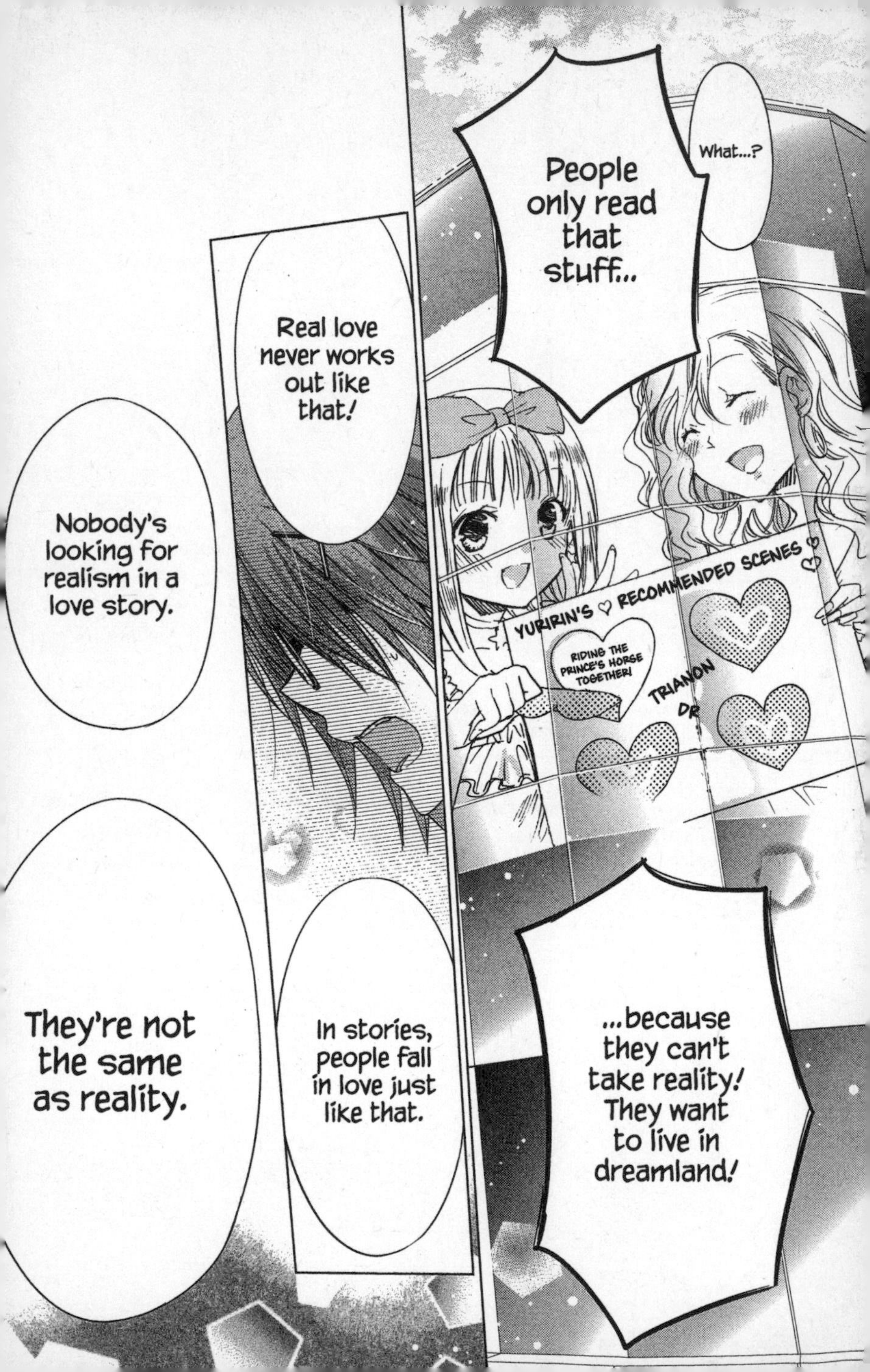
What...?
People only read that stuff...
YURIRIN'S ♡ RECOMMENDED SCENES ♡
RIDING THE PRINCE'S HORSE TOGETHER!
TRIANON OR
...because they can't take reality! They want to live in dreamland!
Real love never works out like that!
In stories, people fall in love just like that.
Nobody's looking for realism in a love story.
They're not the same as reality.

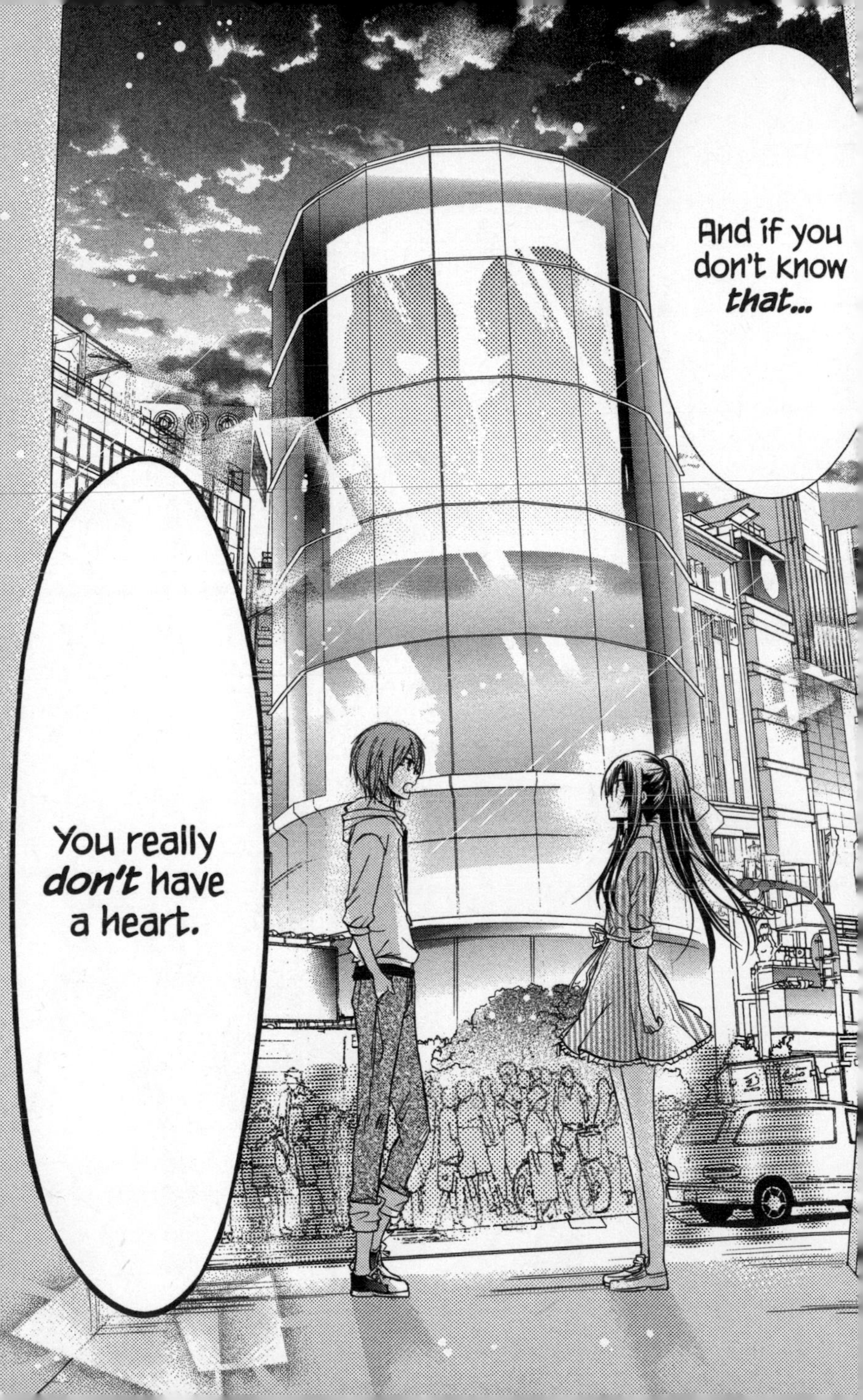
And if you don't know *that*...
You really *don't* have a heart.

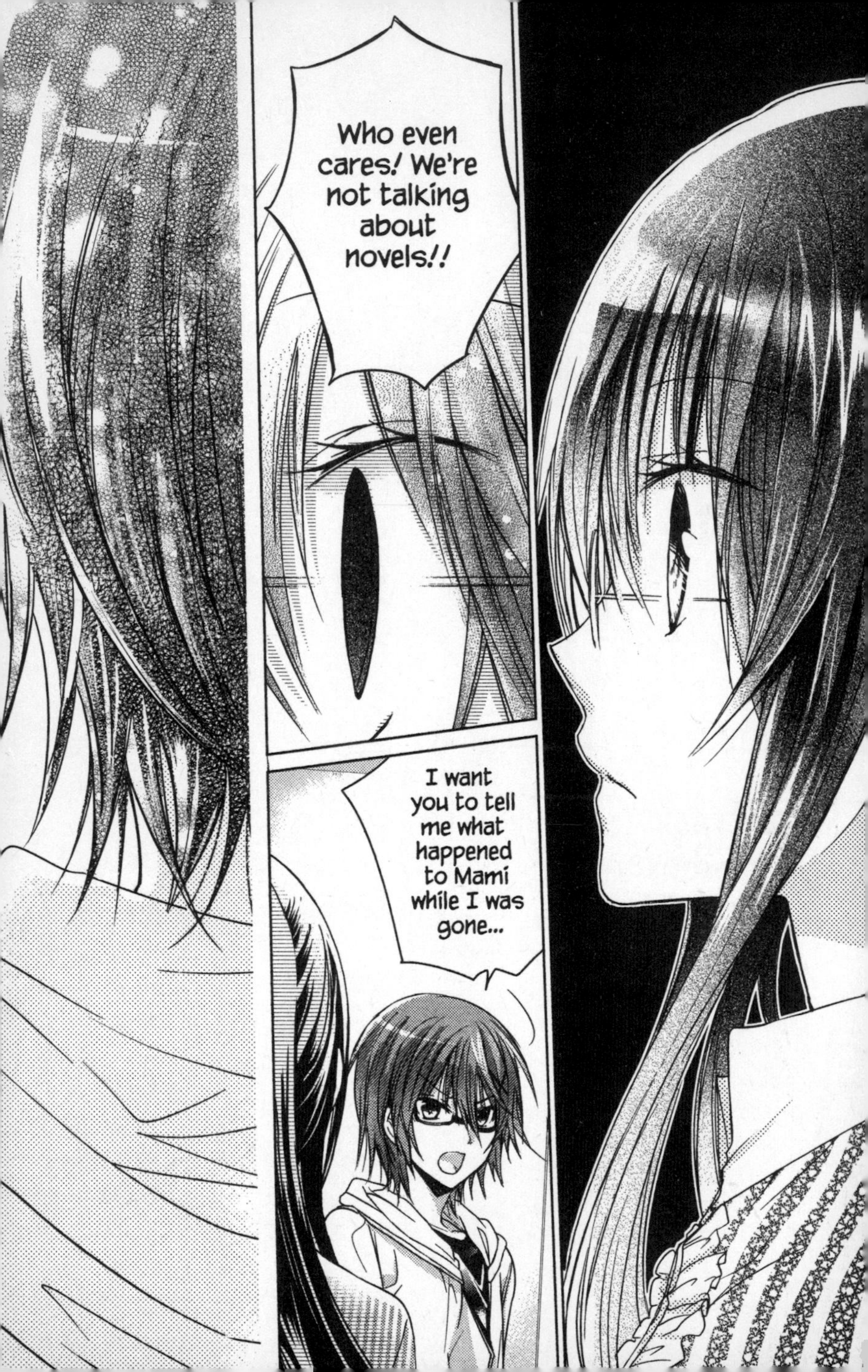
Who even cares! We're not talking about novels!!
I want you to tell me what happened to Mami while I was gone...

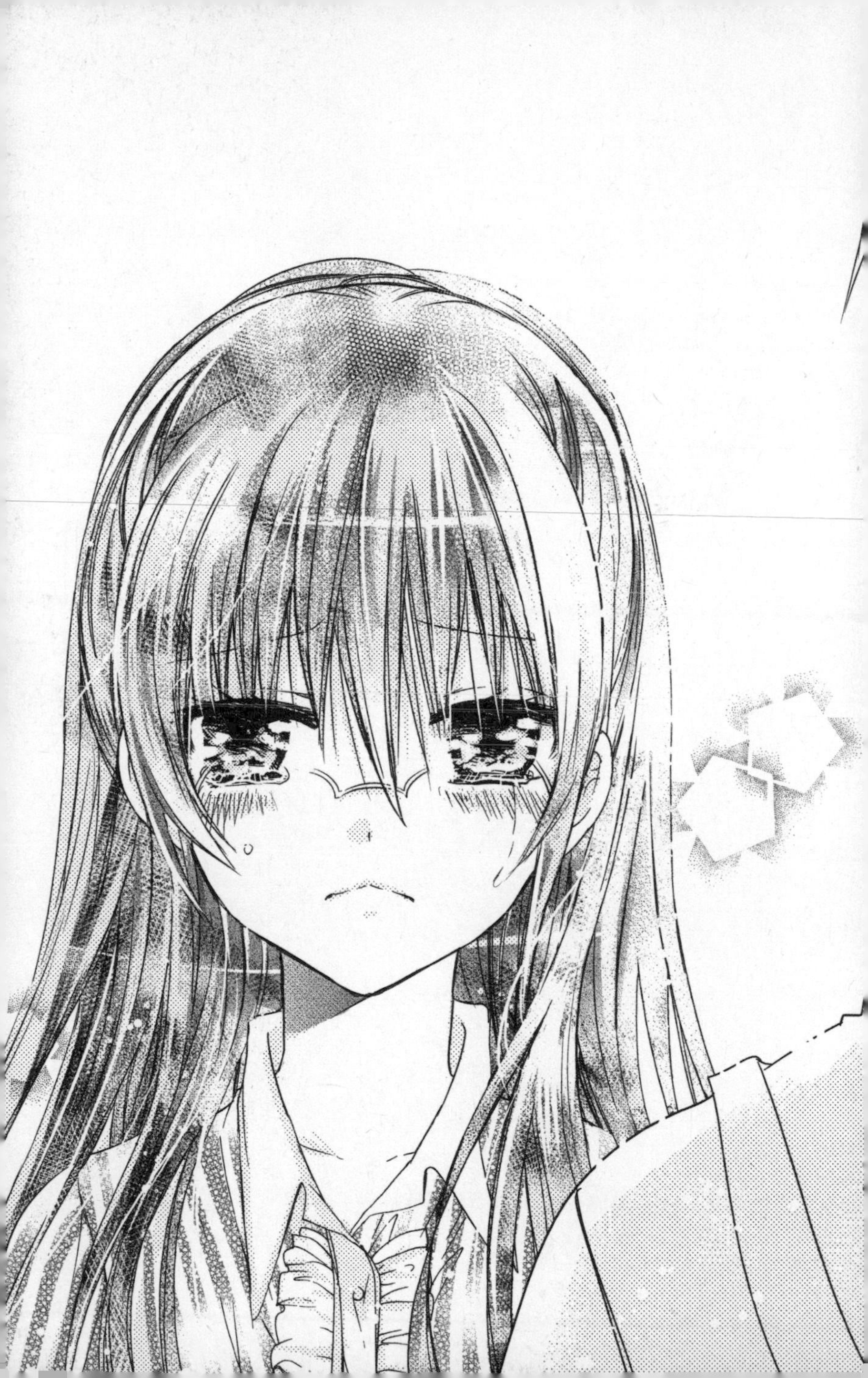

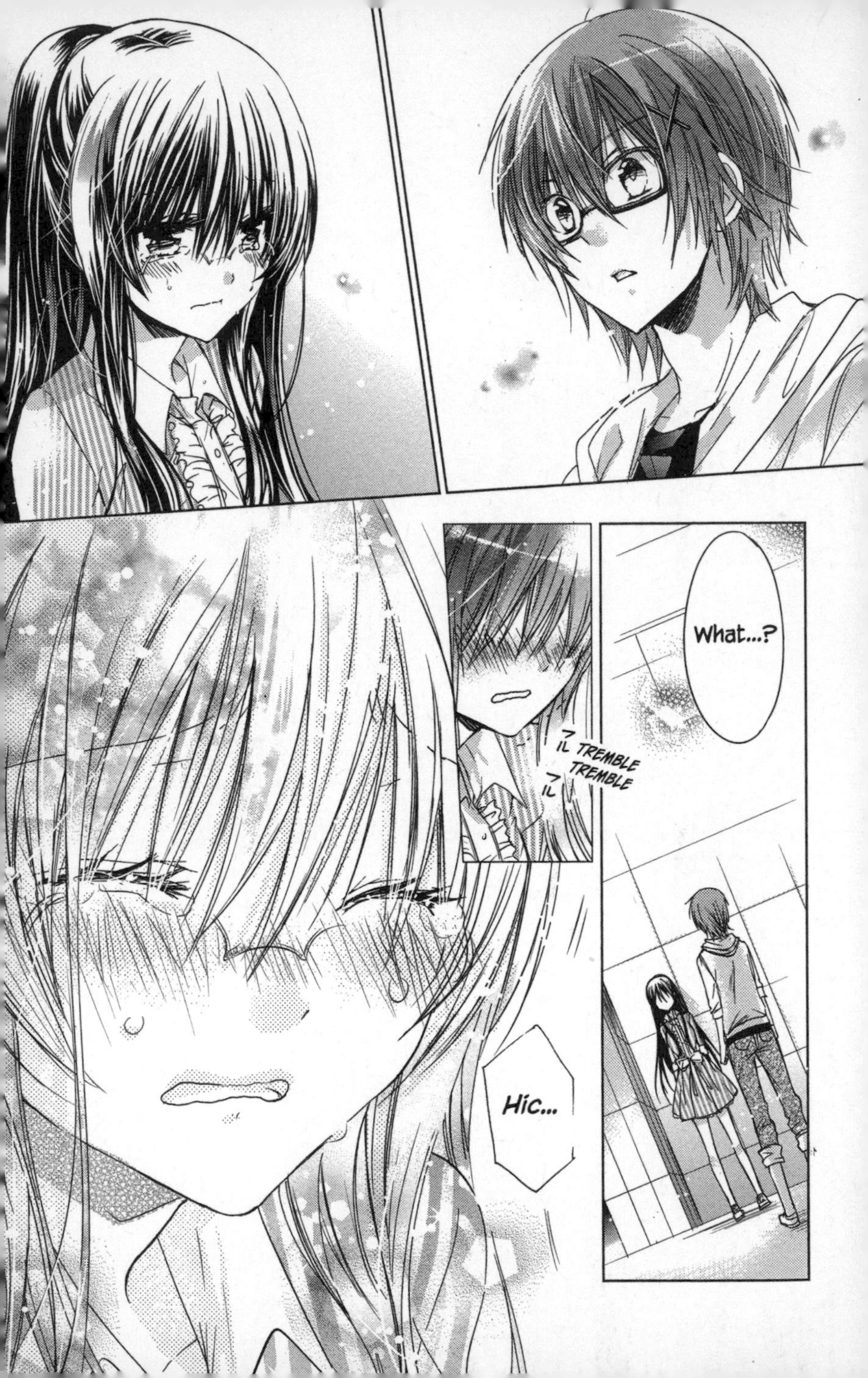
What...?
TREMBLE
TREMBLE
Hic...

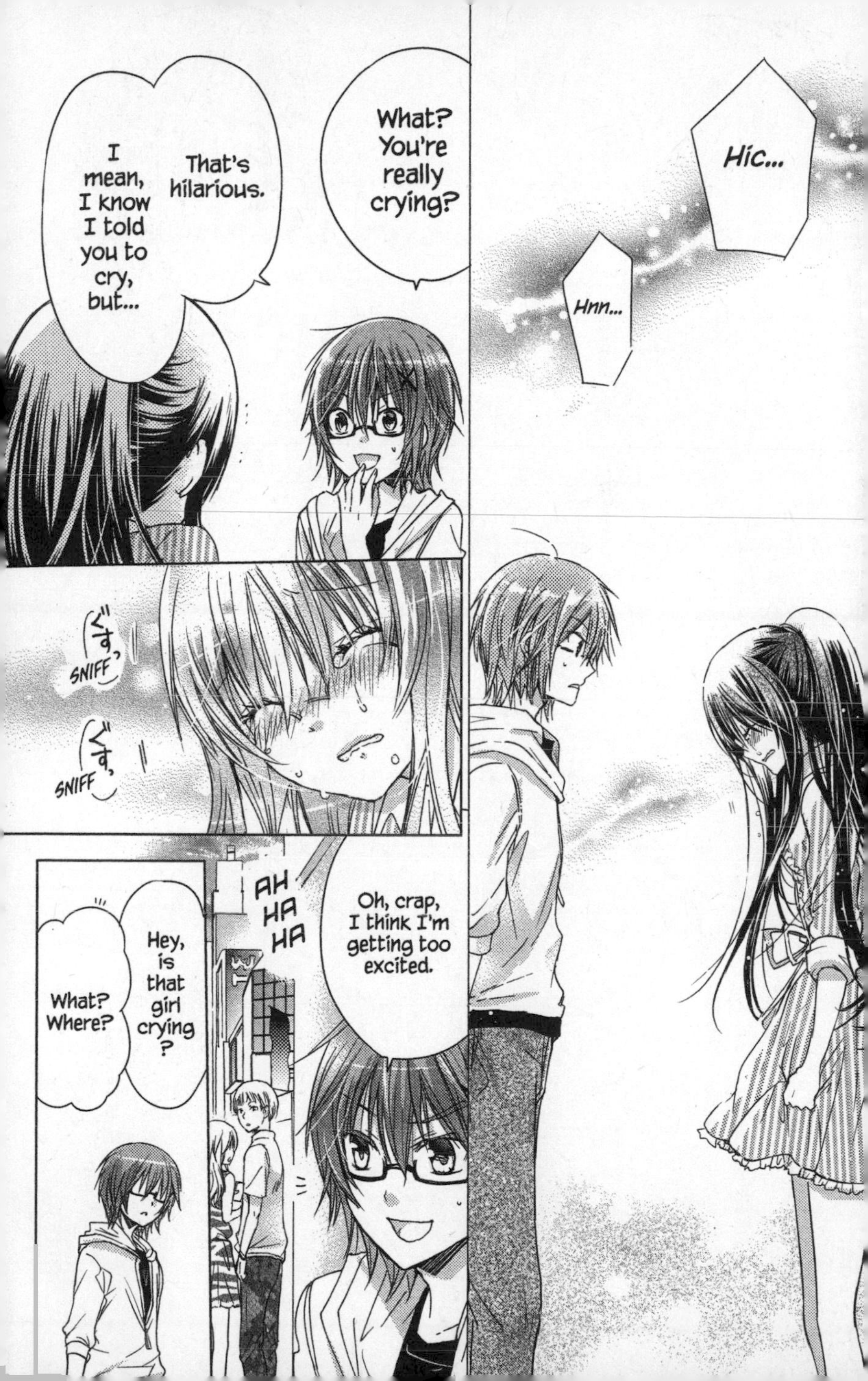
Hic...
Hnn...
What? You're really crying?
That's hilarious.
I mean, I know I told you to cry, but...
ぐす、
SNIFF
ぐす、
SNIFF
Oh, crap, I think I'm getting too excited.
AH HA HA
Hey, is that girl crying?
What? Where?

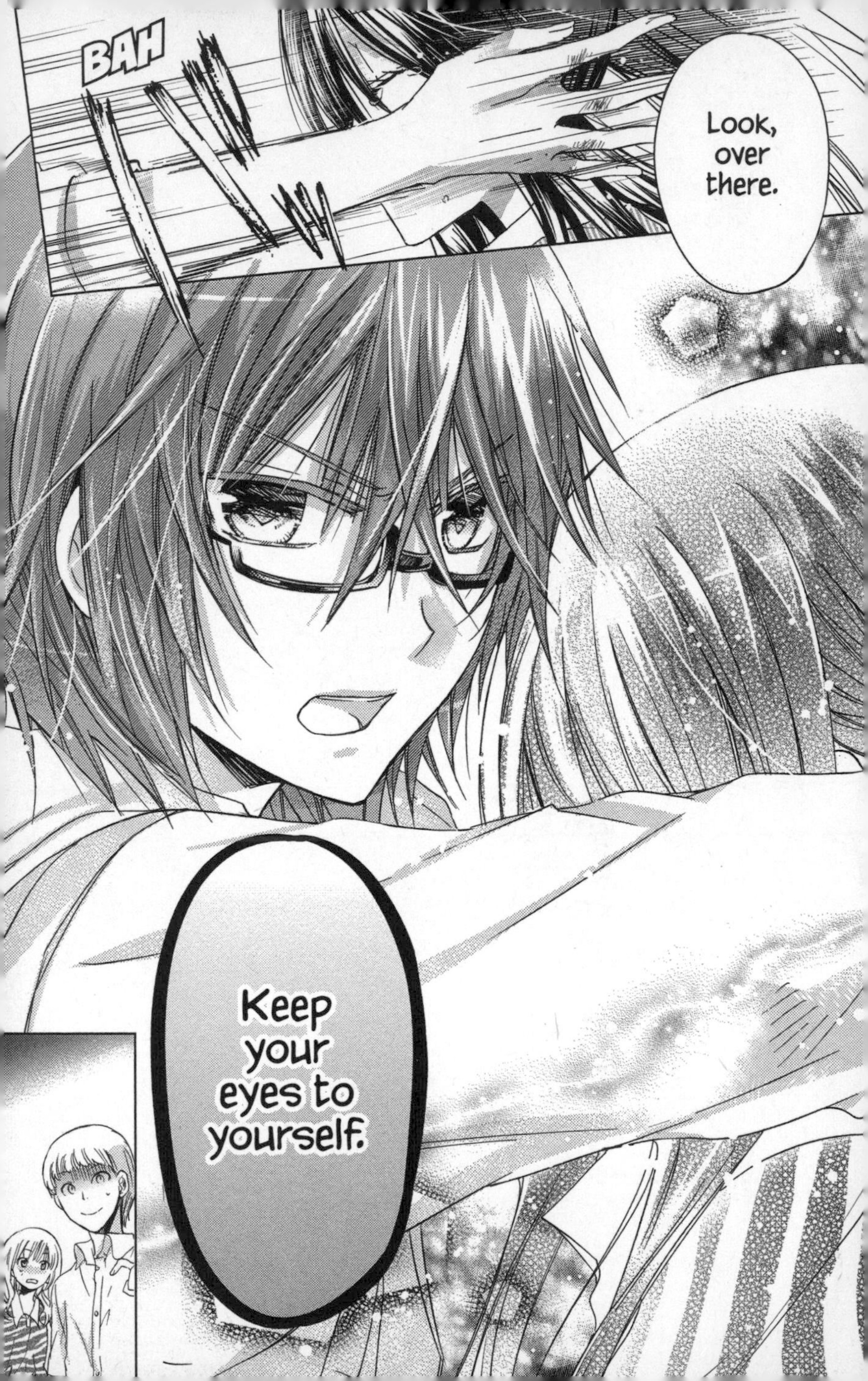
BAH
Look, over there.
Keep your eyes to yourself.

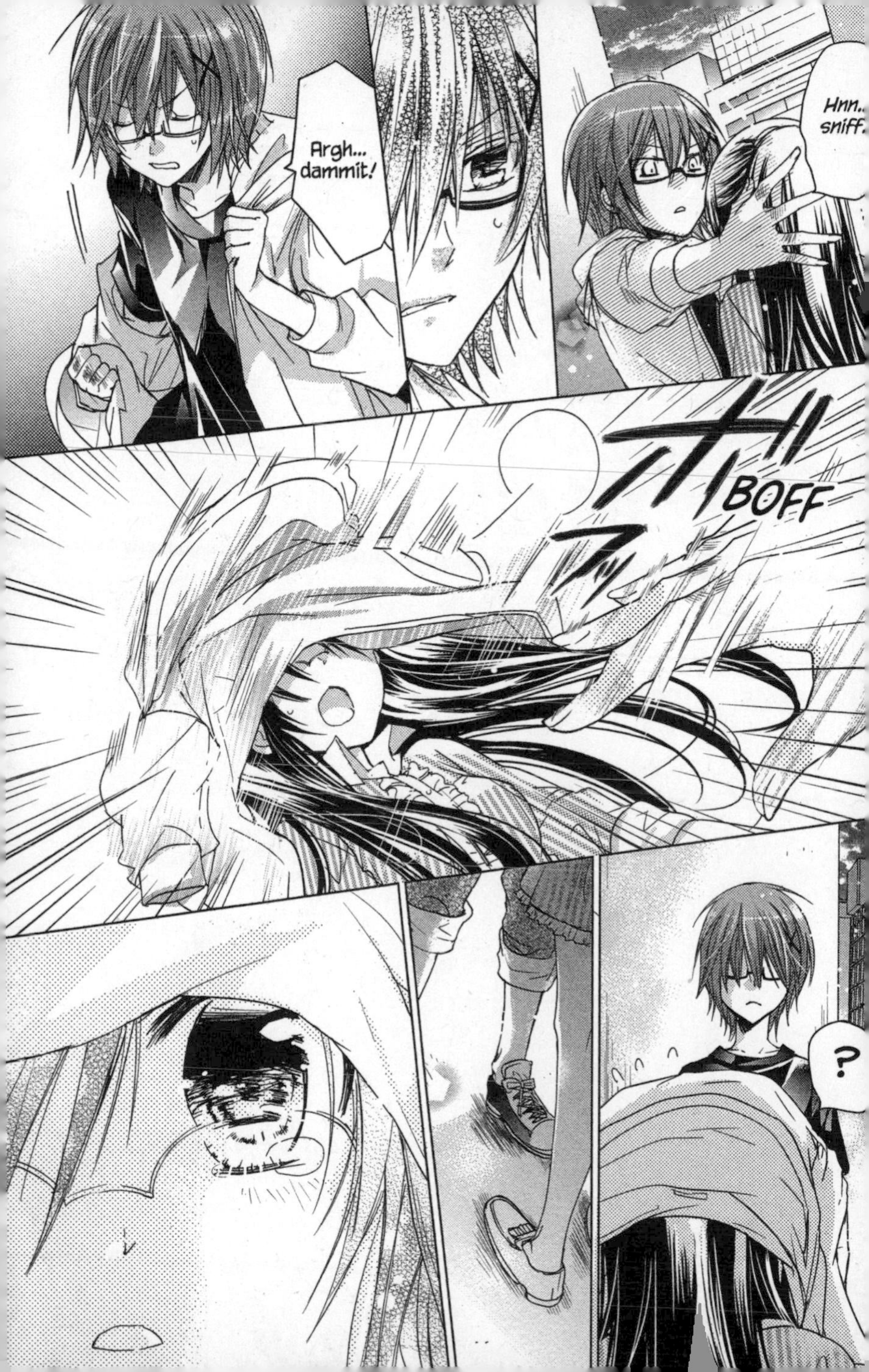
Hnn.. sniff.
Argh... dammit!
BOFF
?

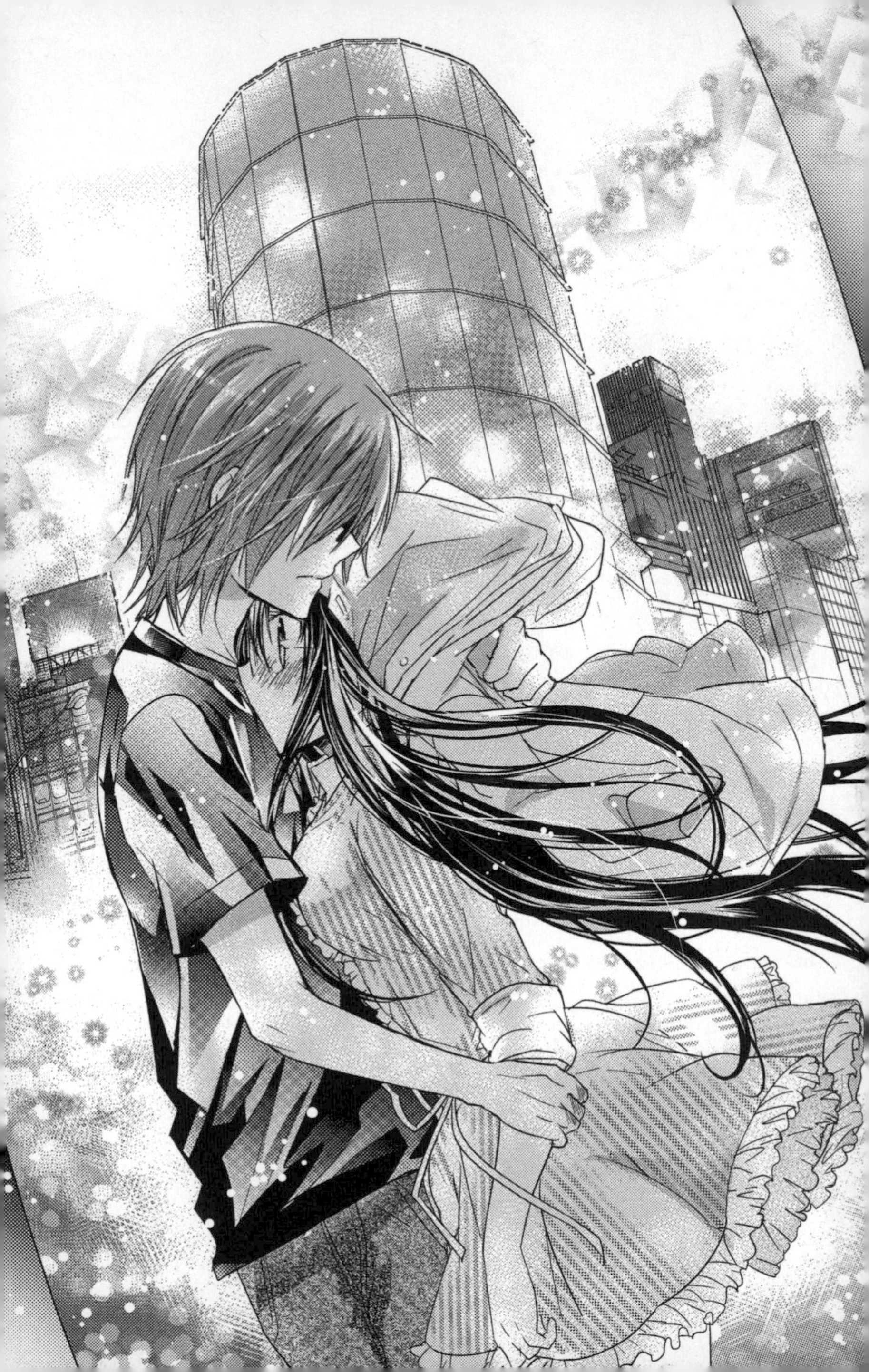

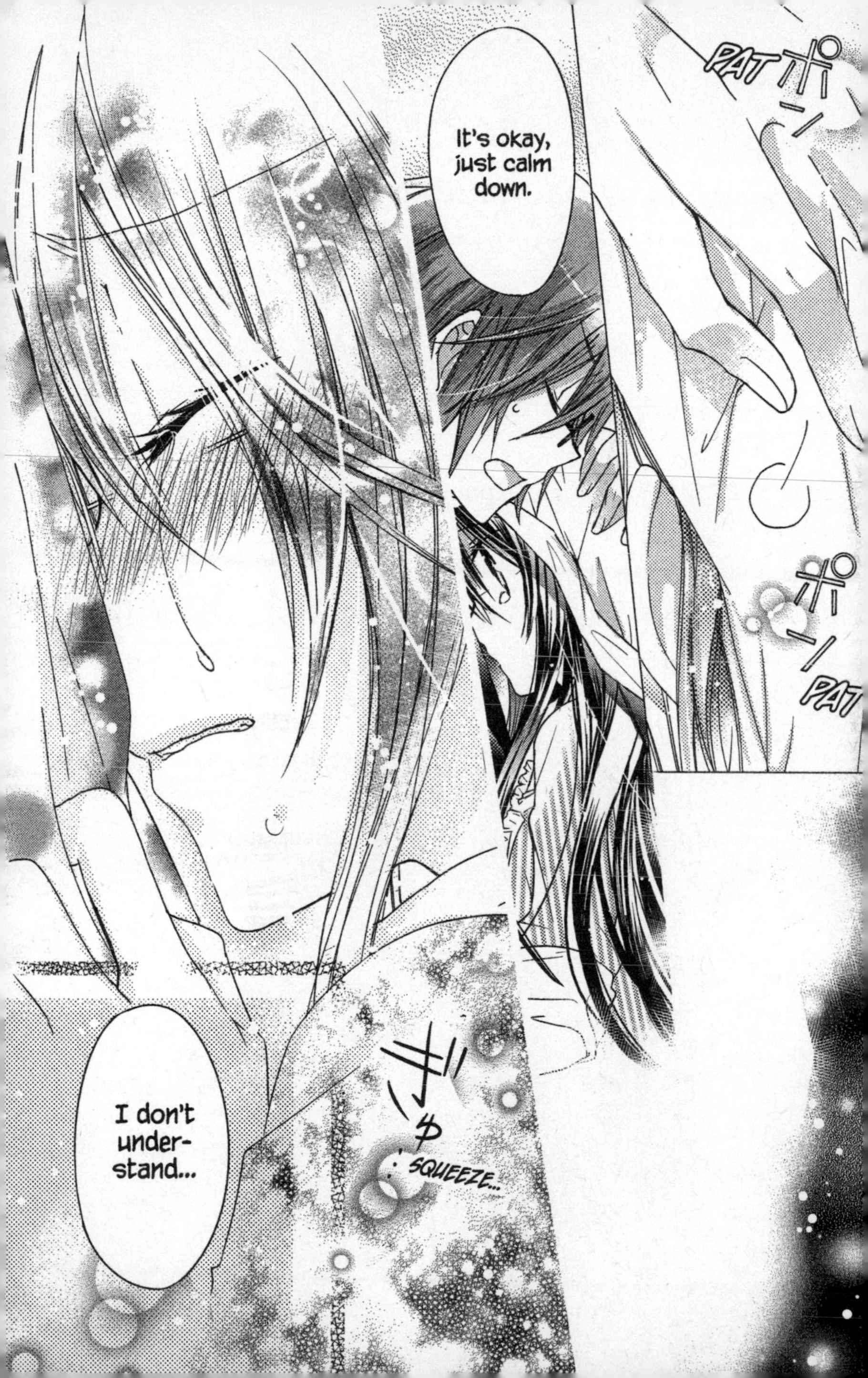
PAT
It's okay, just calm down.
PAT
SQUEEZE...
I don't understand...

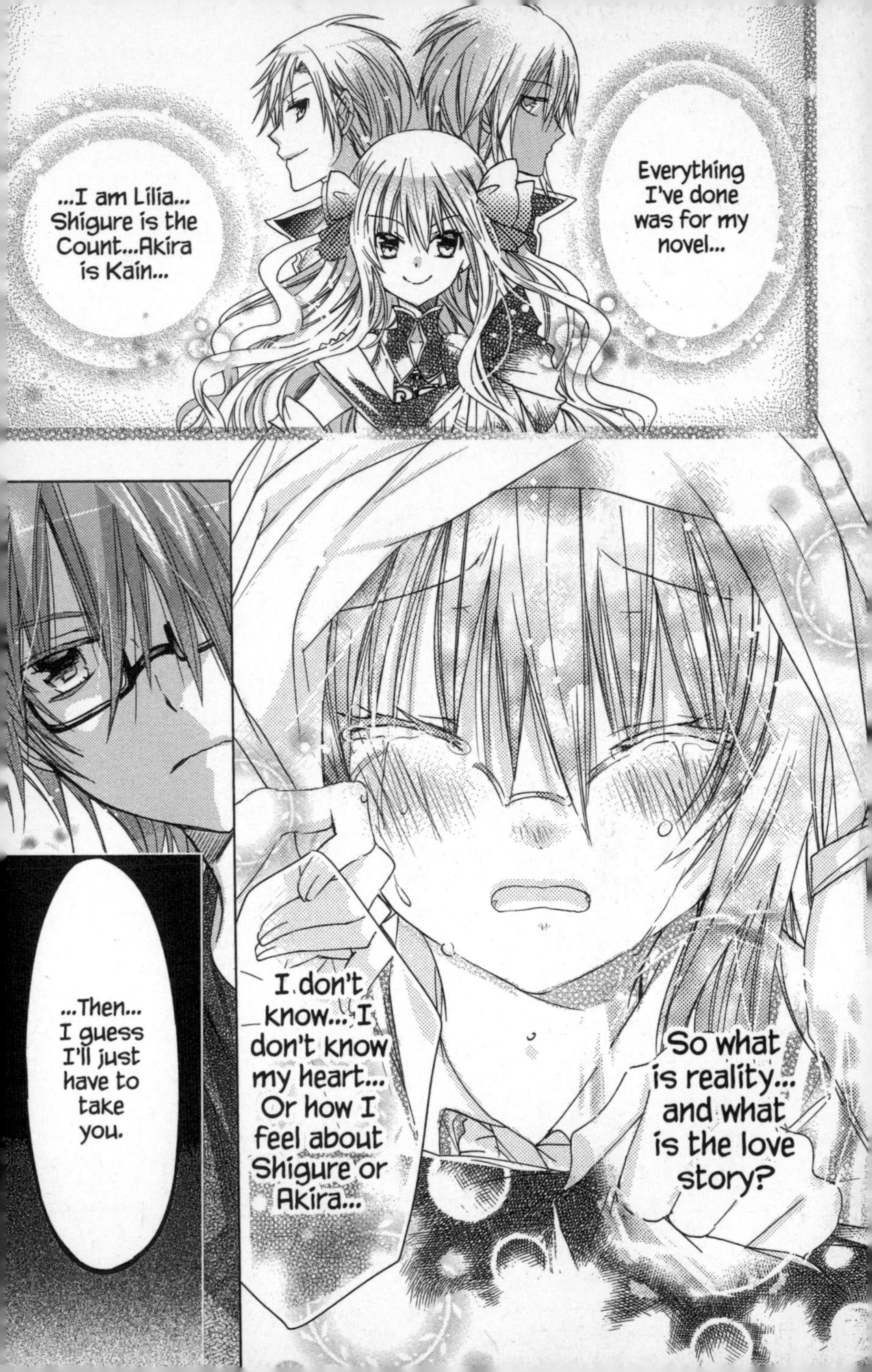
Everything I've done was for my novel...
...I am Lilia... Shigure is the Count...Akira is Kain...
So what is reality... and what is the love story?
I don't know... I don't know my heart... Or how I feel about Shigure or Akira...
...Then... I guess I'll just have to take you.

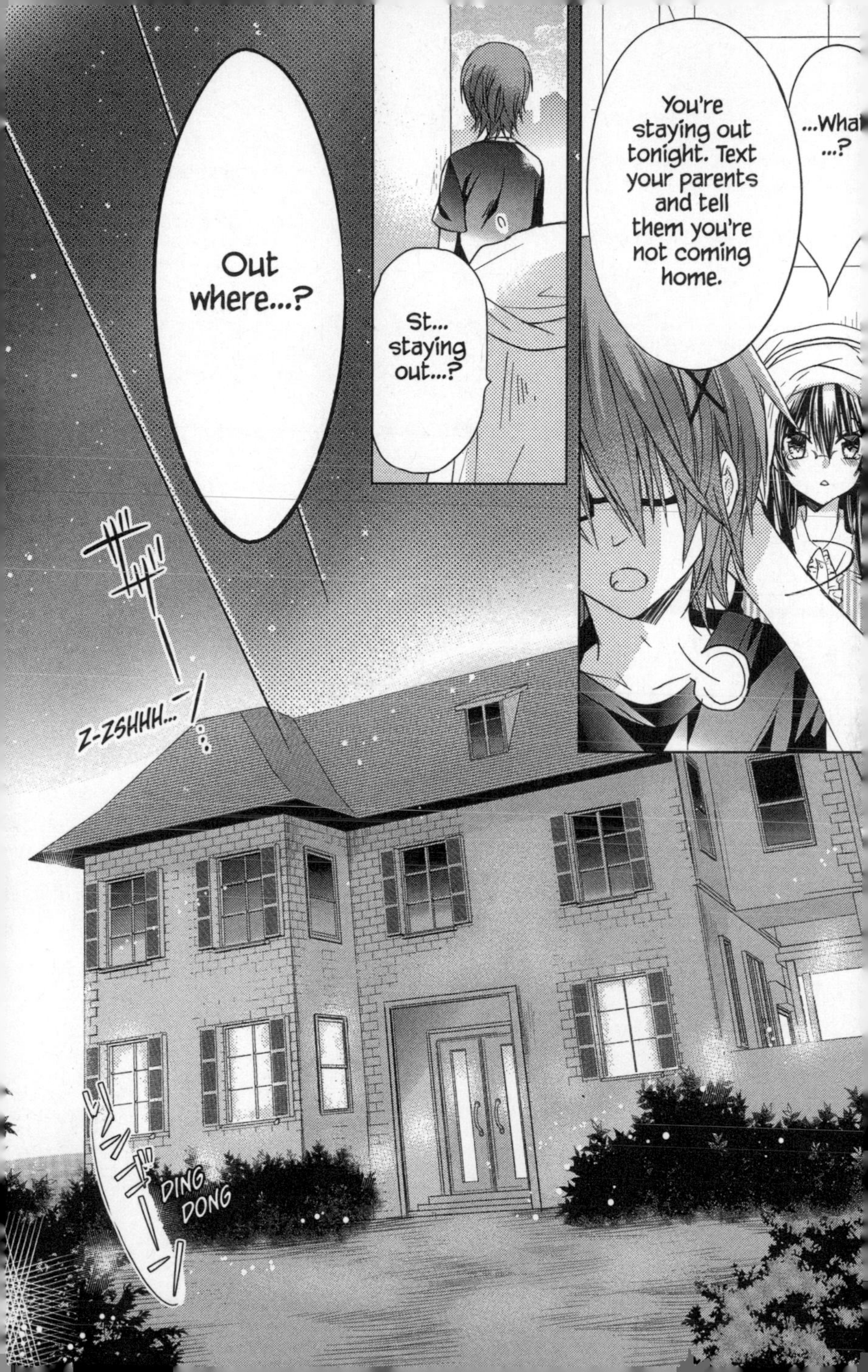
You're staying out tonight. Text your parents and tell them you're not coming home.
...What ...?
St... staying out...?
Out where...?
Z-ZSHHH...
DING DONG

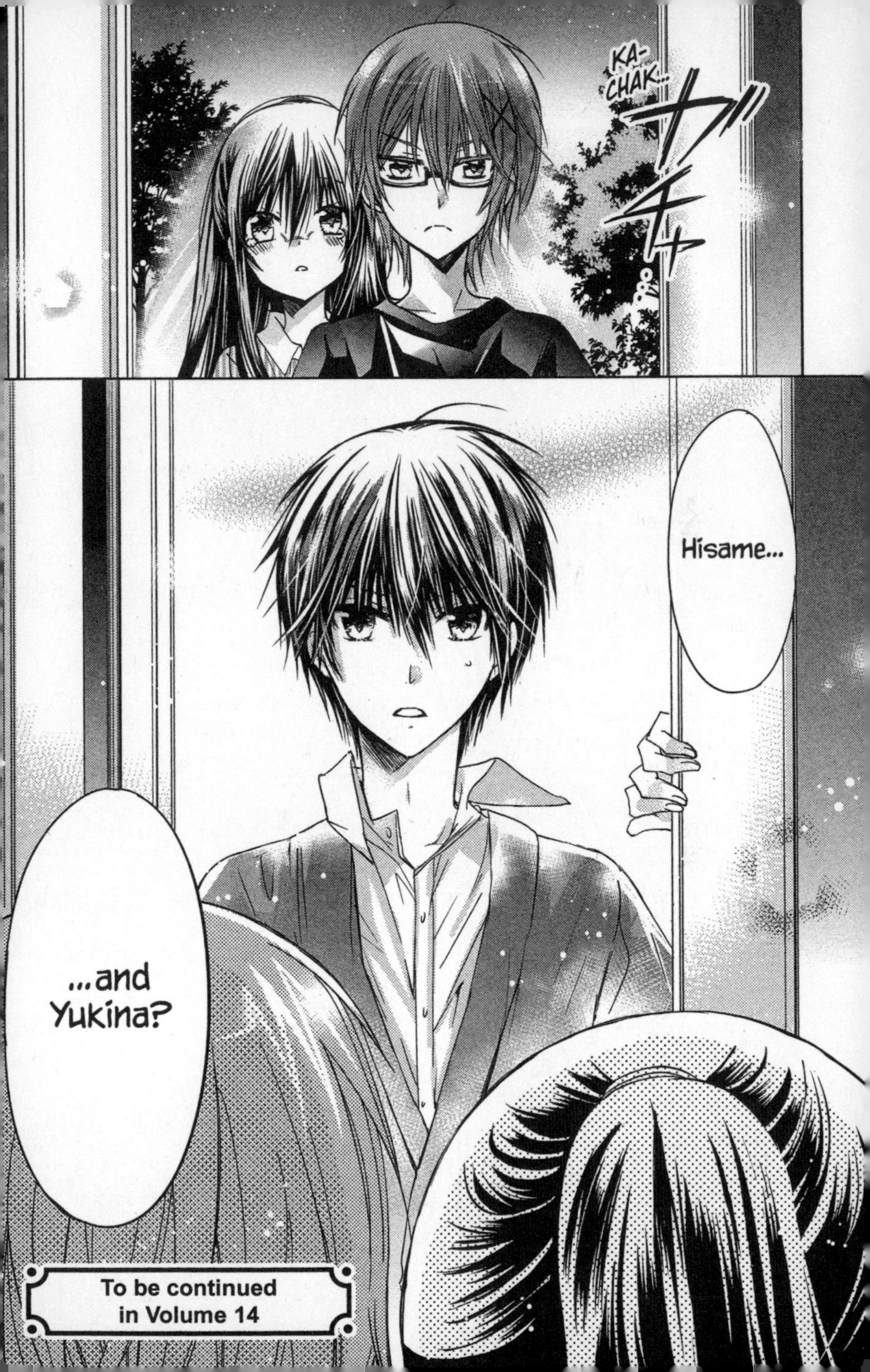
KA-CHAK...
Hisame...
...and Yukina?
To be continued in Volume 14

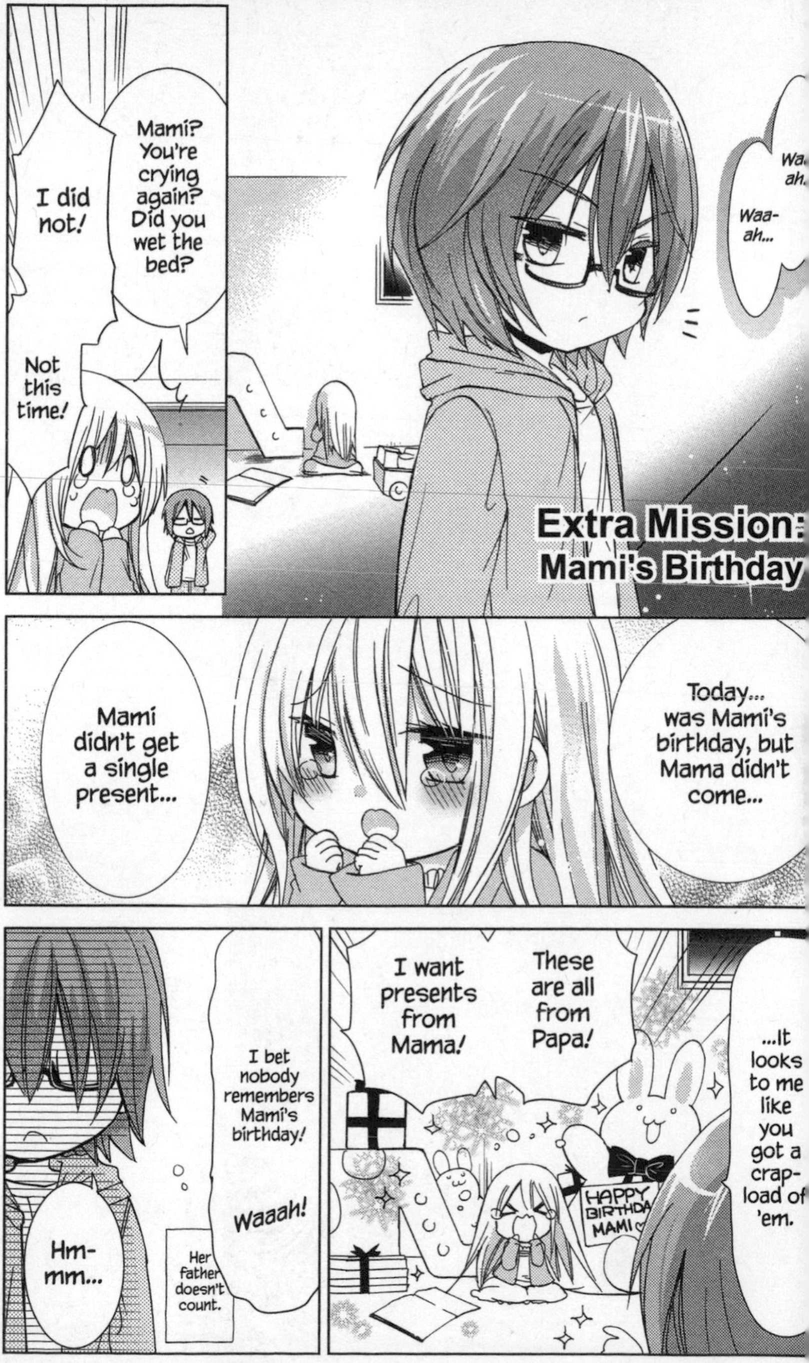
Waa-ah...
Extra Mission: Mami's Birthday
Mami? You're crying again? Did you wet the bed?
I did not!
Not this time!
Today... was Mami's birthday, but Mama didn't come...
Mami didn't get a single present...
...It looks to me like you got a crap-load of 'em.
These are all from Papa!
I want presents from Mama!
HAPPY BIRTHDAY MAMI
I bet nobody remembers Mami's birthday!
Waaah!
Her father doesn't count.
Hm-mm...

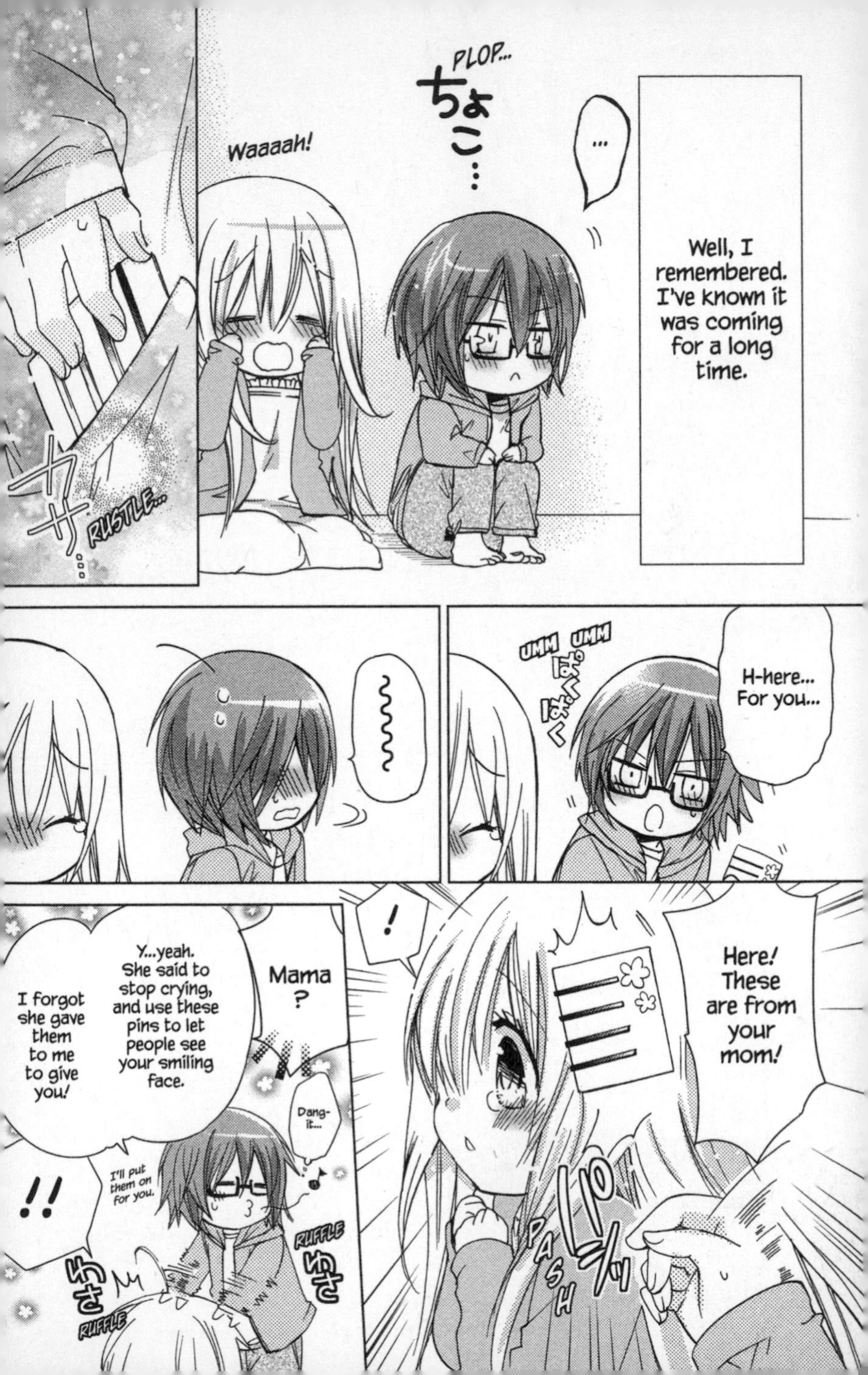
Well, I remembered. I've known it was coming for a long time.
...
PLOP...
ちょこ…
Waaaah!
RUSTLE...
ガサ…
UMM UMM
ぱくぱく
H-here... For you...
!
Here! These are from your mom!
PASH
ぱしっ
Mama?
Y...yeah. She said to stop crying, and use these pins to let people see your smiling face.
I forgot she gave them to me to give you!
Dang-it...
I'll put them on for you.
!!
RUFFLE
ゆさ
ゆさ
RUFFLE

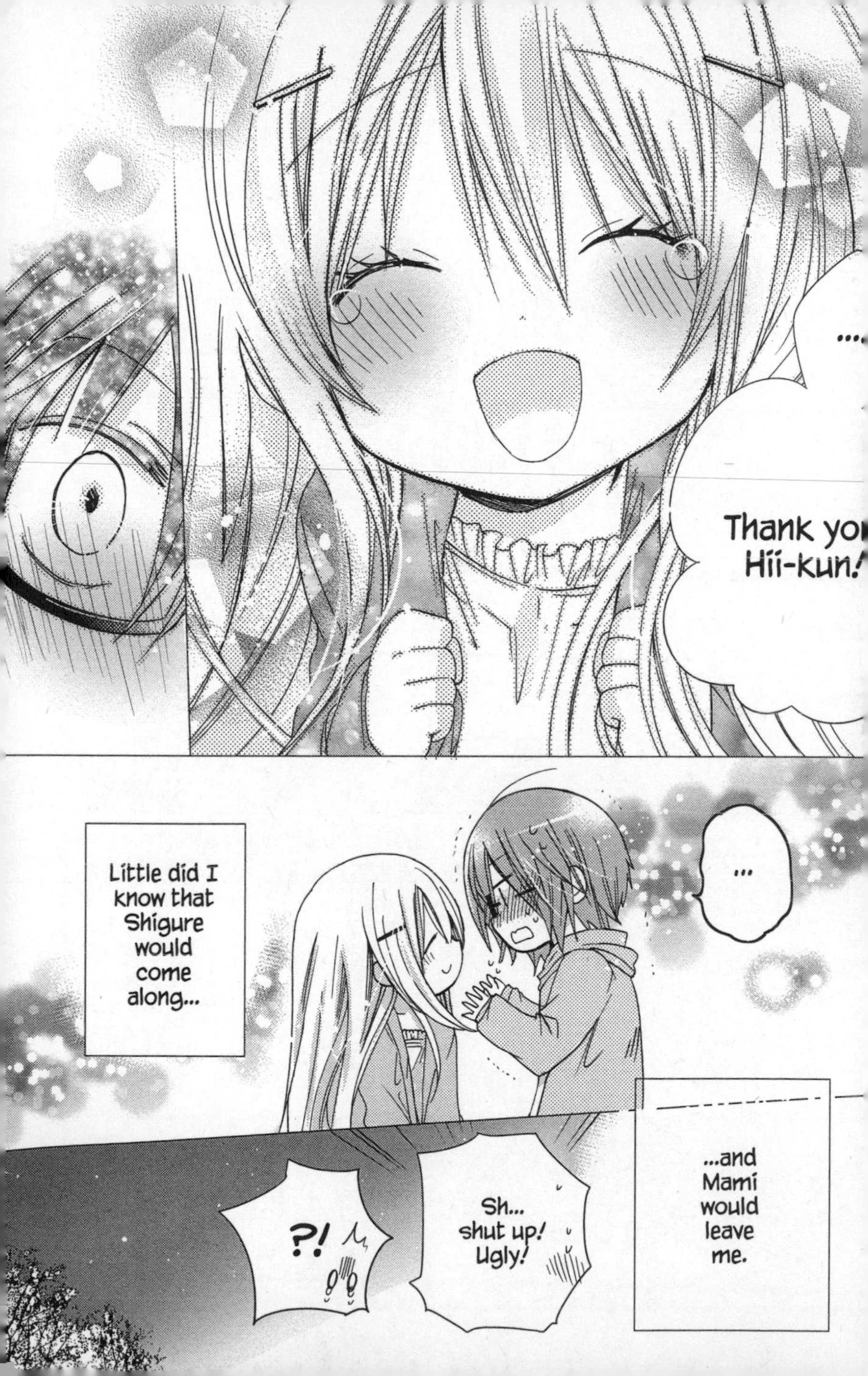
….
Thank yo
Hii-kun!
…
Little did I know that Shigure would come along…
…and Mami would leave me.
Sh… shut up! Ugly!
?!

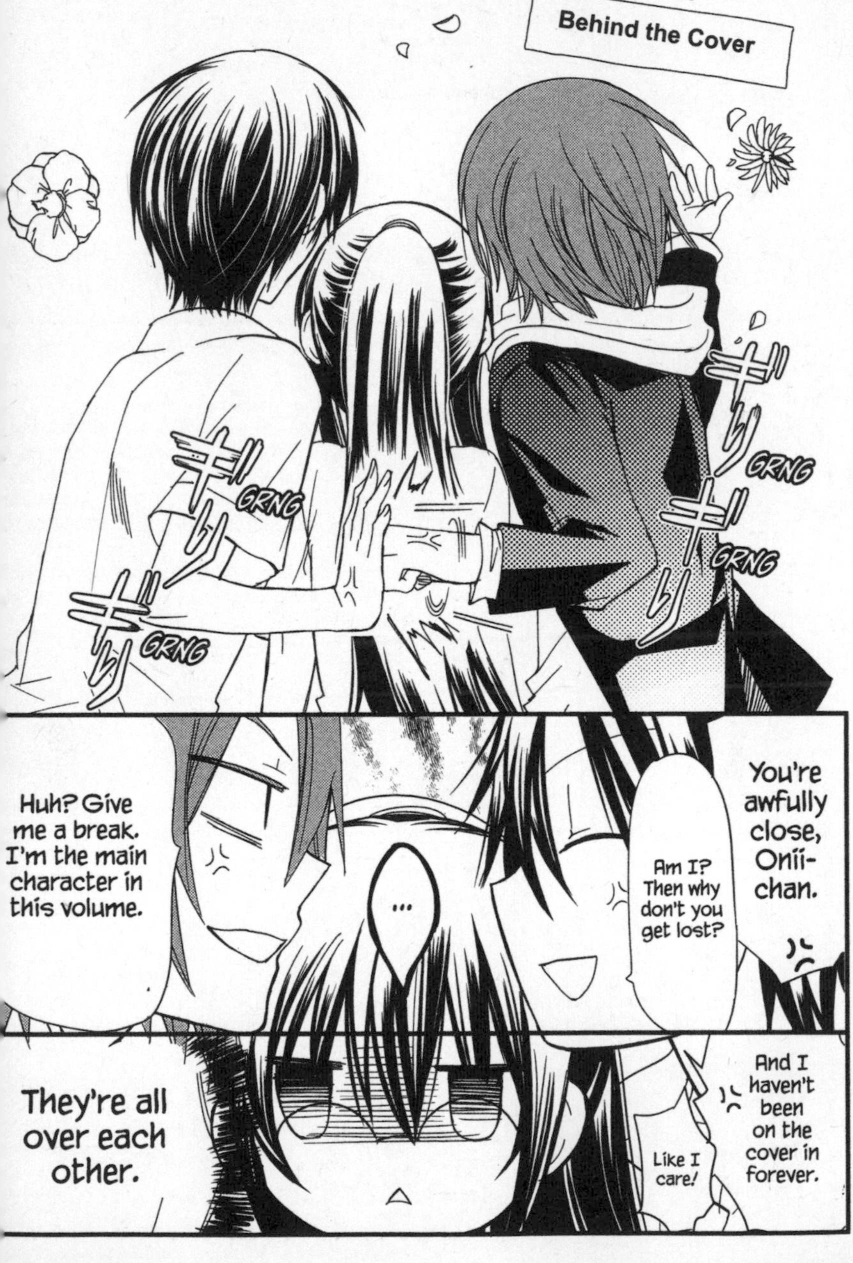
Behind the Cover
GRNG
GRNG
GRNG
GRNG
You're awfully close, Onii-chan.
Am I? Then why don't you get lost?
...
Huh? Give me a break. I'm the main character in this volume.
And I haven't been on the cover in forever.
Like I care!
They're all over each other.

Afterword

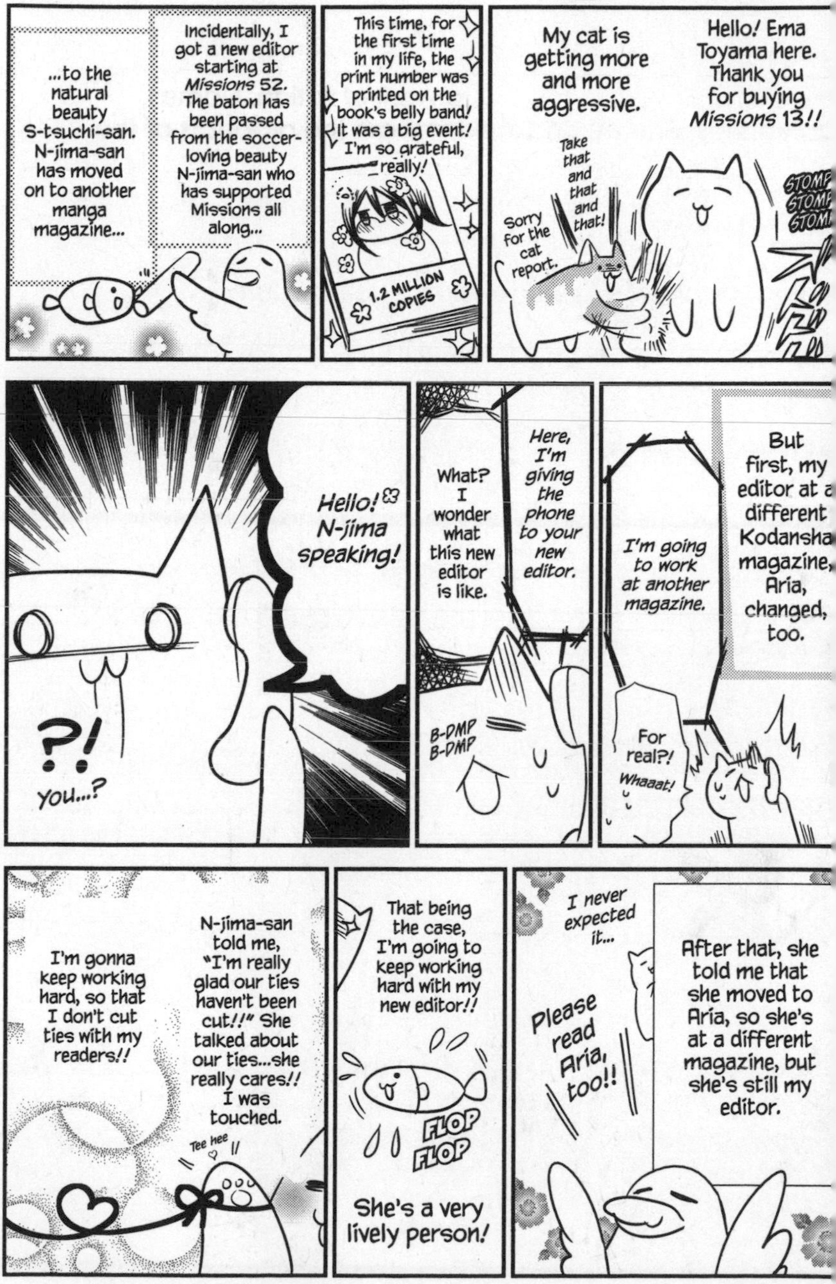
Hello! Ema Toyama here. Thank you for buying *Missions* 13!!
My cat is getting more and more aggressive.
Take that and that and that!
Sorry for the cat report.
This time, for the first time in my life, the print number was printed on the book's belly band! It was a big event! I'm so grateful, really!
1.2 MILLION COPIES
Incidentally, I got a new editor starting at *Missions* 52. The baton has been passed from the soccer-loving beauty N-jima-san who has supported Missions all along...
...to the natural beauty S-tsuchi-san. N-jima-san has moved on to another manga magazine...
But first, my editor at a different Kodansha magazine, Aria, changed, too.
I'm going to work at another magazine.
For real?!
Whaaat!
Here, I'm giving the phone to your new editor.
What? I wonder what this new editor is like.
B-DMP B-DMP
Hello! N-jima speaking!
?!
you...?
After that, she told me that she moved to Aria, so she's at a different magazine, but she's still my editor.
I never expected it...
Please read Aria, too!!
That being the case, I'm going to keep working hard with my new editor!!
FLOP FLOP
She's a very lively person!
N-jima-san told me, "I'm really glad our ties haven't been cut!!" She talked about our ties...she really cares!! I was touched.
Tee hee
I'm gonna keep working hard, so that I don't cut ties with my readers!!

Missions of Love volume 13 is
characters, places, and incid
author's imagination or are used fictitiously. Any resemblance to actual events, locales, or persons, living or dead, is entirely coincidental.

A Kodansha Comics Trade Paperback Original.

Published in the United States by Kodansha Comics, an imprint of Kodansha USA Publishing, LLC, New York.

Publication rights for this English edition arranged through Kodansha Ltd., Tokyo.

First published in Japan in 2013 by Kodansha Ltd., Tokyo as *Watashi ni xx shinasai!,* volume 13.

ISBN 978-1-63236-105-9

Printed in the United States of America.

www.kodanshacomics.com

9 8 7 6 5 4 3 2 1

Translation: Alethea Nibley & Athena Nibley
Lettering: Paige Pumphrey
Editing: Paul Starr
Kodansha Comics edition cover design: Phil Balsman